HOUSING THE NATION
—
A SINGAPORE POLICY STORY

HO, Kim Hin / David

PARTRIDGE

To order additional copies of this book, contact
Toll Free +65 3165 7531 (Singapore)
Toll Free +60 3 3099 4412 (Malaysia)
orders.singapore@partridgepublishing.com

www.partridgepublishing.com/singapore

CONTENTS

FOREWORD

"Over 100 years ago, this (Singapore) was a mud-
flat, swamp. Today, this is a modern city. Ten years
from now, this will be a metropolis. Never fear."
(The first Prime Minister of Singapore Lee Kuan Yew, 1965)

This book highlights the findings, contributions and recommendations made on several crucial issues, concerning the subject of the large and complex physical infrastructural provision. like the ubiquitous yet high quality 'Public Housing' in Singapore. Chapter 1 takes a close look at public housing, i.e. the Housing & Development Board (HDB) housing in Singapore, which has evolved from the provision of basic housing shelter needs to meeting the rising aspirations of Singapore's resident population for a better quality of life. This Chapter develops a unique and state-of-the-art dynamic, structural public housing macroeconomic model (DSPHM), based on an open economy for several key macroeconomic variables, actual and expected, as well as the demand for new HDB flats sold. Through scenario analysis in scenario planning format, The Chapter readily adopts the DSPHM for simulating two scenarios, namely a "no change" first scenario and a public housing "deregulation" second scenario. In both scenarios, there is the same GDP expansion over the next 10 years. The first scenario is conclusive that beyond the optimal point of overwhelming public housing provision, the supply line of additional new HDB flats must rise at a slower pace (and in small doses) at the margin. This optimal point is favorable from an allocative efficiency perspective of scarce public housing resources. The second scenario is conclusive that the deregulation of public housing continues to sustain household affordability for new HDB flats even into the medium term (i.e. the next 6 years) at the least, and before private mortgage interest rates start to rise to become excessive. This second "deregulation" scenario also indicates the possible emergence of several new policy measures for the Singapore public housing sector – a rental HDB housing policy measure, privatization of HDB mortgages as a new policy measure, and private market securitization of HDB mortgages as a further new policy measure.

Chapter 2 explores the relationship between several economic factors and the demand for public housing in Singapore and Hong Kong. This Chapter deploys the innovative and versatile system dynamics model, to shed better understanding on the policy implications of assisted ownership housing, via assessing the demand for new flats in both the Singapore and Hong Kong economies, under certain macroeconomic policy changes that are suitable for their unique situations. In Hong Kong's case, it is found that the HOS/PSPS demand would be around similar levels regardless of the performance of the economy. In a sense, the decision by the Hong Kong Special Administrative Region (HKSAR) government to cease selling HOS/PSPS flats is not justified in this Chapter, given the existing regulations of the Home Ownership Scheme (HOS), launched in 1978 by the Hong Kong Housing Authority (HA), along with another scheme known as the Private Sector Participation Scheme (PSPS). The Chapter suggests a relaxation of regulations regarding the premium arrangements of the resale of HOS/PSPS flats on the open market. Similar to the Singapore government's HDB scheme, that by deferring the premium payment schedule till after the transaction, should not only ease the financial burden of the HA in the construction of new flats, but also help to foster a more developed open market for the HKSAR government's HOS/PSPS flats. In the case of Singapore, the Chapter suggests an opening of the public housing (HDB) mortgage market to private sector mortgages under open competition. The fall in the demand for HDB flats shown in the Chapter can be attributed to rising demand in the secondary HDB housing market, owing to HDB's relatively lenient requirements. The Chapter offers meaningful insights on the the potential, sustainable development of the HDB mortgage market by the private sector under open competition.

Chapter 3 is concerned with the underlying structural relationships that affect Singapore's public housing policy to potentially privatize the HDB concessionary-rate mortgage loans for HDB homebuyers. Such a potential privatization infuses and sustains price competitiveness among the domestic private banks in Singapore, and lead to improved efficiency among them as well as the Singapore economy at large. Two structural relationships are discussed in terms of the mortgage interest rate structure. First, a comparison is made between the HDB hurdle rates and the HDB mortgage yields to examine the notion of the potential privatization of the HDB concessionary rate mortgage loans. The examination reveals that the private banks' interest rates are lower than HDB concessionary rates on average for a 30 year-mortgage term. Therefore, it makes it more attractive for HDB homebuyers to take up the private banks' mortgages rather than the HDB mortgages. The likely reason for the lower interest rates offered by the private banks is primarily due to price competition in terms of the interest rate structure, which the individual banks face among themselves and with the HDB. Secondly, the HDB hurdle rates and the HDB mortgage yields are examined. As the measure of the efficiency of the HDB mortgage financing activity, the examination reveals that the HDB mortgage yields are generally lower than the HDB hurdle rates. Therefore, it is more worthwhile to pass the HDB mortgage financing activity to the private sector, where the Singapore domestic private banks are viable in generating better mortgage yields. Chapter 3 is not without its limitations. First, the private banks' interest rates in Singapore are compared on the assumption that the interest rates would be fixed for a 30 year-loan term. This is because it is not possible to anticipate the floating interest rates offered by the private banks. Such private banks would usually offer fixed interest rate up to a maximum period of two years. Similarly, a fixed interest rate for the HDB concessionary interest rate is assumed and for a much longer 30-year mortgage term. Such a fixed HDB interest rate is not entirely accurate because the HDB offers fixed interest rate but subject to revision every 3 months. Secondly, the estimated hurdle rates may not precisely represent the HDB hurdle rate, as the cost of equity data is solely based on "CapitaLand Limited". Estimates of the HDB hurdle rates can be sourced from other public listed real estate companies to possibly establish a more accurate cost of equity.

Chapter 4 is concerned with real option analysis, inclusive of its option pricing, which is widely debated in the finance and economic literature. The Chapter highlights that the binomial option–pricing model, proposed by Cox, Ross and Rubinstein, CRR (1979), is appropriate to represent the movement of the underlying HDB resale flat prices, subject to private market forces in HDB's large scale public housing secondary resale market. The Housing and Development Board (HDB), the national housing authority, is shifting its wealth redistributive focus to more allocative efficient housing policy initiatives in the presence of scarce resources for public housing. The HDB Main Upgrading Program (MUP) is a heavily subsidized and highly targeted public housing policy. Since its inception in 1992, the HDB has budgeted some S$3 billion to finance the MUP policy. Limited local and anecdotal evidence show that the HDB MUP policy affects public housing households and the affected areas. One positive impact is the asset value enhancement of the HDB flats within the upgraded public housing precincts. The value of the upgraded HDB flat, particularly with the space-adding item (SAI), has improved considerably. The embedded real option premiums for HDB flats under the MUP policy are found to be around S$10,300 for a 3–Room HDB flat and S$2,000 for a larger 4-Room HDB flat. These real option values are estimated from both the binomial real option pricing model and the Samuelson–McKean model. The estimation of the real option value to upgrade may help the homebuying HDB flat owner to better assess his enhanced flat value, and to better appreciate the cost and gain involved. It enables the homebuying HDB flat owner to make a better decision to hold, or to unlock the underlying value of his HDB flat, affected by the MUP policy. A 3-Room homebuying HDB flat owner is more inclined to opt for upgrading while the option premium is deemed to be less attractive for upgrading in the case of the homebuying 4-Room HDB flat owner. Chapter 4's findings can be extended to estimate the value of upgrading at other HDB housing estates like the Bedok, Telok Blangah and Marine Parade HDB estates, provided that there are sufficient transaction data available. It is also possible to examine the option values for more HDB room flat types and their impact on the hold–sell decision.

Chapter 5 recognizes that HDB flats and their amenities in Singapore are by no means poor quality because HDB flats and their amenities provide affordable, high rise and quality housing for resident homebuyers. Housing affordability is always an issue of concern to many Singaporean homebuyers because shelter forms one of the basic life necessities. The corresponding private residential market in Singapore offers quality and premium private residential accommodation for homebuyers, who prefer the private residential market. Rising mortgage rates lower long–run housing affordability. Lowered housing affordability implies lowered residual income for other living expenses and so homebuyers may well choose to become HDB homebuyers for their household–family activities. This Chapter finds that the appropriate affordability model is the appropriate multi-factor housing affordability index (HAI) model of eq (5.2), which considers the ability to provide down payment and to service the mortgage taken up. The model also considers housing accessibility.

HAI = monthly housing income/ (down payment of 20% + mortgage rate)

$$HAI = \frac{AI}{12 \star \{2.5 \star [(0.8 \times Price_j) \star MC_{i,n}] - CPF\}} \times 50 + \frac{RG + Sav + CPF\ Sav}{0.2 \star Price_j + LFSD} \times 50$$

(5.2)

, where $Price_j$ = Price of housing type,

AI = Annual household income

$MC_{i,30}$ = Mortgage constant of housing loan, given n years at prime lending rate i,

CPF = Monthly CPF contributions,

$LFSD$ = Legal fees and stamp duties,

Sav = amount of household savings,

$CPF\ Sav$ = amount of savings in CPF,

RG = Resale gains from previous housing

The multi-factor HAI model traces the footsteps of a typical middle-income homebuying household that conforms to the Singapore social system of going through 16 years of education, to graduate from university with an honors degree, and who then enter the workforce for 40 years before retiring at 65 years old. Special emphasis is placed on the housing types that the homebuying household chooses at different stages of its live, say from 2008 to 2023. Deploying the HAI model, Chapter 5 presents the results in Table 5.4.

Table 5.4. The Housing Affordability Index, Singapore

Housing Affordability Index (HAI):

Housing Type/ Year	2011	2016	2017	2018	2019	2020	2021	2022	2023
4-room HDB Starter (New Estate)	2.036	4.367	4.648	4.978	5.250	5.526	5.815	7.509	7.711
5-room HDB Starter (New Estate)	1.664	3.481	3.701	3.956	4.169	4.385	4.611	5.928	6.086
Exec HDB Starter (New Estate)	1.375	2.819	2.994	3.196	3.365	3.538	3.717	4.760	4.886
4-room HDB Starter (Old Estate)	1.675	3.506	3.728	3.986	4.200	4.418	4.645	5.972	6.132
5-room HDB Starter (New Estate)	1.286	2.618	2.780	2.966	3.122	3.282	3.447	4.409	4.526
Exec HDB Starter (New Estate)	1.144	2.305	2.447	2.608	2.745	2.884	3.028	3.866	3.968
5-room HDB Resale	1.017	2.184	2.326	2.481	2.618	2.757	2.900	3.744	3.844
Exec HDB Resale	0.892	1.901	2.024	2.157	2.276	2.396	2.520	3.248	3.335
Exec Condo	0.669	1.150	1.174	1.199	1.213	1.225	1.235	1.520	1.497
Private Condo (Outside Central)	0.430	0.686	0.692	0.697	0.697	0.695	0.693	0.841	0.818
Private Condo (Rest of Central)	0.306	0.464	0.464	0.463	0.459	0.454	0.449	0.539	0.520
Private Condo (Core Central)	0.162	0.194	0.185	0.177	0.167	0.158	0.149	0.171	0.157

Source: Author, 2020

The simulation estimates focus on the hypothetical homebuying household purchasing its first HDB home, while satisfying the compulsory 5-year minimum occupancy period, before they decide to upgrade. The greater the HAI, then the more affordable the housing choice is for the household. It is assumed that the homebuying household buys a 5-room flat in the newer HDB estates. The homebuying household's 5-room flat choice is factored into the resale proceeds upon liquidation from say 2016 onwards when the household is given the legal freedom to upgrade. Once the compulsory 5-year minimum occupancy period is fulfilled, the hypothetical young homebuying household is comfortable with moving into a median priced resale HDB flat of their choice or purchase an executive condominium or purchase a flat under the HDB design, build and sell scheme (DBSS), if the homebuying household so chooses. Unfortunately, the price of a median private condominium or other private housing types are generally unaffordable for such a household, even with the fortuitous gains that it may enjoy from liquidating its HDB starter flat. The gap between the private and public housing market widens even further, as the HAI for private condominiums within the Central area stays persistently out of the reach of the homebuying household. In the prime core central area and its prime direct real estate (DRE) developments, the homebuying household would find its HAI for a unit there to be even beyond their financial reach as time goes by. The corresponding Monti Carlo model simulations (MCMSs) affirm that the critical (maximum) price of housing at a certain period hinges largely on mortgage rates, the amount of mortgage taken and the repayment period. Gross monthly household income is another vital factor. Housing affordability of public housing for the middle class, represented by a HDB 5-room starter flat, is heavily correlated with the maximum mortgage taken up and the rate of price rise. Regular monthly savings also play a key role in determining whether-or-not the homebuying household can pay the outlay i.e. the initial down payment of 20% of the buying flat price (including CPF). For public housing and for the upper-middle income group, who qualify for an executive condominium, the expected annual price rise is more crucial than the mortgage amount taken up. Regular monthly savings are relevant but are overshadowed by the earlier two factors of the price rise and the mortgage amount taken up.

The main factors determining housing affordability for upgrading to the executive condominium comprise the rate of its annual price rise and the mortgage amount obtainable. However, the expected price rise of the HDB starter flat, which the homebuying household first purchases is a relevant factor, influencing housing affordability. Because the sale proceeds of the first flat purchase and of benefiting from the price appreciation of public housing, such sale proceeds can typically pay the down payment of the next (upgraded) flat, to improve housing affordability and accessibility. For homebuying households seeking to upgrade to the private condominiums, such households also benefit from the sale proceeds of their first flat purchase and from the price appreciation of public housing. The sale proceeds can pay the down payment of the next private condominium apartment, to improve housing affordability and accessibility. The fortuitous wealth for such homebuying households is evident in selling their starter HDB housing to upgrade to better private condominiums.

Lastly, Chapter 6 offers the book's conclusion.

Happy reading.

Yours sincerely,
Professor (Dr) HO, Kim Hin / David
Singapore
December 2020.

ACKNOWLEDGEMENTS

The Author wish to extend their most sincere appreciation to the School of Design & Environment, under the highly able Deanship of the Provost & Chair Professor (Dr) LAM Khee Poh, of the National University of Singapore. The same wish is extended to the University of Cambridge and the University of Hertfordshire in Hatfield, UK. These three tertiary institutions of higher learning and research are globally leading Universities, inspiring and encouraging both modern and contemporary studies of large and complex physical infrastructural provision, in particularly public housing.

ABOUT THE AUTHOR

Dr HO Kim Hin / David is Honorary Professor in Development Economics & Land Economy, awarded by the UK public university, the University of Hertfordshire. He retired end-May 2019 as Professor (Associate) (Tenured) from the National University of Singapore. Professor HO spent the last thirty-one years across several sectors, which include the military, oil refining, aerospace engineering, public housing, resettlement, land acquisition, land reclamation, real estate investment, development and international real estate investing. He spent six years in the real estate career as part of the executive management group of Singapore Technologies at Pidemco Land Limited, and as part of the senior management team of the Government of Singapore Investment Corporation's GIC Real Estate Private Limited. Seventeen years are spent in the National University of Singapore at the then School of Building and Estate Management, the Department of Real Estate, School of Design and Environment, where his research expertise is in two areas.

First is international real estate in the area of risk–return behavior behind international real estate investing in direct and indirect real estate. Secondly, is urban and public policy analysis involving real estate, sea transport, public housing, land and land use. Schooled in development economics and in land economy at the University of Cambridge, England, he has effectively extended these disciplines to examine his two expertise areas. Apart from being well versed in econometrics, his quantitative interests include real estate demand and supply, investment and finance, artificial intelligent modeling in real estate and system dynamics modeling for real estate market analysis and public policy analysis. He is the Member of the Royal Economics Society (U.K.), Academic Member of the National Council of Real Estate Investment Fiduciaries (U.S.), Fellow of the American Real Estate Society (U.S.), member of the American Economic Association (U.S.) and member of the Economic Society of Singapore and the Singapore Institute of Management. He holds the degrees of Master of Philosophy (1st Class Honors with Distinction), Honorary Doctor of Letters and the Doctor of Philosophy from the University of Cambridge, U.K. He has published widely in top international journals and conferences, in chapters of international academic book publishers. Professor HO has written 13 major books (including this book), undertaken many consultancies and funded research projects. He has written a total of about 275 published works (with 91 in peer reviewed, reputable international journals). He is an editorial board member of the Journal of Economics & Public Finance, Real Estate Economics journal, Journal of Property Research, Journal of Property Investment & Finance, Journal of Real Estate Finance & Economics, the Property Management journal and the International Journal of Strategic Property Management. He has published widely in conferences, Finance, chapters of international academic book publishers, undertaken many consultancies and funded research projects. He is an immediate past Governor of the St Gabriel's Foundation that oversees nine schools in Singapore; and a District Judge equivalent member of the Valuation Review Board, Ministry of Finance, Singapore, and the Singapore Courts.

INTRODUCTION

Housing The Nation - A Singapore Policy Story

Chapter 1 is concerned with the Singapore government's overall policy of economy-wide and financial sector deregulation, the privatization of public enterprises. Without exception, the Housing and Development Board (HDB) introduced the policy on 1 Jan 2003 for the domestic private banks to originate the HDB market-rate mortgages. Banks are permitted to provide mortgages to HDB homebuyers who are still eligible for the HDB concessionary rate mortgages but have opted instead for the private bank mortgages. This Chapter examines the feasibility of implementing the policy for the full privatization of the HDB mortgages. Such a privatization of the HDB concessionary rate mortgages infuses and sustains the price competitiveness among the private domestic banks, resulting in improved efficiency for the banking sector and the economy. In terms of structural relationships, the Chapter compares the loan interest rate structure of the private domestic banks, which provide mortgages to HDB homebuyers, as against the HDB concessionary interest-rate structure. Through scenario analysis in scenario planning format, Chapter 1 readily adopts the DSPHM for simulating two scenarios, namely a "no change" first scenario and a public housing "deregulation" second scenario. In both scenarios, there is the same GDP expansion over the next 10 years.

The first scenario is conclusive that beyond the optimal point of overwhelming public housing provision, the supply line of additional new HDB flats must rise at a slower pace (and in small doses) at the margin. Such an optimal point is favorable from an allocative efficiency perspective of scarce public housing resources. The second scenario is conclusive that the deregulation of public housing continues to sustain household affordability for new HDB flats even into the medium term i.e. the next six years at the least, and before private mortgage interest rates start to rise to become excessive. This second "deregulation" scenario also indicates the possible emergence of several new policy measures for the Singapore public housing sector – a rental HDB housing policy measure, privatization of HDB mortgages as a new policy measure, and the private market securitization of HDB mortgages as a further new policy measure.

Chapter 2 looks at several economic factors and the demand for public housing in Hong Kong and Singapore. These two economies are known for their intensive government housing policies even though the manner of regulating their assisted homeownership schemes is vastly different. This Chapter deploys the system dynamics model to shed a better understanding on the policy implications of assisted ownership housing, via assessing the demand for new flats in both the Singapore and Hong Kong economies, under certain macroeconomic policy changes that are suitable for their unique situations. In Hong Kong's case, it is found that the HOS/PSPS demand would be around similar levels regardless of the performance of the economy. In a sense, the decision by the Hong Kong Special Administrative Region (HKSAR) government to cease selling HOS/PSPS flats is not justified in this Chapter, given the existing regulations of the Home Ownership Scheme (HOS) launched in 1978 by the Hong Kong Housing Authority (HA), along with another scheme known as the Private Sector Participation Scheme (PSPS). The Chapter suggests a relaxation of regulations regarding the premium arrangements of the resale of HOS/PSPS flats on the open market. Similar to the Singapore government's HDB scheme, that by deferring the premium payment schedule till after the transaction, should not only ease the financial burden of the Hong Kong government HA in the construction of new flats, but also help to foster a more developed open market for the HKSAR government's HOS/PSPS flats. In the case of Singapore, Chapter 2 suggests an opening of the public housing (HDB) mortgage market to private sector mortgages under open competition. The fall in the demand for HDB flats shown in the Chapter can be attributed to rising demand in the secondary HDB housing market, owing to HDB's relatively lenient requirements. The Chapter offers meaningful insights on the Singapore government's aims of providing large scale public housing ownership and the potential, sustainable development of the HDB mortgage market by the private sector under open competition.

Chapter 3 examines the underlying structural relationships that affect Singapore's public housing policy to potentially privatize the HDB concessionary-rate mortgage for HDB homebuyers. Two structural relationships are discussed in terms of the mortgage interest rate structure. First, a comparison is made between the HDB hurdle rates and the HDB mortgage yields to examine the notion of the potential privatization of the HDB concessionary rate mortgages. The examination reveals that the private banks' interest rates are lower than HDB concessionary rates on average for a 30 year-mortgage term. Secondly, both the HDB hurdle rates and the HDB mortgage yields are discussed. The HDB mortgage yields are compared against the HDB hurdle rates. As the measure of the efficiency of the HDB mortgage financing activity, the examination reveals that the HDB mortgage yields are generally lower than the HDB hurdle rates. It is inferred that the HDB mortgage yield cannot meet the HDB minimum required rate of return, the HDB hurdle rate, which is HDB's own absolute performance benchmarking. It is more worthwhile to pass the HDB mortgage financing activity to the private sector, where the Singapore domestic private banks are viable in generating better mortgage yields. In term of improved efficiency to the banking sector and the Singapore economy, the notion of potentially passing the HDB mortgage financing activity to the Singapore private sector is acceptable.

Chapter 3 is not without its limitations. First, the private banks' interest rates in Singapore are compared on the assumption that the interest rates would be fixed for a 30 year-loan term. This is because it is not possible to anticipate the floating interest rates offered by the private banks. Such banks would usually offer fixed interest rate up to a maximum period of two years. Similarly, a fixed interest rate for the HDB concessionary interest rate is assumed and for a much longer 30-year mortgage term. Such a fixed HDB interest rate is not entirely accurate because the HDB offers fixed interest rate but subject to revision every 3 months. Secondly, the estimated hurdle rates may not precisely represent the HDB hurdle rate, as the cost of equity data is solely based on "CapitaLand Limited". Estimates of the HDB hurdle rates can be sourced from other public listed real estate companies to possibly establish a more accurate cost of equity. Chapter 4 is concerned with the Main Upgrading Programme (MUP), which is a bold and major policy implemented by the Housing Development Board (HDB) since the 1990s. This heavily subsidized MUP policy is highly targeted to enhance the social and economic value of public housing in Singapore. It benefits HDB households residing in the older HDB housing estates in terms of both an enhanced asset value of the household's HDB flat, and a quality public housing living environment. The HDB flat owner whose precinct is selected for upgrading under the MUP policy is envisaged to be holding a call option to upgrade his HDB flat, because such an option to upgrade is valuable and it has an opportunity to command a higher resale price in the HDB resale market. Chapter 4 estimates the option premiums for upgrading by utilizing the intuitive and explicit numerical-method solution of the binomial real option pricing model and the Samuelson–McKean closed-form solution. The embedded real option values under the MUP policy are estimated at S$10,300 and S$2,000 for the popular 3-Room HDB flat and 4-Room HDB flat respectively. It is also found that government subsidies have a significant impact on the option values.

Chapter 5 that acknowledges the advent of globalization and sustainable moderate economic growth over the past decades to have resulted in the high standard of living in Singapore. However, while economic growth is rising moderately and sustainably, wealth is increasingly concentrated in the hands of the top deciles of homebuying households. Consistent with such economic growth and wealth trends, housing prices and the overall cost of living have risen considerably, prompting concern on the issue of housing affordability. Chapter 5 examines the income patterns and housing choices made by different homebuying households, resulting from different positions of wealth, via deploying model simulation using a hypothetical homebuying household over the next 16 years. An appropriate housing affordability index is adopted to ascertain the critical price for influencing the homebuying housing and home upgrading decisions. A Monte Carlo simulation is conducted to link the vital variables influencing the affordability index and the critical price. It is explicit that income levels, mortgage interest rates, the price of the type of housing, and the amount of fortuitous gains from prior housing, largely influence the homebuyer's buying decision of would be homeowners and upgraders. Chapter 5 concludes by recommending the possibility of the evolution of an increasingly multi-tier structure for the Singapore public housing sector and the private residential market, via adopting the Stock-flow Model by DiPasquale and Wheaton, which reflects expected rising income disparity over the long run of say the next 16 years.

Chapter 6 offers the book's 'Conclusion'.

CHAPTER 1

DEMAND AND ITS STRUCTURAL DYNAMICS OF NEW PUBLIC HOUSING SOLD IN SINGAPORE

The Singapore Government's vision of home ownership for all is realized via its large- scale public housing and through its key statutory board, the Housing and Development Board (HDB). Even though. it is onerous enough to provide a roof over the head of every citizen, Singapore successfully promotes affordable universal home ownership that enables its 5.7 million population to become stake holders in the small 725 sq km (280 sq mile) island-state nation, and with its very high population density of 7,804/ sq km (20,212/ sq mile). Land reclamation increases Singapore's land area from 580 km² (220 sq mi) in the 1960s to 710 km² (270 sq mi) by 2015, an increase of some 22%. Singapore is projected to reclaim another 56 km² (20 sq mi) by 2030. Some projects involve merging smaller islands to form larger, more functional islands as with Jurong Island in South Western Singapore. Sand used for reclamation is found in rivers and beaches, rather than in deserts. In 2010, Singapore imports roughly 15 million tons of sand for land reclamation but that such an import in recent years prompts Indonesia, Malaysia, and Vietnam to restrict or to bar sand export to Singapore. So in 2016, Singapore uses polders for land reclamation, in which an area is enclosed and then pumped dry (Wikipedia, 2015 and 2020; Straits Times, 4 Feb 2018). The extent of Singapore's home ownership to date stands at 85% to 90% of its population in the ballpark, who are housed in public housing, and with 10% to 15% housed in private apartments and landed real estate assets. An impressive and overwhelming 92% home ownership is achieved among all citizens, with about 23 HDB new towns planned and implemented. Virtually all HDB new towns have high rise, high density apartments or flats like the 1-room, 2-room, 3-room, 4-room, the 5-room and the executive-condominium flats. Each HDB new town is meant to enjoy self-sufficiency in retail, educational, sports, swimming complex, recreational, community clubs, town center and greenery amenities, while being integrated with a comprehensive bus, road, bicycle, foot path and mass rapid transit system. In Singapore, political leadership is appropriately and wholly committed to sustainable economic growth and environmental improvement, to enable the island state to achieve a first world economy and with a first world environment.

Since self-government in 1959, the island-state of Singapore has undergone modernization at a substantial economy of scale and at a growth rate unparalleled in the world. The result has been significant and moderate economic growth with concomitant expansion in household income and education levels and enhanced changes in value creation and lifestyles. Accompanying such significant changes is public housing policy, a major government instrument of Singapore's modernization efforts. Public housing has brought about major population redistribution, demographic restructuring and a large scale upgrading of household living conditions. The public housing authority, the Housing Development Board (HDB) is established as a statutory board in 1960, a year after Singapore's self-government.

The HDB has been adequately funded and legally empowered to implement large-scale public housing estates. The HDB is formed by the new government then in response to the serious housing shortage in the post World War II period. The government in the early years of Singapore's nationhood is determined to resolve the housing shortage problem and to commit substantial resources to the housing sector. Public housing policy is meant to provide basic shelter for the population at large. The policy is effectively discharged by the HDB and the policy evolves to offer quality housing and its environment to the lower- and middle- income households. The full home ownership policy objective, meant for virtually all resident citizens and who cannot afford private housing, is achieved in an immense overall wealth redistribution initiative. Since the 1960s, the HDB has completed some 862,918 units of public housing with an estimated 85% of the resident population living in HDB flats, and close to 83% of the residents own HDB flats under the Home Ownership Flat Scheme (policy) instituted by the HDB (HDB annual report, 2001/2002).

The key contributing factor to the success of public housing in Singapore, is strong government support and financial commitment in the regular provision of subsidized housing and additional government loans to fund HDB's operation, from the government's annual operating budget and its annual development budget. The primary policy objective is to house an overwhelming proportion of the population, not with merely a social housing good but with an enhanced asset that has a high social and investment value. The social investment aspect is maintained via reasonable qualifying criteria, to prevent households from abusing public housing benefits. By achieving large economics of scale in the provision of public housing, the HDB offers differentiated but standardized types of HDB flats and incurs low standardized costs for building these flats. Comprehensive facilities in full complement are provided in the public housing new towns across the island-state of Singapore. At the same time, the large-scale HDB housing construction program contributes to high job creation in the construction sector and all other sectors of the Singapore economy, especially in the 1960's through to the late 1980's. Public housing policy on the whole stimulates widespread job creation and favorable income distribution as tangible outputs of the policy, through the multiplier effect on the economy that helps to stabilize the economy.

From a macroeconomic perspective, both the construction sector and the public housing sector play an important role in the gross domestic product (GDP) expansion of the Singapore economy in real terms. With prudential fiscal policy, high Central Provident Fund (CPF) contribution rates, a form of compulsory social private savings, and a stable exchange rate, the HDB is enabled to maintain gradual rises of the controlled pricing of new first-hand HDB flats sold, and to sustain low marginal pricing of HDB flats that serves as a stabilizing influence on the economy. HDB can also offer the basal requirement of HDB rental flats to the underclass, thereby enabling a relatively low-price inflation regime in Singapore.

Nevertheless, in the global high technology meltdown of 2001 and the subsequent economic slowdown worldwide, both the Singapore economy and the demand for new HDB flats sold have been adversely affected. HDB has some 10,300 new flats units remaining unsold, which it hopes to clear within one to two years then. Demand for new flats sold is not expected to differ much from the past financial year when it sold 8.3 percent fewer new flats than the previous year (The Straits Times newspaper, 17 October 2003). Therefore, poor market conditions affect household investment and consumption confidence, and the resultant demand for new HDB flats sold is observed to weaken. There is a decrease of 27 percent in the number of new HDB flat applications received, amounting to 8,377 applications (i.e. HDB flats sold) in Financial Year (FY) 2001/2002, compared with 11,478 in the previous FY. HDB then launched its pilot Build-To-Order (BTO) system on 15 April 2001, as a refinement of the Registration for Flats System (RFS) policy, to offer household applicants more flexibility in the timing and choice of location for the flats to be built. HDB would only build flats if 70% of the total units in the HDB development project have been booked, in order that the HDB housing production system keeps in line with the demand for new flats (sold). Therefore, HDB's building policy is subject to enhanced allocative efficiency of its utilized scare resources.

Another instance of HDB's shift towards more intensive allocative efficiency, versus wealth redistribution, would be the latest housing development plan in the Central Area. In such a policy, some 50-storey HDB blocks in the Tanjong Pagar public housing estate may be scrapped to avoid a glut of unsold units. However, the then National Development Minister Mr. MAH Bow Tan reiterates that the HDB should not undertake the massive project to build Singapore's tallest HDB flats, only to have empty and unsold HDB flats upon completion. Such a policy avoids the problem that the HDB would face when demand sharply falls and that the HDB would be left with many unsold HDB flats (The Straits Times newspaper, December 2003). HDB resorts to a detailed waiting list of public housing applicants that indicates the type of flat demanded and the preferred location. The RFS waiting list together with the projections of housing demand from demographic analysis, enables the HDB to anticipate a 10-year flat demand in the long run, and to therefore roll out a 5-year HDB building program, which represents the public housing supply strategy.

Tactical adjustments to such a supply strategy are regularly revisited at least once a year, taking into consideration the BTO system and its results. Thus, the impact and growth of public housing demand due to changing factors, through to the public housing sector, would be reflected in the public housing strategy. As a result, Chapter 1 examines several key determinants that affect the demand of new public housing sold, mainly from a macroeconomic perspective, to address the question as to what are the key macroeconomic and expectational factors that can affect the demand of new public housing flats sold? Chapter 1 seeks to examine the policy implications for new HDB flats sold in the longer run, and that this Chapter is concerned with the first time HDB flat applicants i.e. Singapore citizens, which form a household each, and that they demand new public housing flats. However, the HDB resale market is subject to the forces of the private market mechanism, and that the resale flat prices are determined by free market dynamics and are therefore excluded in this Chapter. Chapter 1's scope is confined to the demand for new

4-room HDB flats, being most sellable at around 46% of all flats sold (HDB annual report, 2001/2002).

Hence, Chapter 1 is organized in five sections in which the first section provides the introduction and rationale. The next (second) section discusses the related literature review concerning the demand and supply sides of public housing, locally and abroad. The third section examines the methodological approach of the Chapter 1 and Keynes' general theory. The concept of system dynamics is also introduced. Section four presents the analysis and validation of the system dynamics macroeconomic model for public housing and scenario analysis for policy implications. Lastly, section five concludes the Chapter's findings.

The Related Literature

There has been limited studies on the structural and dynamic aspects of public housing in Singapore, even though several studies highlight specific public housing policy measures, involving homeownership rules, subsidized pricing policy, affordability, choice behavior and general demand stimulus from public housing construction. According to Lim *et. Al.* (1985), it can be argued that a potential adverse effect of the public housing policy of full homeownership, is the excessive investment in housing. On the basis of housing affordability measured by a CPF member's ability to pay for the purchase of his HDB flat in 1985, it is found then that most dual-income households in Singapore are able to pay for the purchase of a HDB flat through the household's CPF contributions, because more than 80% of a household's accumulated and continued CPF contributions as well as CPF savings, can be used for the purchase of a HDB flat then (CPF Board annual report 1985-1986). With the provision of stable and affordably priced HDB flats, the home ownership policy has acted to reduce general price inflation during Singapore's period of rapid economic growth and excess demand in the 1960s to early 2000.

Meen (2003) highlights that in the late eighties, when a boom in United Kingdom (UK) house prices is observed to coincide with a boom in the macro economy, the relationship between housing and the macro economy did become an important subject of public debate. The literature in recent years identifies several ways in which housing markets affect the macro economy in both the demand and supply sides of the economy. Balchin (1995) reiterates that the economics of house building are predominantly demand determined. It can be argued that Singapore's successful experience in public housing is largely influenced by economic development. The relationship between controlled pricing adjustments for new public housing flats and the ability of household-buyers to pay can be examined, with the likely result that the widespread implementation of the HDB's public housing construction programme has inter alia resolved the acute housing shortage prior to 1960. Such a result has produced several welfare advantages like income generation, economic stabilization and improved income redistribution. The effectiveness of Singapore's public housing programme is largely attributable to robust and sustainable economic growth. In addition, the provision of adequate funds and the required statutory powers for the HDB, are imperative for public housing's effectiveness.

Based on the new town concept of Fig 1A, each HDB town is designed to be self-sustainable. Helmed by a hierarchy of commercial developments, ranging from a town center to precinct-level outlets, there is no need to venture out of town to meet the most common needs of residences. Employment can be found in industrial estates located within several towns. Educational, health care, and recreational needs are also taken care of with the provision of schools, hospitals, parks, sports complexes, and so on. HDB new towns are sub-divided into neighborhoods, with most neighborhoods served by a neighborhood commercial center. There are as many as nine neighborhoods to as little as two, depending on town size. Except for the older towns, estates and consolidated towns, most towns use the first digit of their block numbers to indicate the neighborhood in which the block is located in. Each neighborhood is composed of multiple precincts, which are built on the concept of promoting communal exchanges and which are more secure. While older precincts may merely involve dividing rows of identical blocks in relatively close proximity without any other real interaction with each other, newer precincts are designed to physically envelop a common space, or centered around some kind of communal facility such as a multi-storey carpark. While precinct boundaries may be difficult to physically distinguish in older precincts, they are usually obvious in newer precincts through the physical layout of the block and their unique architectural design. Newer precincts (and upgraded older precincts) also often adopt fanciful names reminiscent of private developments to lend an air of class and belonging, although these names are often not used in reality since they are sometimes not displayed and are not part of official addresses.

Fig. 1A. HDB New Town Structural Model Plan

Source: Author, TAN Eng Khiam; 2012 and 2020

The corresponding land uses in terms of the HDB New Town Planning and Site Standards are summarized and presented in Table 1A. The Table spells out generous enough standards at the town, neighborhood and precinct levels in terms of the number of planning units, of dwelling units per planning unit, of population size per planning unit and of the land area per planning unit.

Table 1A. HDB New Town Planning and Site Standards

Table 1 Hierarchy of planning levels in a new town				
Planning level	No. of planning units	No. of dwelling units per planning unit	Population per planning unit	Land area per planning unit (ha)
Town	1	25,000–50,000	125,000–250,000	625
Neighbourhood	5–6	4000–6000	20,000–30,000	80–100
Precinct	6–7	500–1000	2500–5000	10–15

Source: Author, TAN Eng Khiam; 2012 and 2020

The HDB Precinct

The Housing and Development Board (HDB) precincts are clusters of public housing blocks arranged as a single unit. Comprising an average of 10 blocks per precinct, they are collectively grouped into up to nine neighborhoods per new town. HDB is the sole public housing planner, designer and builder in the city-state, adopting the precinct concept as early as 1978, based on the understanding that social interaction and community bonding can be optimized in a smaller planning unit, as compared to a full neighborhood. Precincts are planned to evoke a stronger sense of security although they are not physically fenced, and do not restrict movements for residents or outsiders in any physical way. Tampines New Town is the first new town to be planned according to this precinct approach in 1980. The approach persists in subsequent application of the model in other towns through to the present, although some modifications are noted in terms of precinct size and physical configuration.

Rising usage of multistorey carpark like in Fig 1B allows flexibility in the provision of open spaces for each precinct, and in the configuration of blocks to separate human and vehicular traffic. While older new towns are not built according to the precinct approach, they are planned and built in batches in the same manner as the precincts. Major town redevelopment and upgrading plans like the Main Upgrading Program and the Interim Upgrading Program in older estates like Queenstown, Toa Payoh and Bukit Merah from the 1990s, involve the enhancement of the precinct approach, including physical upgrading to collective groups of blocks, the re-configuration of public spaces around them, and the possible christening of names to these estates. In other cases, old groups of blocks are completely demolished and rebuilt under the 'Selective *En Bloc* Redevelopment Scheme', encouraging the evolution of such older towns towards the precinct approach.

Fig. 1B. Multi-Storey Carpark Found At Newer HDB Estates In Singapore

Source: Author, 2020

The HDB Block Design

Each public housing block is planned and designed to be a vertical community, with common areas built into the design like in Fig 1C to promote social interaction. Void decks refer to the first level, which are often left devoid of housing units, thus the word "void". These open, sheltered spaces are intentionally left empty to offer convenient spaces for communal activities like weddings, funerals, parties, bazaars and even as polling stations. Selected blocks feature a single stand-alone shop, often referred to as "Mama shops" to provide convenient doorstep service. Other common facilities built in void decks may include 'Resident Committee' facilities and offices, kindergartens, medical centers, Neighborhood Police Posts and fire posts. Older flats have common corridors, some of which may run across the length of slab blocks. Considered public property, older flats are subjected to rules to prevent homeowners from occupying and restricting movement, with exception of flats at far ends of corridors, which may be purchased and incorporated as parts of the corridors into the flats from the HDB. While such corridors are welcome for being the default interaction areas for neighbors and their children, and the added sense of security owing to their open-nature, issues of privacy can crop up and resulting in more contemporary blocks featuring far less units per corridor. Larger units like the 5-room flats are commonly housed in 'Point blocks' that are featured as only four units per floor.

**Fig. 1C. Neighbors In An HDB Block
Usually Share A Common Corridor**

Source: Author, 2020

Early HDB blocks tend to be of a single standard slab design of uniform height, typically averaging 12 stories and arranged equidistant from each other. Blocks of varied heights were subsequently introduced to reduce the uniformity and to cater to differing tastes, like the 4-storey block and the 25-storey point-block. Occasionally, a single block of highly unique design would be built to serve as landmarks like the 14-storey Forfar House (or Block 39) in Queenstown, which is the tallest residential building in Singapore upon its completion in 1956, then Block 53 in Toa Payoh that had a unique 3-sided design and Block 259 in Ang Mo Kio with an unusual circular clover-leaf-like design. The slanting roofs of several blocks in Potong Pasir were considered revolutionary and became instant landmarks for the estate till this day. Today, HDB blocks tend to amalgamate the point and slab block of the former Singapore Improvement Trust (SIT) designs, featuring taller blocks but with slightly more units of about 6-8 units per floor. The façades of public housing blocks evolve over time. While the SIT blocks occasionally feature Art Deco designs, the first HDB blocks are typically plan and standardized. After the initial rush to mass build flats in the 1960s however, varying façades began to appear in subsequent decades, initially only through subtle variations such as colored tiles, but which became full-scaled multi-colored paintwork complete with bright motifs from the 1990s. After several elaborate designs, some of which subsequently presented logistical headaches during maintenance, more subdued and contemporary designs began to emerge from the 2000s. For hanging out clothes, residents use bamboo sticks and hang them out of the window clipped onto the pole supports. For blocks built in the late 1990s to mid-2000s, HDB made bamboo pole holders so that hanging clothes out would be safer. For blocks built in the mid-2000s to present, HDB issued all flats with items that residents can clip their clothes on without bamboo poles.

The HDB Flat Types

There are several types of public and semi-public housing available, classified on the number of rooms and flat size, as summarized in

Table 1B. Flat size is denoted by the terms like 4-room or 5-room, and is based on the number of bedrooms inclusive of the living room. Newer 5-room apartments come with only three bedrooms and a dining room. A 3-room flat has two bedrooms in about 70 m² (750 sq ft). A 4-room flat has three bedrooms with about 90 m² (970 sq ft) of space. A 5-room is about 110 m² (1,200 sq ft). Some have an extra room that is used as a study while others have a dining area. An executive apartment has three bedrooms and separate dining and living rooms, with 150 m² (1,600 sq ft) of space. The largest HDB flats (in terms of floor area) ever built are the 2-storey, 'executive maisonettes' built in the 1990s which have a floor area ranging from 160 - 190 m², but which are currently no longer constructed. Semi-public housing like the 'executive maisonette' is governed under HUDC last time instead of HDB and have a much larger floor area. Some newer HDB developed flats in new towns include condominium-like finishes.

Table 1B. The Early HDB Flat Types

Flat type	Typical size	Typical layout	Status
1-Room Emergency	23 m² (250 sq ft)		No longer built
1-Room Improved	33 m² (360 sq ft)		No longer built
2-Room Emergency	37 m² (400 sq ft)		No longer built
2-Room Standard	41 m² (440 sq ft)		No longer built
2-Room Improved	45 m² (480 sq ft)		No longer built
3-Room Standard	54 m² (580 sq ft)		No longer built
3-Room Improved	60 m² (650 sq ft)		No longer built
3-Room New Generation	69 m² (740 sq ft)		No longer built
3-Room Model 'A'	75 m² (810 sq ft)		Derivatives still being built
3-Room Simplified	65 m² (700 sq ft)		No longer built

Source: Author, TAN EK; 2012 and 2020

Ownership and Rental

More than 80% of Singapore's population live in HDB flats, with 95% of them owning their HDB flat. HDB Flats in Singapore are sold on a 99-year lease agreement. The remainder are rental flats reserved for those who are unable to afford to purchase the cheapest forms of public housing despite financial support. HDB maintains a quota system of ethnicities through the Ethnic Integration Policy. By ensuring that each block of units are sold to families from ethnicities roughly comparable to the national average, HDB seeks to avoid physical racial segregation and formation of ethnic enclaves common in other multi-racial societies. In practice, while ethnic enclaves are avoided, some towns remained traditionally popular for specific ethnic groups. For instance, towns like Bedok, Tampines and Woodlands have a slightly larger proportion of ethnic Malays above the national average. Partly in response to public sentiment against the alleged formation of "Permanent resident (PR) enclaves", where some flats appear to be dominated by PRs from a single nationality, the HDB introduces the Singapore Permanent Resident Quota on 5 March 2010. Other than Malaysian PRs, which are excluded from the quota owing to their "close cultural and historical similarities with Singaporeans", all other PRs were subject to a cap of 5% PR households per block.

The New HDB Flats

The primary acquisition avenue is through the purchase of new flats directly from the HDB. Over the years, various forms of sale program has been in place, with the current mode of sale known as the Build-To-Order (HDB) program launched in 2001. This is run alongside the Sale of Balance Flats (SBF) exercise which handles the sale of balance flats from earlier BTO exercises, unsold SERS replacement flats and flats which were repossessed by the HDB. The sale of EC and DBSS flats are conducted separately by the respective private developers. Under the current sales schemes, successful applicants for new BTO flats typically have to wait several years before moving in while the flats were built, since the commencement of construction can only occur when the BTO successfully attains 65~70% sales. Applicants, who wish to move in immediately or earlier, required to participate in the SBF exercise (although some flats may still be under construction) or go for Resale Flats.

HDB Flat Affordability

Several local studies emphasize the importance of the affordability of new public housing flats that are sold by the HDB. In particular, the controlled (subsidized) pricing of the 3-room and 4-room HDB flats is readily affordable to the lower income families. One local study is concerned with the utility of the household's demand for public housing, under a dynamic utility optimization behavior model of households. The household is assumed to have prefect knowledge of future economic conditions. The utility model that analyzes household's demand for public housing can be extended to explain the household's decision to forecast public housing demand. The utility model helps to reduce the risks associated with central planning in the supply of public housing. Another local study has evaluated the factors that influence the household's decision to purchase a new public housing flat in Singapore and Hong Kong. Affordability, pricing, waiting time and location are found to be the main factors. On the subject of the financing of public housing flats for home ownership, such financing in Hong Kong largely depends on the banks therein, which charge relatively high interest rates of 9% to 9.5% p.a. Singapore's HDB loans merely charge a relatively low interest rate of around 3% p.a. that substantially enhances the affordability of Singaporean households to purchase public housing flats.

It can be argued that a marketing plan and strategy can well be optimized under marketing research for sold public housing in Singapore, to improve the take-up rate. The most influential factor affecting the demand for public housing may well turn out to be the affordability issue. Nonetheless, Ho *et. al.* (1997) emphasize that successful environmental management is a dynamic one, and that it operates up and down the hierarchy of the government, community, the family and the individual. The outcome of both the state and private participation then consists of high quality and large-scale physical infrastructure and facilities to be provided by the state like public housing, transport, schools, hospitals, public utilities and the recreational amenities. Ho *et. al.* adds that the Singapore government has adopted a balanced approach between environmental management and economic development, to sustain economic growth.

Liu (2002) highlights the interesting observation that given the large scale of public housing development in Singapore and under a high degree of homeownership, public housing activities do not unduly tie-up scarce capital in the aggregate, which would otherwise be available for investment formation. Liu attributes this unique situation to Singapore's strong and regular net domestic savings, non over-investment in HDB flat purchases by households, and the economic spin-offs from public housing through multiplier effects into the economy at large. Liu reiterates that as the world population grows relentlessly, aggravated further by rural-urban migrations in the 20th century, many more megacities are emerging. The threat of the megacity is a pressing issue in a rapidly urbanized Asia, with its huge and teeming population. A mega-city enjoys the concentration of talent, entrepreneurship, opportunities and resources. However, such mega cities are associated with high stress and alienation of nature in the daily lives of people. The unavoidable reality is that the rise of world population in the 20th century is substantial and problematic to resolve. There is the need to re-scrutinize the tools available for planners, to meet the need of massive urbanism in the world today. In such a foregoing light, Liu's 'Constellation City' is conceived.

A Highly Recommended Constellation City

Lui's 'Constellation City' should cope more adequately with the needs of megacities. Such a constellation city is a collection of several fully independent cities within a megacity, each with a population size of around 1.5 million to 2.5 million people and with its own central business district (CBD), new towns, mass rapid transit (MRT) system, cultural and institutional facilities. In close physical proximity, such fully independent cities are connected to one another by the MRT or commuter trains. Among the nearest precedents is the Hague-Rotterdam-Amsterdam cluster, totaling 4 million people. Constellation cities give inhabitants the best of two worlds. By virtue of its size, a constellation city attracts talents, technical progress, high and new technologies and finance to generate powerful synergy. The relative independence of each city within a megacity provides less stressful, convenient and simpler lifestyle. Therefore, and for newly emerging megacities, they should be planned at the outset as constellation cities. New towns are too blunt a tool for such a challenge. Existing megacities should upgrade their regional commercial centers into full-fledged CBD's, carving out land areas surrounding each CBD, to create a city of 1.5 to 2.5 million people. Within each city, there are still regions and new towns. Between cities, there should preferably be green belts.

The Methodological Approach

Chapter 1's main contribution is the introduction of a dynamic structure of public housing demand that adopts an integrated system dynamics and econometric model, through the formulation of a conceptual causal loop framework. Such a conceptual causal loop framework is essentially a comprehensive conceptual cause and effect framework, which is concerned with the feedback processes and the dynamic structure of the demand for new public housing sold in the Singapore context. This integrated dynamic and structural model is unique and innovative in helping to identify the structural demand of new public housing sold but within a dynamic setting. Chapter 1 adopts a comprehensive macroeconomic model involving the multiplier concept and expectation augmentation, that are important in the Keynesian analysis of the economy. The Chapter then examines the formulation of a dynamic and structural public housing macroeconomic (DSPHM) model. The period chosen for Chapter 1 is available for say a sufficiently long period of 18 years between 1984 and 2002 for only demonstration purposes. The data set represents that period's seven key factors (variables):

1. New HDB Flats Sold in Singapore,
2. The Then Prevailing New HDB Flat Prices,
3. HDB Lending Rate,
4. Total GDP Growth,
5. Government Expenditure,
6. Aggregate Investment And
7. Aggregate Consumption.

Secondary data where necessary are sourced from the annual reports of the HDB, the Department of Statistics and Economic Review Survey reports from Singapore's Ministry of Trade and Industry as well as annual reports of the Central Provident Fund Board (CPF Board), under the Ministry of Finance.

The System Dynamics Approach

System dynamics extends control theory to the analysis of industrial systems to analyze economic, social and environmental systems (Richardson 1985). The algorithm of system dynamics can best be leveraged to analyze complex systems where there are multiple sources of uncertainties. One of the most powerful features of the system dynamics lies in its analytic capability that can provide an analytic solution for complex and non-linear systems (Kwak, 1995). System dynamics is designed to be a practical tool that identifies a problem, focusing on feedback processes involved in a system, and makes it useful in devising and testing alternative policies, which resolve the pressing problems that may confront an organization.

(Sterman, 2000). For the foregoing concerns and over the last decade, many top companies, consulting firms, and governmental organizations have used system dynamics to address critical strategic issues. Kwak (1995) reiterates that system dynamics modeling is both a continuum and an iteration of activities that range from the structuring of the conceptual model to the technical requirements. In practice, this continuum can be broadly structured into five main steps as outlined below:

Step one: System Understanding – It begins with the process of deepening the modeler's understanding of a system under study with relevant information, on which the systems dynamics model is conceptualized. The modeler would take a step back in space and time to appreciate the underlying web of ongoing, reciprocal relationships that are cycling to produce the patterns of behaviors that a system is exhibiting.

Step Two: Conceptualization – The translation of the systems perspectives into something more specific that would reflect the implementation viewpoint. At this stage, causal loop diagrams are drawn to show the relationships of the dynamics of the variables involved in the system. The objective is to depict the model to resemble the real world as closely as possible. Usually, more than one generation of causal loop diagrams are developed to arrive at one that is manageable, and such causal loop diagrams should be within the constraints of finite data, while ensuring that the model remains realistic.

Step Three: Model formation and equation simulation – A few variables are organized into a set of equations that characterize the nature of the relationships, as depicted in the casual loop diagrams. Step three also includes assigning numerical values to define the direction and strength of these relationships.

Step Four: Model validation – Model testing and validation are in accordance with the model purpose. Completing this step enables the confirmation that the system loop is 'closed'. It should be noted that in this Chapter 1, model validation is conducted with the ordinary-least-square estimation of eleven estimated equations, eqs (1.1) to (1.11) using time series data, under the subsequent section on the 'DSPHM Model and Equations'. All the eleven equations should attain high goodness-of-fit and the Durbin-Watson test statistic of around 2.0, signifying low serial correlation error (as observed in the Appendix). Principal among these estimated equations would be eq (1.10), where the change in public housing sold is estimated to have a negatively signed relationship with the public housing price variable in a time-lagged form.

Step Five: Policy analysis – the validated model is applied to solve the given problem or to support scenario planning.

The modeling steps two to five in the above outline are deployed in the development of a dynamic and structural public housing (DSPHM) model in the context of Singapore. Among the diverse views concerning "The Great Depression" in the 1920s, Keynes had proposed a profound and seminal thesis, attributing the depression to a speculative boom in production and investment. Therefore, there are more factories and transportation networks that could be used, relative to the prevailing current ability of individuals to pay. The focus is on the "insufficiency of demand" and that the formalism Keynes propounds, enable governments to monitor the crucial components of an economy, and did create a wave of following for Keynes. Arrayed against the Keynes thesis have been economists, who insist that business confidence and not the lack of demand in the aggregate, is the root of economic depression. The corrective course of action is to slash government expenditure to restore private and public investment confidence, for an eventual broad-based economic recovery.

Keynesian General Theory

Keynes explains that the levels of output and employment in the economy are determined by aggregate demand. Agregate demand is the total demand for goods and services in the economy. In microeconomic theory, adjustment in prices, in particular wage and interest rates, would automatically stimulate aggregate demand towards full employment level. Keynes, pointing to the sharp fall in employment and output, argues that whatever the theory, this self-correcting process did not happen. The central point at issue is whether "demand deficiency" is possible.

According to classical economists, the more generally used term for the practice prior to Keynesian *"General Theory"* is that demand deficits are symptoms, not the causes of recessions and economic dislocation and would not happen in a properly functioning market. In classical theory, the two elements of an economic system are believed to produce a state of full employment. First, the push and pull of supply and demand set the price of goods, and that the constant shifting of price would allow the two forces to equalize. Second, when the system produces extra wealth, such wealth can either be saved for future consumption or invested in future production; and that there is a system of supply and demand that affects such a choice as well. The interest rate on savings behaves like the price, equalizing the supply and demand of investment funds. Even in the worst years of the Depression, this theory defines economic collapse as the loss in incentives to produce. The proper solution is then to reduce the price of labor to subsistence levels, causing prices to fall so that buying (and employment) would pick up. Funds not paid out in wages would be available for investment, perhaps in other sectors. Plant closures and layoffs are a necessary but bitter medicine. The other crucial policy is to balance national budgets, either through increased taxation, or, more usually, through slashing expenditures.

Keynesian theory argues that the foregoing classical economics solution and outcomes would exacerbate the underlying problem: by cutting expenditures or raising taxes, the government would be reducing money in circulation, thereby lowering demand. The resultant is that business owners not only lower prices but also reduce output to maintain previous price. According to Keynes, the classical economic analysis offers no way out of a system wide collapse. Lowering wages would remove capital available for investment, since it would reduce expected profits. Instead, consumption would simply be lower so that total demand for goods would drop. Investment in new production would then become more risky and less likely. Keynes argues that once the expectation of lower prices becomes built into assumptions, then it would spiral downward.

Keynesian theory suggests that active government policy can be effective in managing the economy. Keynes advocates counter cyclical fiscal policies i.e. deficit spending when a nation's economy is sluggish and the suppression of inflation in boom times, by raising taxes or cutting back on government spending. Keynesian macroeconomic analysis offers a way of calculating the equilibrium state of an economy, and then defining inflation and recession as departures from equilibrium. Therefore, economic policy can well be guided by such an analysis. Keynesian macroeconomic analysis sharply contrasts with classical economic analysis of government intervention in the economy. Government can raise wages temporarily and therefore expand the demand for goods, stimulating production. However, there is no reason to believe that such wage stimulation would outrun the side effects that discourages investment i.e. the government, which competes with private interests, would be bidding up the wage rate and lead to no overall economic activity expansion. The underlying assumption is that capital is directed to improving productive capacity, for e.g. a large-scale public works program that may well divert capital, therefore "crowding out" new private capital formation to some extent. Two relevant policy implications of Keynesian general theory comprise the following:

o   First, there is the "Keynesian multiplier." In his way of tracking aggregate national production, Keynes argues that increases in consumption do not equal increases in production. The effect on production is always a multiple of the increase in spending. Therefore, a government can stimulate a great deal of new production with each modest outlay.

o   Second, Keynes re-analyzes the effect of interest rate on investment. In the standard model, interest rates determine the supply of funds available for investment. For Keynes, supply depends on the productivity of the system, the very thing that his fiscal proposals are intended to affect. In Keynes re-definition, interest rate depends on the preference that people have about holding onto money, the ratio of money held to the total amount of money in circulation. Such a re-definition opens the possibility of regulating the economy through changes in money supply but Keynes argues that such a view would be relatively ineffective, compared to the use of fiscal policy.

Therefore, Keynes argues that the economy consists of aggregate supply and aggregate demand. Consumer demand is the largest domestic demand source and drives investment demand, which has come out of the profits in supplying consumer demand; and which also serves as the production of capital. Lower profits lead to lower investment, and lower investments lead to lower employment, which leads to lower consumer demand. Keynes argues that the third sector of demand, the government demand, should be used to cushion the shocks of rapid decrease in consumer demand or to buffer hyperinflationary shocks. Keynesian "General theory" relates the government sector to the control of interest rates, and from there, the supply of available investment and consumer demand.

The DSPHM Model

The conceptual causal loop diagram of a dynamic, structural public housing macroeconomic model (DSPHM) is depicted in Fig 1.1. In the formulation of the DSPHM model, it is initially envisaged that the demand for new HDB flats (sold) depends not only on Keynesian aggregate demand, i.e. the demand of an internal economy, but also on consumers' expectations of their future income. Income expectations, in turn, depend on the total income earned by all households, which because of the inclusion of the entire population, is the total output of the economy (gross domestic product, GDP). Thus, the DSPHM model finally envisages the total demand for an open economy to be like Singapore, without exception.

The result is a positive feedback, represented by the consumption multiplier, in which an increase in GDP would boost income and raise consumption; thereby further expanding aggregate demand with a short time lag. Consumer expectations of future income would also adjust to the actual income (GDP) with a delay (i.e. time lag).

The total demand of new flats adjusts with a short delay to the rate of aggregate demand in the economy. A first-order exponential smoothing is assumed, a common autoregressive assumption in many macroeconomic models. As expressed in the following equations, with the initial value of GDP set to its equilibrium value, the aggregate demand (AD). When GDP=AD, the change in GDP is zero:

GDP = INTEGRAL(Change in GDP, AD).....................(1.2)

Change in GDP = (AD-GDP)/Time to Adjust Production......(1.3)

Fig 1.1. The Dynamic Structural Public Housing Macroeconomic (DSPHM) Model

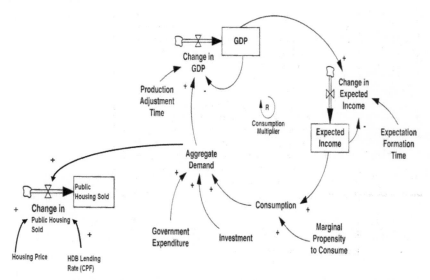

Fig 1: Conceptual Causal Loop Diagram Of The Dynamic Structural Public

Source: Author, 2020. _NB_. *Housing Price in short refers to the Public Housing Price.*

Aggregate demand is the sum of consumption C, government expenditure G, and investment I:

$$AD = C + I + G \dots\dots\dots\dots\dots\dots\dots\dots\dots\dots\dots\dots\dots\dots\dots(1.4)$$

Consumers spend a fraction of their expected income, the Marginal Propensity to Consume (MPC):

$$C = MPC \star \text{Expected Income}\dots\dots\dots\dots\dots\dots\dots\dots\dots\dots$$
(1.5)

, where MPC is the marginal propensity to consume out of expected income.

Keynes assumes that expected income is greater than zero but less than 1 in regard to the least-square relationship between expected income and the GDP. In other words, if the GDP is anticipated to increase by S\$1 in expected income it would spend some, but not all of the increase in aggregate consumer demand. The marginal propensity to sprnd (MPC) is estimated from the coefficient a_o in the following least-square multiple regression analysis (MRA) of equation (1.6).

$$GDP = C + a_o \text{ Consumption} + a_1 \text{ Consumption}_{t-1} + GDP_{t-1} \dots\dots\dots\dots (1.6)$$

Expected income adjusts to actual income, which in the aggregate is the GDP. The 1st order exponential smoothing is again taken to model the adjustment process. The initial value of expected income is set to the GDP, its equilibrium value:

Expected Income $= INTERGAL$ (Change in Expected Income, GDP) $\dots\dots\dots$ (1.7)

Change in Expected Income $= (GDP - \text{Expected Income})/\text{Expectation Formation Time}\dots\dots$ (1.8)

Public housing (i.e. HDB flats) sold adjusts to actual Public Housing Sold but along time lags in eqs (1.9) and (1.10). The initial value of Public Housing Sold is taken to be the current volume sold of say some 800,000 HDB home-ownership flats.

Public Housing Sold = INTERGAL (Change in Public Housing Sold, PHS_{t-dt})....(1.9)

, where PHS is the public housing units sold in time t and dt is the time step increment.

Change in Public Housing Sold = a_0 * DELAY(AD,t) + a_1 * DELAY(HDB Lending Rate,t) - a_2 * DELAY(Housing Price, t) .... (1.10)

, where Housing Price denotes the public housing price of public housing sold.

Eq (1.10) can be re-expressed involving aggregate demand, the HDB Lending Rate and the average HDB Housing Price in equation (1.11). The method of least-squares is deployed in combination with the Cochrane-Orcutt procedure, to correct for the auto regression error in the equation system. (Details of the results of the econometric analyses are provided in the Appendix for reference.)

Public Housing Sold = $C + a_0$ GDP + a_1HDBLendingRate + a_2Housing Price (Ave).... (1.11)

, where Public housing sold = change in the public housing sold.

After the formulation of the foregoing several key equations, a subsequent analysis is carried out to estimate the correlation between GDP in eq (1.6) and the change in public housing sold.

The DSPHM System Dynamics

The DSPHM model depicted in Fig 1.1 represents the model's conceptual framework in conjunction with the required feedback loops. A loop in the causal loop framework in effect depicts the feedback structure of the HDB (public housing) flats sold within the wider macroeconomic framework. The loop is a map that shows the causal links among the key variables of interest, with arrows from a cause to an effect. The effect can be a positive sign or a negative sign at the end of arrow. For the positive sign, the loop is a reinforcing loop (i.e. a positive feedback loop), which can turn into a runaway situation i.e. a loop that is out of control in the extreme situation. For the negative sign, the loop is a negative feedback loop that stabilizes the loop into a steady state to some extent.

On the loops' feedback strategy, the positive sign in a loop dominates some occasion while the negative sign dominates in others. The principle of loop dominance is observed and that a mix in between can occur. Therefore, the loops illustrate the structure of a sector's dynamics at work, i.e. a diagram of the causal loop framework. In addition, stocks and flows that are connected through the loops, emphasize the underlying structure of the DSPHM model. Stocks and flows track accumulations of material, the price and information as they move through a sector (itself a system,). Stocks can represent inventories of a product, debt and employment. Stocks also characterize the state of an economic sector or variable and generate the information (with or without time delays), upon which decisions are based. The decisions then alter the rate of flow, altering the stocks and closing the feedback loops in a system of selected variables of interest. The DSPHM model's feedback loops are readily illustrated in Fig 1.1 in which the dominant reinforcing loop (R) interconnects expected income, aggregate consumption, aggregate demand, change in GDP and GDP itself.

Model Estimation and Policy Analysis

The final DSPHM model is represented as a causal loop flow diagram in Fig 1.2 in terms of the stock and flow structures, the control and feedback structures. This flow diagram interprets the conceptual causal loop diagram of the DSPHM model of Fig 1.1 in terms of a computerized programmable format, to carry out scenario analysis for public housing policy implications. Each scenario is generated using the DSPHM model that is estimated to run a set of forecasts for a long-run period of some 18 years from the present (i.e. time t = 0). The associated set of equations in a software syntax form is provided in the Appendices for reference.

Fig 1.2. Causal Loop Flow Diagram of the DSPHM Model

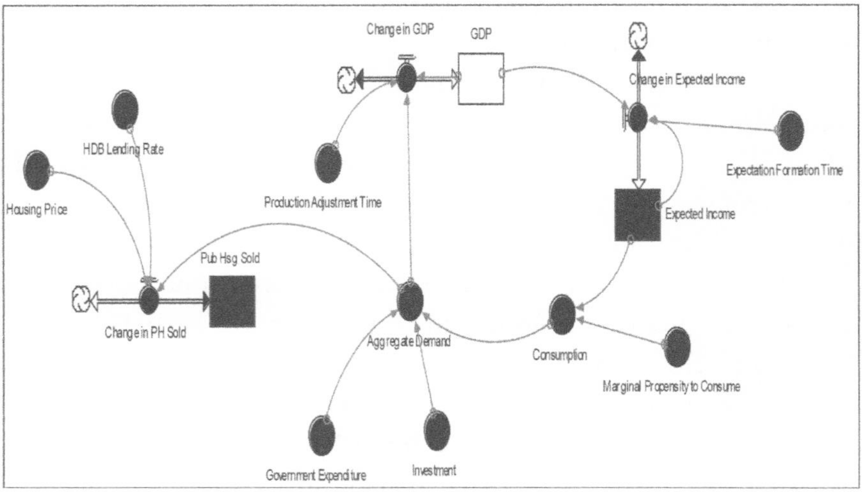

Source: Author and iThink program, 2004 and 2020.

NB. Housing Price in short refers to the Public Housing Price.

The dynamic structure of the demand for new public housing (HDB) flats sold is represented by Fig 1;2's DSPHM model. The model can be adopted for various scenarios to enable policy analysis. The recent decline in the number of new public housing applications of say −26.3% between FY 2000/2001 and FY 2001/2002, is a substantial fall. A key question to pose is whether-or-not the public housing price on the whole and the HDB lending rate, are having an adverse impact on the demand. of the new HDB flats sold? This question can be framed in a first scenario (i.e. a minimal change scenario), which attempts to see how the number of new public housing sold responds, if there is no further increase in the HDB lending rate and the average public housing price. Assuming there is a conjunctural growth in GDP for the next 10 years, then government expenditure and aggregate investment would grow in general in relation to GDP. The results of the first scenario are depicted in Fig 1.3.

Fig 1.3. Scenario 1 – Housing Price and Lending Rate Remaining Unchanged

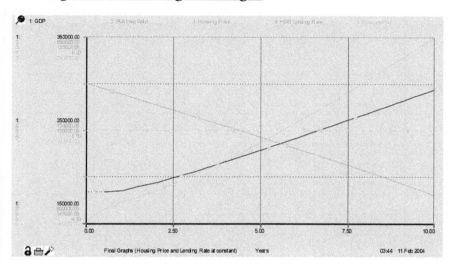

1. GDP, S$ Million per year
2. Public Housing Sold, dwelling units
3. Housing Price, S$ per 4-room flat
4. HDB Lending rate, Percent per annum
5. Consumption, S$ Million per annum

Source: Author and iThink program, 2004 and 2020.

The corresponding forecasts are summarized in Fig 1.3 while Table 1.1 indicates that without further and continuous rise in the HDB lending rate and the average public housing price, then the number of additional new public housing sold would not increase in the aggregate, but would stay below the initialized level of the 800,000 flats sold. The attributable factor is the negative sign relationship between the change in public housing sold and the average public housing price of the 4-room HDB flats. It can be inferred that beyond the optimal point of overwhelming public housing provision in the aggregate, the future supply line of additional new public housing flats would have to rise at a slower pace (and in small doses) at the margin.

Table 1.1. Scenario 1 – Table of the Public Housing Sold vs. Public Housing Price and Lending Rate Remaining Unchanged

Year	GDP	No. of Public Housing	Lending rate	Average price of public housing	Consumption
Initial	183,239,990.00	800,000	5.00	150,000.00	
0	184,519,620.00	788,445.73	5.00	150,000.00	9,794,180.00
1	193,396,560.00	776,891.45	5.00	150,000.00	7,223,920.00
2	203,912,260.00	765,337.18	5.00	150,000.00	8,167,730.00
3	215,854,630.00	753,782.91	5.00	150,000.00	9,379,600.00
4	228,221,660.00	742,228.63	5.00	150,000.00	10,540,550.00
5	241,031,250.00	730,607.54	5.00	150,000.00	11,387,950.00
6	253,968,210.00	718,495.99	5.00	150,000.00	12,016,500.00
7	267,199,650.00	706,055.58	5.00	150,000.00	12,453,750.00
8	280,588,530.00	693,256.45	5.00	150,000.00	12,810,130.00
9	293,825,320.00	680,121.26	5.00	150,000.00	13,036,880.00

Source: Author and iThink program, 2004 and 2020.

The second scenario, which is depicted in Fig 1.4 and presented in Table 1.2, assumes a deregulation scenario in which the GDP would grow at a continuous and gradual rate. HDB is then deemed to review the price of new HDB flats annually, and to adopt the market lending practice of no concessionary lending interest rate for first-time HDB flat buyers, starting from year 2. HDB is envisaged to be opening-up its housing loans to the private banks as a public housing loan privatization policy measure. Such opening-up should benefit private banks with a new line of housing mortgage business, which is substantial, and prompt the banks to perhaps consider a viable mortgage backed securitization (MBS) for such public housing mortgages in the future.

From Fig 1.4 and Table 1.2, it can be observed that the incremental and continuous rise in the HDB lending rate and the average public housing price, have resulted in the number of new public housing sold to gradually fall in the next 5 years. However, after year 6, new public housing demand falls off sharply through to year 10. This may well indicate that despite gradual GDP expansion, the resultant moderate price rise of new HDB flats and the possible, viable privatization of public housing mortgages would occur. Singaporean households are then still able to afford the purchase of a new flat from the HDB.

Fig 1.4. Scenario 2 – Fluctuating Public Housing Price and Lending rate)

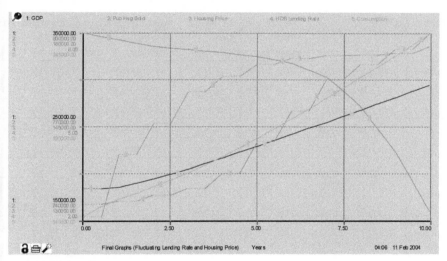

1. GDP, S$ Million per year
2. Public Housing Sold, dwelling units
3. Housing Price, S$ per 4-room flat
4. HDB Lending rate, Percent per annum
5. Consumption, S$ Million per annum

Source: Author and iThink program, 2004 and 2020.

However, by the end of the medium term (around year 6) when private lending rates reach as high as 7.5%, then the demand for new public housing dampens and chokes off. This may well revive the rental HDB market that is consistent with recent government policy changes, like the HDB rule that permits flat owners to rent out their public housing, in part or whole (Reuters News, 2003). The market for transitional housing may well develop in the longer term as more households are engaged in the regional and international business ventures abroad, as well as foreign direct investments as the accompanying inflow of expatriates continue to revisit Singapore.

Table 1.2. Scenario 2 – Table on Public Housing Sold vs Incremental Adjustment to Public Housing Price and Private Bank Lending Rate

Year	GDP	No. of Public Housing	Lending rate	Average price of public housing	Consumption
Initial	183,239,990.00	800,000	2.50	135,000.00	147,109,990.00
0	184,519,620.00	797,891.82	2.60	140,500.00	156,067,360.00
1	193,396,560.00	795,783.64	2.80	145,500.00	162,674,070.00
2	203,912,260.00	794,767.56	3.00	150,500.00	170,143,940.00
3	215,854,630.00	793,834.50	3.50	153,000.00	178,722,150.00
4	228,221,660.00	792,521.44	4.50	155,000.00	188,362,120.00
5	241,031,250.00	790,488.53	5.50	156,000.00	198,777,080.00
6	253,968,210.00	785,868.45	6.50	156,500.00	209,766,890.00
7	267,199,650.00	776,398.42	7.00	156,600.00	221,156,590.00
8	280,588,530.00	761,994.03	7.50	156,850.00	232,872,230.00
9	293,825,320.00	742,634.21	8.00	157,850.00	244,795,240.00

Source: Author and iThink program, 2004 and 2020.

Concluding Remarks

Public housing, i.e. the Housing & Development Board (HDB) housing, in Singapore evolves from the provision of basic housing shelter needs to meeting the rising aspirations of Singapore's resident population, for a better quality of life. HDB's roles in mortgage financing and social management have gone beyond the normal ambit of public housing functions to address changing housing needs. Singapore's success in housing around 85% of the resident population in HDB flats enables around 83% of Singapore's resident population to own their HDB flats. It has therefore prompted new directions for public housing policy.

Chapter 1 develops a unique and state-of-the-art dynamic, structural public housing macroeconomic model (DSPHM), based on an open economy for several key macroeconomic variables, actual and expected, as well as the demand for new HDB flats sold. Through scenario analysis in scenario planning format, Chapter 1 readily adopts the DSPHM for simulating two scenarios, namely a "no change" first scenario and a public housing "deregulation" second scenario. In both scenarios, there is the same GDP expansion over the next 10 years.

The first scenario is conclusive that beyond the optimal point of overwhelming public housing provision, the supply line of additional new HDB flats must rise at a slower pace (and in small doses) at the margin. This optimal point is favorable from an allocative efficiency perspective of scarce public housing resources. The second scenario is conclusive that the deregulation of public housing continues to sustain household affordability for new HDB flats even into the medium term (i.e. the next 6 years) at the least, and before private mortgage interest rates start to rise to become excessive. This second "deregulation" scenario also indicates the possible emergence of several new policy measures for the Singapore public housing sector – a rental HDB housing policy measure, privatization of HDB mortgages as a new policy measure, and private market securitization of HDB mortgages as a further new policy measure.

Acknowledgement: *The Author wish to gratefully acknowledge the initial work carried out for Chapter 1 by* Ms Wong Kah Feng, *a graduate of the NUS Department of Real Estate, and in consultation with Honorary Professor (University of Hertfordshire, Hatfield, UK), Dr HO Kim Hin / David, during their meaningful brain storming sessions before Professor HO retired from the NUS SDE Departments of Real Estate and Building in May 2019.*

Appendix

Estimated AREG Results

MODEL: MOD_1

Model Description:

Variable: GPD
Regressors: CONSUMPT
               V5
               V3

95.00 percent confidence intervals will be generated.

Split group number: 1 Series length: 18
Number of cases skipped at beginning because of missing values: 1

Termination criteria:
Parameter epsilon: .001
Maximum number of
iterations: 10

Initial values:

Estimate of Autocorrelation Coefficient

Rho   0

Cochrane-Orcutt Estimates

Multiple R	.99454637
R–Squared	.98912248
Adjusted R–Squared	.98661228
Standard Error	4381.0556
Durbin–Watson	2.2989081

Analysis of Variance:

	DF	Sum of Squares	Mean Square
Regression	3	22689293083.3	7563097694.4
Residuals	13	249517426.3	19193648.2

Variables in the Equation:

	B	SEB	BETA	T	SIG T
CONSUMPT	1.0294	1.66947	.1340861	.6166021	.54814377
V5	-2.6632	1.50975	-.3120449	-1.7640256	.10119738
V3	1.1638	.12985	1.1618472	8.9629060	.00000063
CONSTANT	4753.4153	3992.16489	.	1.1906861	.25506507

—

Iteration History:

Iteration	Rho	SE Rho	DW	MSE
1	-.28162128	.26612453	2.1823941	17806731.6
2	-.36644659	.25805737	2.1427232	17430175.0

3	-.37933770	.25662048	2.1369968	17395607.7
4	-.38097774	.25643352	2.1362765	17391644.3
5	-.38118100	.25641029	2.1361874	17391159.9
6	-.38120610	.25640741	2.1361764	17391100.2
7	-.38120920	.25640706	2.1361750	17391092.9
8	-.38120959	.25640702	2.1361749	17391091.9

Conclusion of estimation phase.

Estimation terminated at iteration number 9 because:

All parameter estimates changed by less than .001

FINAL PARAMETERS:

Estimate of Autocorrelation Coefficient

| Rho | -.38120963 |
| Standard Error of Rho | .25640701 |

Cochrane-Orcutt Estimates

Multiple R	.99760324
R-Squared	.99521222
Adjusted R-Squared	.99361629
Standard Error	4170.2628
Durbin-Watson	2.1361748

Analysis of Variance:

	DF	Sum of Squares	Mean Square
Regression	3	43379975100.4	14459991700.1
Residuals	12	208693102.0	17391091.8

Variables in the Equation:

	B	SEB	BETA	T	SIG T
CONSUMPT	.91456	1.51815	.1157552	.602415	.55810979
V5	-3.21668	1.46401	-.3634299	-2.197177	.04838126

V3	1.24471	.09628	1.2345925	12.928576	.00000000
CONSTANT	2882.74390	2763.07757	.	1.043309	.31736819

The following new variables are being created:

Name	Label
FIT_2	Fit for GPD from AREG, MOD_1
ERR_2	Error for GPD from AREG, MOD_1
LCL_2	95% LCL for GPD from AREG, MOD_1
UCL_2	95% UCL for GPD from AREG, MOD_1
SEP_2	SE of fit for GPD from AREG, MOD_1

REG

MODEL: MOD_8

Model Description:

Variable: CHANGE_O
Regressors: HOUSING
                   AVEPHPL1
                   HDBLEL2
                   CHPHSDF
                   GDPL5

95.00 percent confidence intervals will be generated.

Split group number: 1 Series length: 14
Number of cases skipped at beginning because of missing values: 5

Termination criteria:
Parameter epsilon: .001
Maximum number of iterations: 10

Initial values:

Estimate of Autocorrelation Coefficient

Rho   0

Cochrane-Orcutt Estimates

Multiple R	.85659105
R-Squared	.73374822
Adjusted R-Squared	.54356838
Standard Error	4698.0022
Durbin-Watson	1.0471079

Analysis of Variance:

	DF	Sum of Squares	Mean Square
Regression	5	425773886.3	85154777.3
Residuals	7	154498574.5	22071224.9

Variables in the Equation:

	B	SEB	BETA	T	SIG T
HOUSING	.13409	.07372	.71271274	1.8190360	.11172624
AVEPHPL1	-.05574	.10443	-.32811075	-.5337234	.61005419
HDBLEL2	2130.57695	2855.01974	.17939190	.7462565	.47981894
CHPHSDF	.48335	.12497	.75610057	3.8675777	.00615091
GDPL5	-.04802	.11287	-.20259210	-.4254694	.68326931
CONSTANT	-13960.08460	12015.85741	.	-1.1618051	.28339226

Iteration History:

Iteration	Rho	SE Rho	DW	MSE
1	.39126184	.34783292	1.3362124	19198070.9
2	.57481550	.30928192	1.5251216	17845417.0
3	.63520746	.29191767	1.5892335	17689584.2

4	.64886484	.28759456	1.6032873	17677786.6
5	.65169155	.28668004	1.6061658	17676480.7
6	.65226751	.28649286	1.6067510	17676263.0
7	.65238451	.28645480	1.6068698	17676220.7
8	.65240826	.28644707	1.6068939	17676212.2
9	.65241309	.28644550	1.6068988	17676210.5

Conclusion of estimation phase.

Estimation terminated at iteration number 10 because:

Maximum number of iterations was exceeded.

FINAL PARAMETERS:

Estimate of Autocorrelation Coefficient

Rho	.65241406
Standard Error of Rho	.28644518
Cochrane-Orcutt Estimates	
Multiple R	.94471104
R-Squared	.89247895
Adjusted R-Squared	.78495789
Standard Error	4204.3085
Durbin-Watson	1.6068998

Analysis of Variance:

	DF	Sum of Squares	Mean Square
Regression	5	880328738.8	176065747.8
Residuals	6	106057260.9	17676210.2

Variables in the Equation:

	B	SEB	BETA	T	SIG T
HOUSING	.11638	.06387	.26362033	1.8219627	.11829820
AVEPHPL1	-.10921	.07524	-.26305830	-1.4514990	.19684168
HDBLEL2	4630.27538	2173.48756	.34881577	2.1303436	.07717272
CHPHSDF	.46633	.07916	.81953553	5.8912502	.00106146

GDPL5	.02611	.11109	.03537357	.2350875	.82195864
CONSTANT	–20802.47495	12392.14915	.	–1.6786818	.14422038

The following new variables are being created:

Name	Label
FIT_8	Fit for CHANGE_O from AREG, MOD_8
ERR_8	Error for CHANGE_O from AREG, MOD_8
LCL_8	95% LCL for CHANGE_O from AREG, MOD_8
UCL_8	95% UCL for CHANGE_O from AREG, MOD_8
SEP_8	SE of fit for CHANGE_O from AREG, MOD_8

DSPHM Model Equations In Programmable Format under the "iThink" Program

Expected_Income(t) = Expected_Income(t - dt) + (Change_in_ Expected_Income) ⋆ dt
INIT Expected_Income = GDP

INFLOWS:
Change_in_Expected_Income = (GDP - Expected_Income)/ Expectation_Formation_Time
GDP(t) = GDP(t - dt) + (Change_in_GDP) ⋆ dt
INIT GDP = Aggregate_Demand

INFLOWS:
Change_in_GDP = (Aggregate_Demand - GDP)/Production_ Adjustment_Time
Households(t) = Households(t - dt) + (- Change_in_Households) ⋆ dt
INIT Households = {Place initial value here...}

OUTFLOWS:
Change_in_Households = {Place right hand side of equation here...}
Aggregate_Demand = Consumption+Government_ Expenditure+Investment

Consumption = Expected_Income*Marginal_Propensity_to_ Consume

Expectation_Formation_Time = 2

Government_Expenditure = 90+step(10,1)

Investment = 10

Marginal_Propensity_to_Consume = .8

Production_Adjustment_Time = 1.

THE MACROECONOMIC DYNAMICS OF ASSISTED HOME OWNERSHIP IN SINGAPORE AND HONG KONG

Government policies tend to be tenure biased in many countries, often favoring ownership, as for instance in the provision of discounts on the sale of social housing (Forrest and Murie, 1988; Bacher, 1993; Pickvance, 1994; Hays, 1994; Balchin, 1996; Ching and Tyabji, 1991). Singapore and Hong Kong are two of the best examples offered. In Hong Kong, the Home Ownership Scheme (HOS) is launched in 1978 by the Housing Authority (HA), along with another scheme known as the Private Sector Participation Scheme (PSPS). The PSPS shares the same eligibility requirement as the HOS but with the only difference that those flats under the PSPS are constructed by private real estate developers, and then sold at a concessionary price set by the government (Lee, 2003). According to La Grange & Pretorius (2000), encouraging the transfer of wealthier public tenants to assisted homeownership, to accommodate needy families and so reduce the length of the queue for public housing, has been one of the goals of public housing policy since the mid 1980s. La Grange's (1998) study suggests that public ownership housing are "massively oversubscribed" by families renting in the private sector. The HOS in effect shifts housing resources allocation from the well-off public residential household (PRH) tenants to the more needy family-households in the process, and so enabling such households to own their flats (Yeung and Wong, 2003). Apparently, the HOS has been working thus far, as 189,500 PRH flats have been recovered by both the HOS/PSPS and related schemes. The mechanism of such schemes is that the well-off PRH tenants have either to pay a required double rent or to shift to HOS/PSPS housing.

Owners of HOS flats in Hong Kong are not allowed to sell their homes in the open market within a certain period. Before 1999, the HOS flats can only be resold to the HA at the original selling price in the first 5 years. However, in the next 5 years, the HOS flats can be resold to the HA at a discounted price, based on the prices of private properties at the time. The restrictions are modified in 1999, permitting buyers of HOS/PSPS flats to resell them in the open market in 5 years instead of 10 years. Also, the HA was only willing to buy back the HOS/PSPS flat at the original selling price within the first 2 years instead of 5 years. Thereafter, the HOS/PSPS flats can be resold either in the second-hand HOS/PSPS market, which implies a lower selling price, or in the open market. Unlike the condition imposed on Singapore's Housing and Development Board (HDB) flats, a premium is paid to the Hong Kong government *before* the transaction if an HOS/PSPS owner decides to go for the second option (the open market). On face value, there is a risk-sharing mechanism on the HOS/PSPS flats especially when property prices are falling. However, the arrangement on the premium acts as a barrier for HOS/PSPS owners to sell the flats in the open market.

The arrangement of mortgages for Singapore's HDB flats and Hong Kong's HOS/PSPS flats are different as well. In Hong Kong, mortgages for the HOS/PSPS flats are generally obtained through banks, grounded on the best lending rate or the prime interest rate at the time. Naturally, the mortgages in Hong Kong would be much more costly than in Singapore, given Hong Kong's higher property prices and interest rates. Singapore has a longer mortgage term than Hong Kong, where the mortgages last 20 years in most cases. In Singapore, by contrast, a Housing and development Board (HDB) flat buyer can obtain a loan from the HDB for as long as 65 years minus the age of the applicant. The implication is a negative relationship between the age of applicants and the duration of the mortgage terms. The longest term under such a mortgage term policy can be 44 years, owing to HDB's minimum permitted age of the applicant of 21 years. Such a mortgage term policy insinuates that the younger the applicant, the lower the cost of admission for the HDB home purchasing in Singapore. Table 2.1 summarizes the key differences between Singapore's 'HDB Home Ownership Flat Policy' and Hong Kong's 'HA HOS/PSPS'.

Table 2.1. Arrangements of the HDB & HOS/PSPS Schemes

HDB (Singapore)	HOS/PSPS (Hong Kong)
1. Sold freely in the market.	1. Only sold to HA in the first 5 years. Resold to the market thereafter.
2. Loans obtained from HDB	2. Loans provided by banks in general.
3. No risk-sharing	3. Risk sharing (see point 1)
4. Able to use CPF as payments for an HDB flat (up to 16% of the property price).	4. No arrangement thus far in the use of MPF for home buying.
5. 20% down payment rate.	5. Down payment as low as 5% of selling price.
6. Mortgage term depends on the age of applicants.	6. Mortgage term fixed at 20 years in general.
7. Constructed solely by the government.	7. Constructed by the government (HOS) and private developers (PSPS).
8. Resale levy required after the resale of HDB flats.	8. Premium required before any transaction of HOS/PSPS takes place.

Source: Housing Development Board (HDB), Singapore, Housing Authority (HA), Hong Kong; 2002, 2004 and 2020.

There is another noticeable difference in the case of Hong Kong. Since 1995, a private property purchaser is required to put 30% of the selling price as down payment when he/she buys a private property. The reason for the relatively high down payment rate is the underlying Hong Kong government's measure to curb speculations in the property market, after realizing the huge spike in property prices a year before. Nevertheless, household applicants for HOS/PSPS flats in Hong Kong are required to put as low as 5% of the selling price as down payment. In short, it is a lot easier for Hong Kong citizens to obtain their HOS/PSPS flats once they pass through the income requirements, because the cost of assisted homeownership is much lower than that of a private property ownership.

To sum up and on the one hand, the Singapore government provides a more direct form of assistance for HDB home ownership, via mortgage loans at concessionary rates and high-quality subsidized housing. On the other hand, the Hong Kong government only constructs subsidized dwellings for its eligible population, while leaving the mortgage business to private enterprises. Owing to the different institutional settings of the two housing schemes between Singapore and Hong Kong, the objectives of the case studies are slightly different. In Singapore's case and given the control in the mortgage business by the government, one may ask what would happen once the mortgage loan market is completely open under various macroeconomic conditions. In Hong Kong's case and inspired by its government's decision to cease the sale of HOS/PSPS flats in 2003, Chapter 2 attempts to find out whether or not the demand for new HOS/PSPS flats under different macroeconomic conditions is economically justified. Hence, the Chapter is divided into five sections. The first section provides the related literature on the relationship between macroeconomic factors and assisted ownership housing. The next (second) section discusses the methodologies adopted in the Singapore and Hong Kong studies are introduced and compared. The third section discusses the scenarios for this Chapter. The fourth section provides the results obtained from the scenario analyses and their implications. The fifth section concludes the Chapter.

The Related Literature

As previous studies on assisted ownership housing primarily emphasize the choice of ownership itself and in other words, tenure decisions, then most of the studies have tried to explain the reasons affecting the rate of home ownership in an area. It is stated by Saunders (1990) that ontological explanations typically commence from the premise that ownership is the innately preferred tenure form while affordability and preferences are secondary considerations in tenure decisions. At least many governments share similar ideas, as ownership has been pursued as a desirable social objective since the mid-1970s, formalized with a 'Long Term Housing Strategy in 1987' (Housing Branch, 1987). However, it is argued by La Grange & Pretorius (2000) that the "ontological perspectives of home-ownership do not sit easily with a highly sophisticated market economy."

Conversely, from the consumers' point of view, strong preferences for homeownership are closely related to many households' retirement strategy, despite major affordability constraints. Simply put, homeownership is favored as a form of retirement saving (Lee, 1996). This notion of homeownership as a form of investment is supported by La Grange & Pretorius (2000) in that the high rates of ownership can be explained by two factors that are introduced by investment preferences. The first factor is the high returns on residential investment (the demand factor). The second factor is the low and often negative user cost of housing capital over extended periods, for most of the past decade (the financing mechanisms). The investment factors are relating to and rather independent from the general financial sector institutions and the foregoing regulatory imperatives identified. The insinuation is the impact of market factors on tenure choice decisions. Regarding the impact of general economic conditions on homeownership, Meen (2003) highlights that in the late 1980s, when a boom in United Kingdom (UK) house prices coincided with a boom in the macro economy as a whole, the relationship between housing and the macro economy did become an important research subject. Such booms affect both the demand and supply sides of the UK economy. Balchin, Bull and Kieve (1995) even reiterate that the economics of house building are predominantly demand determined.

Some other researches, though limited, have attempted to explore the interactions between the public housing market and various economic factors. Ong and Sing (2002) found that the prices of private housing and the prices of public housing determined in the open market are interrelated. The reason is that the public housing market is more regulated and is consequently less responsive to economic forces, as noted by the market forces hypothesis. The private housing market has the tendency to respond to changes first and it results in the returns in the private market leading those in the public housing market. Furthermore, the upgrading hypothesis states that homeowners are enabled to upgrade to private property due to strong enough capital appreciation on their public flats (Lum, 1996; Ong, 1999). Because of such enabling upgrading, the price changes in the Singapore private housing market should be affected by those in the public housing market. Chua (2000) mentions that public housing is considered an "investment of a large part of [flat-owners'] long term savings", or simply, a source of wealth.

Nevertheless, one of the major problems concerning the literature of public housing dynamics is that most studies primarily focus on the British and North American housing markets (see the review given by Meen and Andrew, 1998), while only a few studies, which look at the Asian housing markets, are highly diversified and much different from the housing markets of those developed countries. Therefore, the inferences from the previous literature are not directly applicable to the Asian housing markets (Wong, 1998; Tu, 2004). Hence, the main theme of Chapter 2 is to bridge to knowledge gap of the possible ramifications on assisted ownership housing demand, subject to different economic conditions.

The Methodology in Brief

Chapter 2 adopts a comprehensive macroeconomic model involving the multiplier concept that is important in the Keynesian analysis of the economy, for both the cases of Singapore and Hong Kong. The Chapter examines the formulation of a dynamic and structural public housing macroeconomic (DSPHM) model. However, it should be noted that due to the differences in the institutional settings of the respective housing policies and the questions that need to be answered, there would be slight differentiations in the model presented for this Chapter. Before entering the discussion of the models used in the Chapter, the two primary concepts of the model would be introduced in the following sub sections.

The System Dynamics Approach

System dynamics applies control theory to the analysis of industrial systems and is being extended to analyze economic, the social and environmental systems. The algorithm of system dynamics can best be leveraged to analyze complex systems where there are multiple sources of uncertainties. According to Lyneis (2000), system dynamics models can provide more reliable forecasts of short- to mid-term trends than usual statistical models, and better decisions can be reached. It also helps to understand the causes of industry behavior, thus allowing early detection of changes in industry structure and factor determination, to which forecast behavior are significantly sensitive. Furthermore, it allows reasonable scenarios to be determined and analyzed as inputs to decisions and policies.

System dynamics is also designed to be a practical tool that identifies a problem, focusing on feedback processes involved in the system, and makes it useful in devising as well as testing alternative policies that alleviate the pressing problems they may confront organization (Sterman, 2000). It have been proven in other industries that the use of well-calibrated structural models, such as system dynamics simulators, can do a reasonable job of forecasting in situations where regression and trend forecasts have proven their individual weaknesses (Sterman, 1988; Sterman, 2000; Lyneis, 2000), but the use of such theories in direct real estate markets has been very sporadic. Vennix (1996) offers a case study to illustrate the dynamics of the housing market from the perspective of housing associations. It is argued by Tonelli, Cowley and Boyd (2004) that system dynamics will accentuate the forecasting module by reflecting the casual relationships and dynamic interaction of market variables better, surpassing the existing static models that mainly rely on multiple regression equations.

The DSPHM Model: A Study of Singapore's Public Ownership Housing

The conceptual causal loop diagram of a dynamic structural public housing macroeconomic model (DSPHM) is depicted in Fig 2.1. In the formulation of the DSPHM model, it is envisaged that the demand for new HDB flats depends on consumers' expectations of their future income. Income expectations, in turn, depend on the total income of all households, which because of the inclusion of the entire population, is the total output of the economy (GDP). The result is a positive feedback, represented by the consumption multiplier, in which an increase in GDP would boost income and raise consumption, thus further expanding aggregate demand with a time lag. Consumer expectations of future income would also adjust to the actual income (GDP), with a delay (i.e. time lag).

The total demand for new flats adjusts with a delay to the rate of aggregate demand in the economy. A 1st order exponential smoothing is assumed, a common autoregressive assumption in many macroeconomic models. As expressed in the following equations, the initial value of GDP is set to its equilibrium value, the aggregate demand (AD). When GDP=AD, the change in GDP is zero:

Change in GDP = (AD-GDP)/Time to Adjust Production......(2.1)

Aggregate demand is the sum of consumption C, government expenditure G, and investment I:

AD = C + I + G..(2.2)

Using the expected income as the budget constraint, consumption expenditure would be a fraction of the expected income. That fraction is represented by the Marginal Propensity to Consume (MPC), which lies between zero and one.

C = MPC ⋆ Expected Income......................................(2.3)

Fig. 2.1. Structure Map of The DSPHM Model Analyzing The Public Housing In Singapore

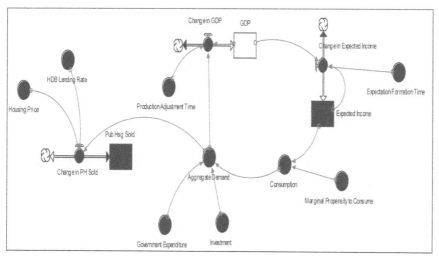

Source: Author, 2020.

Expected income adjusts according to actual income, which the aggregate of such is the GDP. The 1ˢᵗ order exponential smothering for the adjustment process is typically represented in many models. The initial value of expected income is set to the GDP, its equilibrium value:

Expected Income = INTERGAL (Change in Expected Income, GDP).....(2.4)

Change in Expected = (GDP - Expected Income)/Expectation Formation
Income   Time.. (2.5)

Public Housing Sold = INTERGAL (Change in Public Housing Sold,
            PHS_{t-dt})...(2.6)

, where PHS is the public housing units sold in time t and dt is the time step increment.

Public housing (HDB) sold adjusts to actual Public Housing Sold, along with time lags in eqs (2.79) and (2.810). The initial value of Public Housing Sold is taken to be the current volume sold say, for demonstration purposes, of 800,000 HDB homeownership flats.

Change in Public = a_0DELAY (AD,t) + a_1DELAY (HDB Lending Rate,t) –
Housing Sold a_2DELAY (Housing Price, t) ....(2.7)

Eq (2.7) can be re-expressed involving aggregate demand, the HDB Lending Rate and the average HDB Housing Price in eq (2.8). The method of least-squares is adopted in combination with the Cochrane-Orcutt procedure to correct for the auto regression error in the equation system.

Change in Public = $C + a_0$GDP + a_1HDBLendingRate + a_2Housing
Housing Sold   Price...(2.8)

After the formulation of the several foregoing key equations, a subsequent analysis is carried out to estimate the correlation between GDP in eq (2.4) and the change in public housing sold.

The Model to Analyze the Situations of HOS/ PSPS Housing in Hong Kong

To further explore the development of the HOS/PSPS schemes in Hong Kong, Chapter 2 would deploy a model similar to the DSPHM model, with slight modifications, to explore the dynamics of the demand for the HOS/PSPS housing under certain economic situations.

This model, as mentioned before, is inspired by the DSPHM model, which takes the macroeconomic factors into consideration. However, the model used for Hong Kong's case would be a bit more detailed. Data used in the model are gathered from the Hong Kong Census & Statistics Department, the Rating and Valuation Department, the Housing Authority (HA) and the Hong Kong & Shanghai Banking Corporation (HSBC) during say the long enough period of 1984 to 2002. With the help of the *iThink* software, the structure map of the model is illustrated in Fig 2.2.

Fig. 2.2. The Structure Map For The Model Used In Hong Kong's Case

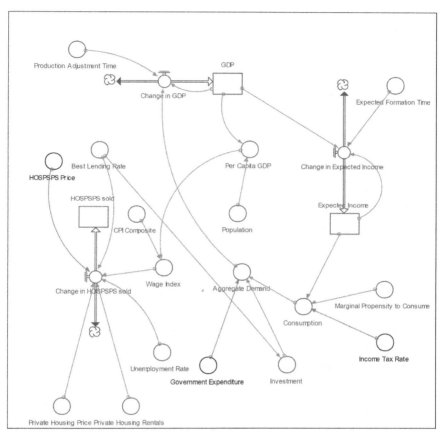

Source: Author, 2020.

The right-hand side of the Fig 2.2 structure map is essentially the same as the DSPHM model, which is grounded on Keynes' *General Theory*. The multiplier effect from the changes of consumption, the investment and government spending, is kept intact in such a model. The equations involved in the macroeconomic side of this model are described in the next paragraphs.

Essentially most of the equations used in the Hong Kong model are the same as the ones proposed in the DSPHM Model but with a few exceptions. The government expenditure is assumed to be constant, while investment (I) is a function of best lending rate, the cost of raising capital. It is because businesses would judge the profitability of a project in terms of its cost and return. The interest payments for a loan is the primary source of cost, which must be taken into consideration. Investment only takes place if the expected return outweighs the lending rate, which is a proxy for the cost. As a result, investment is assumed here to be a time–series function of the best lending rate.

$$I = f(\text{best lending rate})\dots\dots\dots\dots\dots\dots\dots\dots\dots\dots\dots (2.9)$$

Consumption expenditure, as mentioned above is a fraction of expected income, which is determined by the Marginal Propensity to Consume (MPC). One thing worth noting is that an income tax rate of say 15% is being put into the model, which is the maximum income tax rate in Hong Kong, to make the situation more realistic. However, one may argue that income tax, as a part of government revenue, should have a relationship with government spending. It is true but the situation is that income tax is one of the many sources of government revenue, along with other taxes and charges. So, it is reasonable to assume that the explanatory power of income tax on government spending is limited. Moreover, it is assumed that people would use a fraction of their savings, rather than the whole 15% of their incomes, to handle the income tax. As a result, the adverse effect from the tax on consumption would be a bit smaller than that on the income level. The equation of consumption (C) is as follows:

$$C = \text{Expected Income} \star \text{MPC} \star (1 - \text{Income Tax Rate})\dots\dots\dots\dots.2.10)$$

Since an individual's decision to purchase is within the context of microeconomics, the nominal wage indices are utilized via the change in nominal wage to represent the budget constraint of a consumer. An individual buys a HOS/PSPS flat only if he can afford at least the monthly mortgage payment. The addition of the CPI composite (the price index) in the formation of a nominal wage index is due to the use of real values in the model. The equation for the 'Nominal Wage Indices' is expressed to be a function of per capita GDP and the CPI composite, based on time-series data.

Nominal Wage Indices = f(Per Capita GDP, CPI Composite)…………..
(2.11)

Per capita GDP is the relationship between GDP and the population, which is shown in (2.13). It should be noted that per capita GDP is in terms of HK$ million.

Per Capita GDP = GDP / Population………………………… (2.12)

The change in the HOS/PSPS units sold is much different from the equation used in Singapore's case study. Such change is denoted as a time-series function of economic variables like private housing price, private housing rent, unemployment rate, wage index and the price of the HOS/PSPS flats previously.

Change in HOS/PSPS sold = f (wage index, best lending rate, price of private housing, rent of private housing, price of HOS/PSPS, unemployment rate)…………….. (2.13)

The inclusion of private housing prices and rents is meant to offer an alternative for individuals, who are eligible for buying the HOS/PSPS flats. As mentioned before, owners of HOS/PSPS flats are not allowed to sell their flats on the open market in the first 5 years. In addition, HOS/PSPS owners do not have letting rights. In other words, the HOS/PSPS in Hong Kong is a form of constrained ownership, which cannot be used to extract income. As a result, private housing prices and rents serve as the determinants of the opportunity cost for purchasing a HOS/PSPS flat by eligible individuals.

The DSPHM Scenario Planning Analysis

The relevant question posed can be framed in Singapore's first scenario (a minimal change scenario) of the dynamic structural public housing macroeconomic model (DSPHM), which attempts to see how the number of new public housing sold would react, if there are no further rise of the HDB lending rate and the rise of the average public housing (HDB) price. Assuming there is a conjunctural growth in GDP for the next 10 years, then government expenditure and aggregate investment would grow generally in relation to the GDP. The results of the first scenario are depicted in Fig 2.3.

Fig 2.3. Scenario 1 – HDB Price and Lending Rate Remain Unchanged

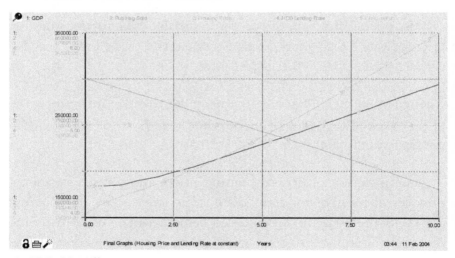

6. GDP, S$ Million per year

7. Public Housing Sold, dwelling units

8. Housing Price, S$ per 4-room flat

9. HDB Lending rate, Percent per annum

10. Consumption, S$ Million per annum

Source: Author, 2020.

The corresponding forecasts are depicted in Fig 2.3 while Table 2.1 presents the forecasts, without further and continuous increase in the HDB lending rate and the average public housing price, then the number of additional new public housing sold would not increase in the aggregate but would stay below the initialized level of 800,000 flats sold.

The attributable factor is the negative relationship between the change in public housing sold and the average housing price of the 4-room HDB flats. It can be inferred that beyond the optimal point of overwhelming public housing provision in the aggregate, the future supply line of additional new public housing flats would have to increase at a slower pace (and in small doses) at the margin.

Table 2.1. The Scenario 1 Table of Public Housing Sold By HDB vs. Public Housing (HDB) Price and Lending Rate Remaining Unchanged

Year	GDP	No. of Public Housing Sold	Lending rate	Average price of public housing (HDB)	Consumption
Initial	183,239,990.00	800,000	5.00	150,000.00	
0	184,519,620.00	788,445.73	5.00	150,000.00	9,794,180.00
1	193,396,560.00	776,891.45	5.00	150,000.00	7,223,920.00
2	203,912,260.00	765,337.18	5.00	150,000.00	8,167,730.00
3	215,854,630.00	753,782.91	5.00	150,000.00	9,379,600.00
4	228,221,660.00	742,228.63	5.00	150,000.00	10,540,550.00
5	241,031,250.00	730,607.54	5.00	150,000.00	11,387,950.00
6	253,968,210.00	718,495.99	5.00	150,000.00	12,016,500.00
7	267,199,650.00	706,055.58	5.00	150,000.00	12,453,750.00
8	280,588,530.00	693,256.45	5.00	150,000.00	12,810,130.00
9	293,825,320.00	680,121.26	5.00	150,000.00	13,036,880.00

Source: Author, 2020.

Singapore's second scenario of the dynamic structural public housing macroeconomic model (DSPHM), which is depicted in Fig 2.4 and presented in Table 2.2, assumes a deregulation scenario in which the GDP would grow at a continuous and gradual rate. HDB is then deemed to review the price of new HDB flats annually and to adopt the market lending practice of no concessionary lending interest rate for first-time HDB flat buyers, starting from year 2. HDB is envisaged to be opening-up housing loans to of HDB housing loans to the private banks as a public housing loan privatization policy measure. Such opening up of HDD loans should benefit private banks with a new line of housing mortgage business, which is substantial, and to consider mortgage back securitization for these public housing (HDB) mortgages in future.

Fig 2.4. Scenario 2 – Fluctuating Public Housing (HDB) Price and Lending rate

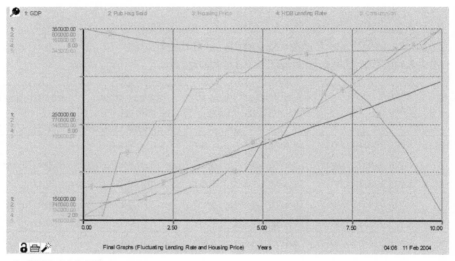

6. GDP, S$ Million per year

7. Public Housing Sold, dwelling units

8. Housing Price, S$ per 4-room flat

9. HDB Lending rate, Percent per annum

10. Consumption, S$ Million per annum

Source: Author, 2020.

From Fig 3.4 and Table 2.2, it can be observed that the incremental and continuous rise of the HDB lending rate and the average public housing price, have resulted in the number of new public housing

(HDB) sold to gradually fall in the next 5 years. However, and after the year 6, new public housing demand by HDB falls off sharply through to year 10. Such a sharp fall may well indicate that despite a gradual GDP expansion, a moderate price rise of new HDB flats and a public housing mortgage privatization, the Singaporean households are still able to afford a new flat from HDB.

However, and by the end of the medium term (around year 6) when private lending rates reach as high as 7.5%p.a., then the demand for new public housing dampens and chokes off. The optimal demand for new public housing (HDB) sold may fall to about 742,000 flat-units by end year 9 (i.e. year 2020) from 800,000 units sold (demanded initially in year 2002). Such a dampening and choking demand may well revive the rental HDB market, which is consistent with recent government policy changes, like the HDB rule that permits HDB flat owners to rent out their public housing, in part or whole (Reuters News, 2003). The market for transitional housing may well develop in the longer term as more households are engaged in the regional and international business ventures abroad, while foreign direct investments and the accompanying inflow of expatriates continue to revisit Singapore.

Table 2.2. Scenario 2 – Table of Public Housing (HDB) Sold vs. Incremental Adjustment to Public Housing Price and Private Bank Lending Rate

Year	GDP	No. of Public Housing (HDB) Sold	Lending rate	Average price of public housing	Consumption
Initial	183,239,990.00	800,000	2.50	135,000.00	147,109,990.00
0	184,519,620.00	797,891.82	2.60	140,500.00	156,067,360.00
1	193,396,560.00	795,783.64	2.80	145,500.00	162,674,070.00
2	203,912,260.00	794,767.56	3.00	150,500.00	170,143,940.00
3	215,854,630.00	793,834.50	3.50	153,000.00	178,722,150.00
4	228,221,660.00	792,521.44	4.50	155,000.00	188,362,120.00
5	241,031,250.00	790,488.53	5.50	156,000.00	198,777,080.00
6	253,968,210.00	785,868.45	6.50	156,500.00	209,766,890.00

7	267,199,650.00	776,398.42	7.00	156,600.00	221,156,590.00
8	280,588,530.00	761,994.03	7.50	156,850.00	232,872,230.00
9	293,825,320.00	742,634.21	8.00	157,850.00	244,795,240.00

Source: Author, 2020.

Scenario Planning Analysis for Hong Kong's HOS/PSPS

The relevant focus of the Hong Kong government's HOS/PSPS policies is examined from a macroeconomic perspective. The reason is that, unlike Singapore, there is no concessionary mortgage loans provided for the purchase of assisted ownership housing. In hindsight, the question of whether-or-not the mortgage loan market should be privatized is basically out of the question. Instead, what suits the situation for Hong Kong is the government's crucial decision to cease the supply of HOS/PSPS flats with effect from 2003. From a macroeconomic perspective, Chapter 2 explores whether-or- not are there any economic justifications of such a crucial government decision by closely looking at the demand for new HOS/PSPS flats under different economic conditions. Hence, the scenarios under the dynamic structural public housing macroeconomic model (DSPHM) are related to the crucial 2003 decision of the government of the Hong Kong Special Administrative Region (HKSAR government) to cease the sale of HOS/PSPS. So, the DSPHM scenarios would simulate possible situations right after year 2002. It should be noted that to conduct the model simulation estimates, starting values are required for important factors like government expenditure, unemployment rate, the HOS/PSPS prices, private property prices and rents, population and expected income. Primary data for year 2002 and thereafter of the afore mentioned variables are sourced from the Hong Kong Census & Statistics Department and the Housing Authority.

In scenario 1, the DSPHM simulation estimates envisage that Hong Kong is gradually recovering from a declining economy in the aftermath of the '1997/1998 Asian Financial Crisis'. Briefly, the crisis is known as the Asian contagion and is a sequence of currency devaluations and other events. which began in summer 1997 and spread through many Asian markets. The currency markets first fail in Thailand resulting from the government's decision to no longer peg the local currency to the US$. Currency declines rapidly spread throughout East Asia, in turn causing common stock market declines, sharply falling import revenues and government upheavals. Therefore, the Hong Kong unemployment rate in the DSPHM simulation estimates is to fall constantly until the end of the simulation (set to be 10 periods). Interest rate would be rising, as the Hong Kong economy is postulated to perform better. The price and rent of private housing would climb under this situation, so also the price of the HOS/PSPS flats but only to a lesser extent. Moreover, the population is assumed to be going up constantly. Lastly, the Marginal Propensity to Consume (MPC) is assumed to be 0.8, which means that individuals would have to make use of 80% of their income each for consumption while leaving the remaining 20% as their savings each.

It should be noted that because there is no intention of any expansionary or recessionary government policies, the government expenditure is assumed to be constant throughout the simulation, and be at the same level that the HKSAR government did spend in 2002. Changes in the variables mentioned above are applicable in scenario 1 for Hong Kong, as presented in Table 2.3, and in the subsequent scenario 2.

Table 2.3. Various Assumed Changes Of Economic Variables Applicable To Both Scenario Studies.

Year	Best Lending Rate (%)	Unemployment Rate (%)	HOS/ PSPS price	Private Housing Price	Private Housing Rents	Investment
Initial	5	7	24,700.00	24,556.00	106	242,098.57
1	5.5	6.7	25,700.00	26,056.00	111	242,874.59
2	6	6.4	27,200.00	28,056.00	121	243,650.62
3	6.5	6.1	28,950.00	30,556.00	136	244,426.64
4	7	5.8	30,450.00	33,306.00	146	245,202.66
5	7.5	5.5	32,450.00	36,306.00	158	245,978.68
6	8	5.2	33,450.00	37,806.00	173	246,754.71
7	8.5	4.9	34,200.00	42,806.00	183	247,530.73
8	9	4.6	35,700.00	46,306.00	193	248,306.75
9	9.5	4.3	36,200.00	47,806.00	208	249,082.77

Source: Author, 2002 and 2020.

NB. Price/Rents of private housing and price of HOS/PSPS housing are prices per sqm. Investment is in terms of HK$ million.

Scenario 2 of Expansionary Government Fiscal Policies on The Model

Scenario 2 is depicted with two noticeable changes. This time, the government decides to do something to further heat up the Hong Kong economy described in scenario 1. Therefore, an expansionary Hong Kong Special Administrative Region (HKSAR) government fiscal policy is proposed. The government can focus on adjusting either government expenditure or income tax rate or both. The HKSAR government proposes an annual rise in government spending by 15%, to further stimulate the demand for goods and services in the whole economy. Also, to encourage consumption, a tax cut is proposed in scenario 2. The income tax rate falls from 15% to 10%, starting from period 5 of the scenario. It is expected that the multiplier effect from a tax reduction would be smaller than that from an increase in direct government spending, based on the notion that the consuming household–individuals would use their savings to pay for a part of their tax payment each. In short, a fall in the tax rate normally brings about a positive effect in consumption, although not as much as the impact brought by the rise in government spending.

The Scenarios Results

The resulting simulation estimates of the Hong Kong scenarios 1 and 2 are summarized in Tables 2.4 & 2.5 and depicted in Figs. 2.5 & 2.6, respectively. From the simulations different results would be obtained for seven variables under the two scenarios – the number of HOS/PSPS (flats) sold, consumption, wage index, the GDP, aggregated demand, government expenditure, and expected income.

Table 2.4. Results From The System Dynamics Model of The HK Scenario 1

Year	HOS/PSPS sold	Consumption	Wage Index	Change in HOS/ PSPS sold	GDP	AD	Government Expenditure	Expected Income
Initial	0	900,082.00	23.21				130,481.00	1,323,650.00
1	8,391.88	885,411.69	22.83	8,391.88	1,272,661.57	1,272,661.57	130,481.00	1,302,076.02
2	17,687.21	874,631.54	23	9,295.33	1,267,644.27	1,258,767.29	130,481.00	1,286,222.86
3	27,215.46	865,607.84	22.54	9,528.25	1,258,028.75	1,248,763.16	130,481.00	1,272,952.71
4	36,595.14	857,834.83	23.15	9,379.69	1,248,754.40	1,240,515.48	130,481.00	1,261,521.80
5	46,912.60	851,117.18	23.31	10,317.45	1,240,593.47	1,233,518.49	130,481.00	1,251,642.91
6	57,763.74	845,327.70	22.98	10,851.15	1,233,570.84	1,227,576.86	130,481.00	1,243,128.97
7	68,063.67	840,361.78	23.64	10,299.93	1,227,587.62	1,222,563.41	130,481.00	1,235,826.15
8	82,103.48	836,127.94	23.36	14,039.81	1,222,533.73	1,218,373.51	130,481.00	1,229,599.91
9	97,886.02	832,545.10	23.92	15,782.54	1,218,307.25	1,214,915.69	130,481.00	1,224,331.03
					1,214,816.79	1,212,108.87		

Source: Author, 2002 and 2020

64

Fig. 2.5 Graphical Presentation Of The
Results of The HK Scenario 1

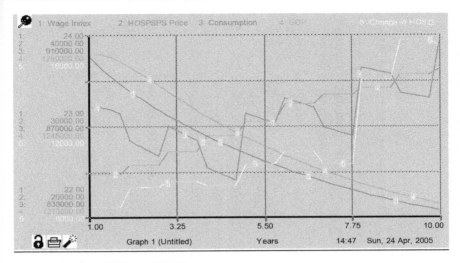

Source: Author, 2002 and 2020

Table 2.5. Results from The System Dynamics Model of Scenario 2 (For Expansionary Fiscal Policies)

Year	HOS/ PSPS sold	Consumption	Wage Index	Change in HOS/PSPS sold	GDP	AD	Government Expenditure	Expected Income
Initial	0	900,082.00	23.21		1,272,661.57	1,272,661.57	130,481.00	1,323,650.00
1	8,389.96	885,772.60	22.97	8,389.96	1,273,697.11	1,278,700.34	150,053.15	1,302,606.76
2	17,664.76	878,362.12	23.53	9,274.80	1,281,323.03	1,294,573.86	172,561.12	1,291,709.00
3	27,137.57	877,155.08	23.65	9,472.81	1,297,601.70	1,320,027.00	198,445.29	1,289,933.93
4	36,413.49	934,006.01	25	9,275.92	1,323,293.71	1,407,420.76	228,212.08	1,297,230.57
5	46,537.36	951,392.06	26.92	10,123.88	1,395,704.75	1,459,814.64	262,443.90	1,321,377.87
6	57,072.22	981,514.45	28.13	10,534.86	1,460,670.44	1,530,079.64	301,810.48	1,363,214.52
7	66,936.32	1,019,359.62	30.47	9,864.10	1,533,596.35	1,613,972.40	347,082.05	1,415,777.25
8	80,407.77	1,064,691.82	32.09	13,471.45	1,618,450.12	1,712,142.93	399,144.36	1,478,738.64
9	95,471.59	1,118,242.31	34.96	15,063.82	1,717,357.20	1,826,341.10	459,016.02	1,553,114.32

Source: Author, 2002 and 2020

Fig. 2.6. Graphical Presentation of The Results of The HK Scenario 2

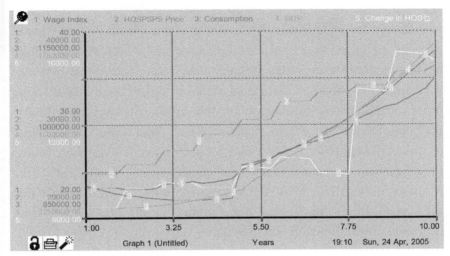

Source: Author, 2002 and 2020

It can be observed in HK scenario 2 of Table 2.5 and Fig 2.6 that the multiplier effects from consumption, investment, and government spending are taking place. It is because the GDP is experiencing a gradual growth, whereas such a situation does not exist in the previous HK scenario 1. The multiplier effect also makes its presence felt in terms of the wage levels of individuals. It can be envisaged that the wage index in the HK scenario 2 constantly rises, while such a rising wage index in the previous HK scenario 1 is hovering around a certain level. Variables like the expected income and aggregated demand are also higher than that in the HK scenario 1. The implication is that expansionary fiscal policy has already manifested its ramifications through the HK economy. Optimal demand for HOS/PSPS sold may rise sharply to about 95,500 flats by end year 9 (i.e. year 2020) from about 8,400 flats sold in year 2003.

Surprisingly, total demand for new HOS/PSPS flats in the HK scenario 2 is slightly lower than that without the extra government policies (in the HK Scenario 1 of about 97,900 flats by year 2020), even though the difference is not that noticeable. It can be explained by a higher income level, courtesy of a better HK economic condition. Since there is a statutory income requirement for HOS/PSPS users, a rise in income insinuates that a portion of the HOS/PSPS applicants would lose their eligibility. Meanwhile, there would be some lower income applicants that now are eligible to purchase HOS/PSPS flats, benefiting from a growing HK economy. The difference between such an income rise insinuation of some HOS/PSPS applicants losing their eligibility and some lower income applicants becoming HOS/PSPS eligible are uncertain. Still, once the general income level gets to rise, an applicant is perceived to prefer private housing owing to a right to extract income through the rental market. Still, the simulation estimates from the system dynamic model suggest that there would be a certain level of demand for the HOS/PSPS flats, no matter how the economy performs.

The Implications

One may ask why there is a sustainable demand for HOS/PSPS flats regardless of the performance of the Hong Kong economy. The reason is regarding the rules on the resale of HOS/PSPS flats within the first 2 years. Even if the private housing market is plummeting, a HOS/PSPS ownership would be able to reclaim the whole housing price by selling the flat back to the HK Housing Authority (HA). Such a HOS/PSPS ownership serves as a risk-sharing function between the HKSAR government and the owner, which is non-existent in the private housing market. In a sense, and with the downside housing price risk basically out of the question, the ack up of demand for assisted-ownership housing in Hong Kong is likely, in comparison to its private housing market.

Another reason is that, given the restrictions on the resale of HOS/PSPS flats 5 years after the original selling day, the supply of HOS/PSPS in the secondary market and the open market are expected to be relatively low. The setting of a premium payment *before* a transaction in the open market generates higher transaction cost for HOS/PSPS owners to sell their flats. Furthermore, it would guarantee a lower price if a HOS/PSPS owner sells the flat on the secondary market, in which the applicants are limited to the tenants of rental housing estates and to the residents of interim housing, managed by the Hong Kong HA, and the Green Form Applicants for public tenants (HA, 2005). Therefore, it is recommended that a relaxation should be made regarding the arrangements of the premium. Instead of paying a premium before a HOS/PSPS is resold, Hong Kong should follow the case of Singapore, where the premium can be paid *after* the transaction.

In the case of Singapore, the demand for new public housing (HDB) flats would drop only when the interest rates are getting relatively too high. Owing to the decree of a resale levy *after* the transaction of HDB flats, this makes it a lot easier for buying and selling activities on the open market. Also, as the requirements of purchasing a HDB flat in the secondary market are a lot lenient, in comparison to the purchase of new direct allocated HDB flats, the privatization of the HDB mortgage market should further enhance the development of the said market. In general, the suggestions from Chapter 2 not only reduces the financial burden of the Hong Kong HA and the Singapore HDB on the possible construction of new ownership housing, but also help to nurture a more mature open market for the Hong Kong HOS/PSPS and the HDB flats.

Concluding Remarks

Chapter 2 aims at exploring the relationship between several economic factors and the demand for public housing, both in Singapore and Hong Kong. These two economies are known for their intensive government housing policies even though the manner of regulating their assisted homeownership schemes is vastly different. Therefore, two different public housing systems are addressed subject to Singapore's and Hong Kong's government-policy initiatives.

Chapter 2 deploys the system dynamics model, a rather innovative concept in direct real estate studies, to shed a better understanding on the policy implications of assisted ownership housing, via assessing the demand for new flats in both the Singapore and Hong Kong economies, under certain macroeconomic policy changes that are suitable for their unique situations, and instead of analyzing the effectiveness of government housing policies via the use of static models.

In Hong Kong's case, it is found that the HOS/PSPS demand would be around similar levels regardless of the performance of the economy. In a sense, the decision by the Hong Kong Special Administrative Region (HKSAR) government to cease selling HOS/PSPS flats is not justified in this Chapter, given the existing regulations of the Home Ownership Scheme (HOS) launched in 1978 by the Hong Kong Housing Authority (HA), along with another scheme known as the Private Sector Participation Scheme (PSPS). Therefore, Chapter 2 suggests a relaxation of regulations regarding the premium arrangements of the resale of HOS/PSPS flats on the open market. Similar to the Singapore government's HDB scheme, that by deferring the premium payment schedule till after the transaction, should not only ease the financial burden of the Hong Kong government HA in the construction of new flats, but also help to foster a more developed open market for the HKSAR government's HOS/PSPS flats.

In the case of Singapore, Chapter 2 suggests an opening of the public housing (HDB) mortgage market to private sector mortgages under open competition. The fall in the demand for HDB flats shown in the Chapter can be attributed to rising demand in the secondary HDB housing market, owing to HDB's relatively lenient requirements. The Chapter offers meaningful insights on the Singapore government's aims of providing large scale public housing ownership and the potential, sustainable development of the HDB mortgage market by the private sector under open competition.

Acknowledgement: *The Author wish to gratefully acknowledge the initial work carried out for Chapter 2 by Professor (Dr) Eddie Chi Man HUI and Mr Ka Hung YU, both from the Department of Building and*

Real Estate, The Hong Kong Polytechnic University, Hung Hum, Kowloon, in Hong Kong; and in consultation with Honorary Professor (University of Hertfordshire, Hatfield, UK), Dr HO Kim Hin / David, during their meaningful brain storming sessions before Professor HO retired from the NUS SDE Departments of Real Estate and Building in May 2019.

CHAPTER 3

THE PRIVATIZATION OF THE HDB (HOUSING AND DEVELOPMENT BOARD) MORTGAGE

The Housing Development Board (HDB) is set up 1960 as a statutory board within the Ministry of National Development (MND), Singapore, under the Housing and Development Act (1997 Revised Edition). HDB had been established to build residential building, which meets the housing needs of households, and with HDBs' core mission of providing affordable basic housing in the form of highly subsidized HDB flats. The board is exempted from local taxation under section 13(e) of the income Tax Act (Cap 134, 1999 Revised Edition), and is committed to good corporate governance, self-regulatory and monitoring-mechanisms like the monthly reporting of HDB's performance, proper accounting records, internal audit and the annual financial audit that is reported to MND. Interim and full year financial results are reported by the board and disseminated to the public. Government grants are also received by HDB to fully cover its annual operating deficit.

Structure wise, HDB holds a 75% stake in EM (Estate Management) Services Pte Ltd, one of its' subsidiary companies. It is currently the largest management agent for public housing in Singapore that offers estate management, engineering services, contracts administration and project management services to town councils. In addition, the board recently underwent restructuring where it's building and consultancy services are delegated to its new subsidiary – A wholly owned subsidiary of HDB, the HDB Corporation Pte Ltd and now known as 'Surbana Jurong (SJ)'. Other investments in subsidiary companies like CESMA international Ltd and ESMACO Pte Ltd have been transferred to SJ with effect from 1 April 2003 and 1July 2003, respectively. SJ is the holding company for all its subsidiaries and associated companies involved in the Group's local and overseas businesses. Unlike HDB, which is formed as a statutory board, SJ and its subsidiaries are financed through the sale of goods and services and subject to a required return on any investment. The rationale for divesting a part of the HDB to the private sector is to enable HDB to concentrate on its role as the public housing authority while its other related functions are farmed out to SJ its subsidiaries and associated companies.

Policy wise, the Singapore government introduced the "Home Ownership (for the People) Scheme" in 1964 to enable citizens to own housing assets as means of financial security, and as a hedge against inflation. This public housing policy measure for home ownership is also intended to help promote the overall economic, social and political stability of Singapore. Being a government agency, the HDB expanded through the broadening of its public housing policy scope, beyond the Board's original mission. More recent activities include the upgrading and redevelopment of older estates, the granting of mortgage finance to purchasers and managing ancillary facilities like the commercial, industrial properties, carpark, market and other amenities in the public housing estate. Under the policy measure to promote universal home ownership, the HDB provides special interest rates – the "concessionary interest rate" to first- and second- time homebuyers. Each homebuyer, who wishes to upgrade its flat is entitled up to two chances to apply for the HDB loan at concessionary rates. Buyers, who are third time buyers and/ or down graders are no longer eligible for the concessionary interest rate, and have to take up open market rate loans for the purchase of HDB flats.

A key similarity between the US and Singapore experience is the availability of government grants that help to support a stable enough banking asset base for the two countries, so that more attractive loan packages may be offered to homebuyers for minimal interest-rate risk. Both countries are responsible for market transparency in terms of how the grants are managed and in terms of robust and sustainable self-regulatory measures for the banking and financial sector. Lastly, such government grants and loan packages offer special assistance in supporting and monitoring subsidized housing programs nationwide. Chapter 3 has therefore wo objectives that comprise the following:

- To establish the structural relationships that encourage the privatization of the HDB concessionary-rate mortgages to private financial institutions.
- To examine the factors that benefit and support the gradual privatization of the HDB concessionary-rate mortgages.

The scope of Chapter 3 is confined to the 4-room HDB homebuyers, who purchase their HDB flats in the open market i.e. the HDB resale market. Homebuyers, who purchase their flats directly allocated by the HDB and other flat-type homebuyers are excluded from Chapter 3, as the HDB's database consistently reveal that the number of sale transactions made each year are much higher in the HDB resale compared to the HDB direct flat allocation sector. The majority of HDB homebuyers are observed to opt for the purchase of the 4-room flats. The private financial institutions, which currently provide mortgages to HDB buyers, are merely restricted to the three large domestic banks, namely the Development Bank of Singapore (DBS), Overseas Chinese Banking Corporation Limited (OCBC) and United Overseas Bank (UOB). Only the HDB concessionary interest-rate loan is mainly covered in Chapter 3 while the rest of the private sector banks' market-rate loans, apart from those of the three large domestic banks, are not duly covered. Hence, Chapter 3 is organized in the following manner with Sections 1 providing the introduction, to be followed by the related literature in the (next) Section 2. The qualitative and quantitative examinations of this Chapter are discussed in Sections 3 and 4 respectively. Section 5 concludes Chapter 3.

The Related Literature

In the US (i.e. the United States of America), the Federal National Mortgage Association (Fannie Mae) is created by the US Congress in 1938 to bolster the housing industry during the economic 'Depression'. The Federal Home Loan Mortgage Corporation (Freddie Mac) is authorized to purchase first lien, fixed-rate conventional mortgages. It is then chartered by the US Congress in 1970 under Title III of the Emergency Home Finance Act to securitize the conventional residential mortgages. The activities of Fannie Mae and Freddie Mac are different from the HDB Mortgage Financing Loan system but share similar goals, wherein the common mission is to expand the availability and affordability of homeownership for the low and middle-income homebuyers. Fannie Mae and Freddie Mac became publicly traded companies in subsequent years with the mission to help more families achieve the dream of homeownership. Fannie Mae and Freddie Mac are also known as the "Government Sponsor Enterprises" (GSEs). However, Fannie Mae and Freddie Mac do create a secondary market for the US home financial system and are not restricted to offering loans to a specific sector of homebuyers. This is unlike the Singapore case where "public" and "private" housing are clearly demarcated, and hat Singapore's Housing and Development Board (HDB) is mainly responsible as the HDB mortgage lender to the public (i.e. the resident households). Nevertheless, the two nations' public agencies are merely confined to to residential mortgage financing.

Fannie Mae and Freddie Mac have as their primary function of the management of direct loans that they previously issue and underwrite, in which these two agencies are previously allowed to lend money directly to mortgage borrowers, and to hold them in their portfolios, but are specifically forbidden to engage in mortgage origination in recent years. Fannie Mae and Freddie Mac are assigned the public mission to offer special assistance to support certain subsidized housing programs. Such special assistance is the same as the promotional support schemes, which the Singapore Housing and Development Board (HDB) offers to homebuyers. The special assistance support that Fannie Mae and Freddie Mac currently offer are the "default insurance" or "loan guarantee" to mortgage investors, commonly known as "Mortgage-back security (MBS)". Such an MBS protects mortgage investors from losses owing to underlying mortgage defaults and late payments. With the assurance that timely interest and principal payments are received, it makes it more attractive for public and institutional investors to so invest in the MBS. The eventuality is that mortgage lenders are enabled to replenish funds to originate new loans. In this way, mortgage funds for home purchase are consistently available and affordable to homebuyers in every state across the US. Fannie Mae and Freddie Mac are viewed as vehicles that readily offer liquidity to the US home financial system, and that both vehicles would assume interest rate risk that is associated with their roles as the intermediary each between mortgage lenders and investors. A fee is received for such as an intermediary to absorb the cost of interest rate risk.

Setting aside the Fannie Mae and Freddie Mac assigned public mission of offering special assistance to support certain subsidized housing programs, both Fannie Mae and Freddie Mac offer lower mortgage rates. They create a wider variety of mortgage products to make them more appealing to homebuyers. Fannie Mae and Freddie Mac have received government sponsorship because the US Congress believes that in the presence of strong monopolies, both Fannie Mae and Freddie Mac may well help to overcome market failure, caused by credit shortage and market instability. Both Fannie Mae and Freddie Mac prevent inconsistent interest rates that can result in the lost opportunity for expanding and creating homeownership. The importance of government subsidies is supported by an added perception that the private market alone is incapable of supporting such financial institutions, like Fannie Mae and Freddie Mac. Government subsidies that Fannie Mae and Freddie Mac and Singapore's Housing and Development Board (HDB) all enjoy are compared in Table 3.1 for reference.

Table 3.1. Government Subsidies Granted To The Government Agencies

US Fannie Mae and Freddie Mac	The Singapore Housing Development Board (HDB)
Their securities are "explicitly government securities" under the Securities Exchange Act of 1934 and the Federal Reserve Act and are exempted from the many state investors protection law.	Not applicable (HDB does not engage in secondary mortgage securities).
They are exempted from registration and reporting requirements of the Securities and Exchange Commission (SEC) whose mission is to protect the investors and maintain the integrity of the securities markets. SEC requires public companies to disclose meaningful financial and other information to public so public can judge if it's a good investment.	Not applicable (HDB does not engage in secondary mortgage securities).
US Fannie Mae and Freddie Mac	The Singaore Housing and Development Board (HDB) Board
They are exempted from state and local income taxation	HBD is exempted from state and local income taxation
Each US agency can receive up to the US$2.25 billion line of credit from the US Treasury Department.	HDB receives government grant that fully covers its deficit annually
They can use the US Federal Reserve (Central bank) as their fiscal support agent.	HDB can use the Ministry of finance as its fiscal support agent

Source: Author, 2005 and 2020.

Fannie Mae and Freddie Mac, known as the US Government Sponsored Enterprises (GSEs) are once deemed to bring stability to the US housing financial sector, but that these two GSEs are criticized for having used their privileges to earn above average profits well in excess of the risk they assumed in the market place. The generous financial benefits that these two GSEs receive from the US Congress have been used to enrich their shareholders and executives, who diverted resources from potentially more productive investments. It is also observed that market interest rates gradually rise over the years, resulting in additional US federal government money being required to provide a financial base to fund the two GSEs. Such a financial base is crucial for each of the two GSEs' survivability, thereby making the GSEs costly to fund, if the US financial market is correct in its belief that the implicit guarantee that the US Government rescues the two GSEs from severe financial distress with like their creditors.

The result is to place the taxpayer at risk if either of both the GSEs should fail. Owing to the undesirable circumstances that many analysts have forecasted, US Congress did feel the importance of credit assessment and the monitoring of the GSEs' fund management, and it prompt the federal government to review the operations of the two GSEs. The result is the Charter Act 1954. The Act imposes the procedure that the GSEs are transformed, over a period into privately owned and managed organizations. Despite many doubts, the GSEs initially hold on to their belief that they can bring substantial benefits. The public perception of Fannie Mae and Freddie Mac, as being sound and stable enterprises, has helped to grow national and global capital investments in support of the US prevailing and future mortgage lending needs.

In the Singapore situation, an important element of its large scale public housing program implemented by the public authority, the Housing and Development Board (HDB), is the public housing finance scheme in the shape of its 'HDB Homeownership Policy'. Such a unique and center piece policy explains how the HDB serves as the key coordinating agency, which handles the flow of funds from different sources. In HDB's financing of public housing, the amount of transactions is vast as briefly summarized in the trend, in which the scale of the HDB homeownership historic trend of (**1970, 1980, 1990 and 2000**) benefitted nine key associated trends respectively i.e. the:

	(1970, 1980, 1990, 2000)
Population of Singapore, million persons	(2.1, 2.4, 3.0 and 4.0)
Population in HDB flats, %	(35, 67, 87 and 85)
Population in owner Occupied HDB flats, %	(21, 64, 87 and 95)
HDB capital expenditure, S$ million	(75, 862, 1,016 and 2,273)
HDB capital expenditure as a proportion of GDP in the	
Construction sector, %	(18.8, 55.2, 28.1 and 22.8)
HDB capital expenditure as a proportion of overall	
GDP, %	(1.3, 3.4, 1.5 and 1.4)
Affordable housing assisted by cross-subsidies.	Yes

Source: Selected HDB Annual Reports (see the References Section)

A primary reason for public housing to grow to such a large scale is that the HDB tailors the apartment sizes and construction costs, according to the affordability levels of the population. The priority is on housing for everyone at the right cost in the right time, while keeping architecture design standards as high as possible under these circumstances. Even then, government subsidies are needed but that amount is set at a level affordable by the government, so that the large-scale public housing program can be sustained. Government subsidies to public housing are slightly reduced by cross subsidies from the profitable commercial and industrial developments in the HDB new towns. The government, as a matter of principle, does not provide cash handouts but in special circumstances gives financial assistance to individuals for asset building, like supplementing payments for purchasing and upgrading of the flats in public housing. Given such a large-scale of development and with such a high degree of home ownership, the question is whether-or-not public housing activities unduly tie up capital, which otherwise would be available for physical infrastructural investment. Economists do not believe so and that their belief is attributable to three perspectives, namely that,

- Singapore regularly experiences strong net domestic savings, made possible from:
  - Sustainable Singapore investments abroad and earning net positive incomes;
  - Favorable Singapore current account surpluses and the building up of foreign reserves;
  - Relatively moderate expansion of domestic investments.

- Singapore households have not over invested in their home ownership purchases.
- The favorable situation achieved as early as end March 2002 is such that the:
  - Conservative and prudent ratio, between the central provident fund (CPF) savings used for homeownership purchase and total CPF savings, is 0.43:1 and with
  - CPF savings used for homeownership purchase = S$ 92.2 billion while total CPF savings = S$214.4 billion;
  - A non-excessive ratio between, the balance in CPF mortgages for homeownership and the balance in the CPF, is 1.10:1 from S$103.4 billion:S$93.7 billion.

- Economic spin-offs from public housing that is highly subsided and carefully managed, are bound to generate wealth expansion in five principal ways:
  - Public housing developments by HDB stimulate demand throughout various economic sectors in Singapore in successive rounds. Industrial outputs of one sector become the inputs of another. The construction sector is greatly expanded by virtue of HDB's large scale public housing program.

- Such stimulated successive rounds of economic activities generate sustainable employment with continual upgrading of the domestic skill pool, and with selective induction of foreign talent in a flexible wage structure.
- The multiplier effect of the construction sector is found to be around 1.4 for the Singapore economy.
- Progressive corporate, property and personal tax regimes generate further income for the Singapore government.
- Public housing developments by HDB also stimulate sustainable expansion of domestic firms and the formation of new firms, with growing opportunities for foreign direct investments. Such firms and opportunities expansions are enhanced by a combination of open competition and friendly policies towards inward investment promotion.

Commercial Banks' Origination of Market-Rate Loan for HDB Flats

By 1 Jan 2003, the Singapore Ministry of National Development (MND) devolves some non-core HDB functions to the private sector by transferring future HDB loans at market rate to the commercial banks. HDB continues to offer subsidized mortgages for first- and second- time homebuyers, who are upgrading from their smaller flats. Before devolving future HDB market-rate loans to the private financial institutions, the HDB offers two type of loans to two groups of buyers. Homebuyers who take up either HDB subsidized rate loans or the market-rate loans would each have a lump sum amount of accrued interest returned, in the event they each sell their mortgaged HDB flats away. Homebuyers taking subsidized interest rate would have the accrued interest returned, based on the prevailing Central Provident Fund (CPF) interest rate of return p.a. Homebuyers who are taking up HDB loans at the market rate of interest p.a. would have their money received back, based on that interest rate, which is pegged at 0.1 percent points below the Development Bank of Singapore (DBS) interest rate.

HDB's Financial Position as the Mortgage Lender

From the HDB annual report as early as FY 2003/2004, the HDB did incur some significant deficit from its operations for the past five years. For year 2004, the deficit before government grant is about S$779 million. Despite the shortfall of funds, the income that HDB earns largely originates from the provision of its home mortgages. The pie chart of Fig 3.1 shows the HDB interest income earnings for FY2003/2004 that constitute 54% of its overall net operational earnings. It can be clearly seen that the HDB income from its operations is largely derived from the "interest" element.

Fig 3.1. HDB Income from Operations

FY2003/2004: S$3,125M

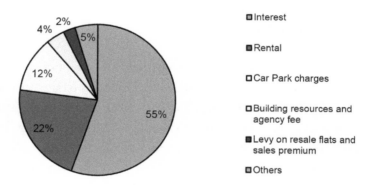

Source: HDB Annual Report, FY2003/2004; Author, 2020

It is inferred that most of HDB's receivable income is generated from the provision of its home mortgages, which are deemed to be its "non-core function". From the HDB Annual Report for FY 2003/2004, most of HDB's funding is being allocated to finance the HDB mortgages that are granted to homebuyers. A smaller proportion of the funding is allocated to finance the development and operational programs of the HDB. Fig 3.2 shows the funding allocation to originate the mortgage finance loans and the housing finance loans.

Fig 3.2. HDB Funding Allocated for Mortgage Finance Loans and Housing Finance Loans, Selected FYs For Trend and Observtions

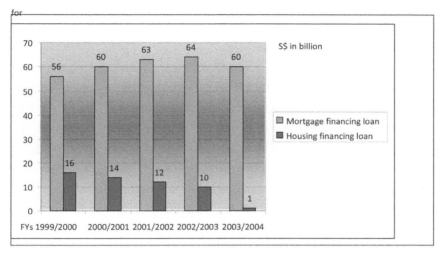

for
Source: Selected HDB annual reports; Author, 2020

HDB has about S\$60 billion of mortgage held under in its portfolio for FY 2003/2004 in Fig 3.2. A substantial amount of its loan portfolio is for the provision of home mortgages. The housing financing loans are separately funded through borrowing from the Singapore Government, bank loans and bonds and that these incur interest expenses to HDB, since interest rate is chargeable to the statutory board for such borrowings. The funding of borrowing from the Singapore government loans occurs even though the HDB conducts a back-to-back financing arrangement for the housing financing loans to household buyers. For such public service, the HDB recovers the required management fee in its housing financing loan rate of interest. By holding these housing financing loans to household buyers in its own portfolio, the HDB faces similar mortgage risks as so faced by the US Fannie Mae and Freddie Mac. The two main risks faced are first the credit risk and secondly the interest rate risk. To minimize the HDB's exposure to interest rate risk, the interest cost of such a risk is managed via rough matching the terms of HDB's government loan with those of its long-term receivables. Besides its role as a public housing authority, the HDB invests and diverts its equity stakes in its subsidiaries and associated companies, as private market entities. HDB also invests overseas under its family of owned entities.

The US experience has prompted Chapter 3 to examine the public housing policy of privatizing HDB mortgages in Singapore. Despite the fact that the US experience has similarities to the HDB mortgage sector, the main difference between the them is that while the US experience is concerned with the secondary market mortgage, the HDB experience is concerned with mortgage origination Like the public housing policies set by the Housing and Urban Development (HUD) in the US, Singapore has adopted a similar mission where extensive effort is expended to encourage the construction and consumption of HDB public housing flats as well as their comprehensive facilities. The associated policy objectives are to encourage homeownership and to enable as many Singaporeans as possible, i.e. an overwhelming majority, to purchase their own home=flats within the nation. The key reason is because homeownership creates positive economic externalities or spillovers to benefit the rest of the economy. A good example would be that homeowners take better care of their flat residences, their HDB neighborhoods and precincts than household tenants. The consequence is that there are desirable improvements in social harmony and the physical living environment.

Hence, the logical linkage to policy from the foregoing externality should be to have policies, which encourage the low- and middle- income households at the margin to own their HDB flats, of instead to rent them. With the mission to encourage affordable homeownership, both the HDB in Singapore and the US experience have adopted similar policies through government sponsorship. One of the core public housing policies adopted is the provision of low interest rate home mortgages, to make it more feasible for households at large to own rather then to rent their homes. Despite federal financial support that the US Fannie Mae and Freddie Mac offer, because these two GSEs promote widespread homeownership, there are positive spillover effects for the US housing market. Whether or not such policies address the spillover effects in a focus way has raised public attention and in recent years. Many doubts have arisen on the effectiveness of transferring tax-payer-funded subsidies to homebuyers, via providing subsidy schemes like those with low interest rates. Such policies have been once deemed to be effective mechanisms to support homeownership, but no longer hold water to the public at large in recent times.

The prime rationale for continuing the subsidy schemes is the need to have a government-based financial agency that supports affordable home ownership. But in the US experience, questions are raised on how well such agencies are performing their missions. Should the political support wane, then such agencies should be abolished. Society's resources are therefore less efficiently allocated if the policy instruments (the agencies) themselves fail to purely address their corporate missions, and to achieve their ultimate policy goals. Although the US experience in terms of its Fannie Mae and Freddie Mac differs in approach to Singapore HDB's key function as a home mortgage lender, the US experience offers several useful insights as to why privatization may potentially bring improved benefits to the Singapore economy.

The Rationale for Privatization

"Privatization" is defined as that process, which alters the balance between the public and private sectors, in favor of the latter sector (Sanker and Venugopal, 1997). Thynne and Ariff (1989) so define the reasons for privatization, in that there are several key motives for privatization and some of the more significant motives include:

- value shifts in favor of private markets and ownership,
- reassessment of the levels of public expenditure after rapid public sector growth of recent decades are partial substitutes for reducing government expenditure,

- reduction of the fiscal and credit pressure,
- reduction of a state's managerial burden,
- promotion of innovation and
- price competition.

They also found that the motive for privatization in Singapore is a unique one as the reasons for privatization cannot be found in inadequate financial returns from the public enterprises, in technical inefficiency and backwardness or in the need for budgetary revenue of such enterprises. The same observation is evidenced by (Asher, 1998) who found that there is a surplus, which impressively ranges from 0.4 percent of GDP as early as 1973 to 7.7 percent in 1985. The Singapore government shares in the nation's savings is unlikely to be reduced through the years to date. The government statutory boards are expected subsequently held accountable to continue to generate surpluses.

Nevertheless, the Economic Committee in Singapore considers public enterprises to be too profitable, with each attempting to maximize profits, without taking into consideration the likely economy-wide repercussion of its actions. The Committee advocates that public enterprises and statutory boards should not strive for profit maximization but should pass on savings, from improved efficiency and productivity, to consuming Singaporeans in the form of lower charges (Ariff, 1989). From the statement made by the Economic committee, two relevant motives to this day for privatization are meaningful:

- value shifts in favor of private markets and ownership,
- promotion of innovation and price competition.

These two relevant motives lead to the enhancement of the "competitive allocation of scare resources" and "economic efficiency" for Singapore. Where there are "value shifts in favor of the private market and ownership" then competition is introduced. An appropriate first example is to devolve the HDB market-rate loan mortgage business, which was implemented in January 2003, to the private banks in Singapore. Such an example has increased competition among the individual banks. Secondly, efficiency is promoted and improved when competition is infused, and in turn "promote innovation and reinforced competition", which result in a greater variety of goods and services that benefit consumers i.e. households and firms. The remaining motives recommended by the Economic Committee, may not be applicable since these motives seek to reduce the government burden in terms of expenditure and managerial burden. The latter may be untrue to a certain extent, as one cannot say for sure that no managerial burden is imposed on a statutory board, if the board has decided to devolve some of its functions to the private sector. It is evidenced in the speech by the then deputy prime minister (DPM) Lee Hsien Loong (2002), relating to the partial privatizing of the HDB market-rate loan. The DPM reiterates that the rationale is to divert some of the HDB's non-core business to the private sector. He even mentions that the homebuyer, who is a third time flat buyer or who is making a lateral transfer, did not fall within the HDB's core objective of promoting universal home ownership. Clearly by diverting the HDB key function, as a key lender for a designated group of homebuyers, should relief the HDB of managerial burden to a certain extent.

To better examine the structural relationships that underpin the potential privatization arguments, let us look at another definition, expressed by another important government committee, the Divestment Committee. It acknowledges that "privatization" denotes not only to "the transfer of ownership of a productive activity from the public sector to the private sector", but also to "the farming out of work to the private sector". From such a definition, two lessons are noteworthy:

- transfer of ownership from the public sector to the private sector, and
- farming out of activity to the private sector.

The two lessons would mean that the devolvement of key public enterprises' activities meant to grow the private sector of such key activities. The word 'productive activity' in the definition suggests that public enterprises are able to generate surpluses, and therefore inadequate funding is not the reason for privatization. Such action of transfer from the public sector to the private sector deepens competition therein. Thereafter, improvement in efficiency and productivity will set in under the presence of competitions. In terms of structural relationship, it can be concluded that "Competition" and "Economic Efficiency" wrote hand in hand, and these are the structural factors that affect the decision for privatization.

Competitiveness

Calomiris (1996) highlights the general perception that the chartering of national mortgage intermediaries offers large potential efficiency gains from economies of scale, where the intermediaries are able to spread the fixed costs over a larger portfolio; and to also achieve superior portfolio diversification via holding a national mortgage portfolio. The Comptroller General of the US (GAO) report of 1996 surfaces the potential rise in interest rate by 15 to 35 basis points if the cost advantage of the GSEs is eliminated, because the enterprise cost is most likely to rise. Such a report, however, cannot justify perpetuating the prevailing US home mortgage market. In fact, the report supports the chartering of competitive banks, nationwide in which new entrants are encouraged into the market. Because of the ability for the economies of scale to be realized when there is competition, there is no need for any government subsidies for the competitive banks.

Competition is needed to achieve optimal efficiency gains and to enable resource allocation decisions to be determined by private sector responses to relative price signals. The lack of competition retards the public enterprise's ability to operate efficiently, respond to market forces and compete against private sector firms. By going onto full privatization, the time and cost for setting the financial target(s) by the public enterprises are eliminated (Waterman, 1992 and Wallison, 2002). Wallison believes that competition among financial institutions is desirable for the public enterprises, like Fannie Mae and Freddie Mac, to transmit some of their cost structure to their customers, under the pressure of competition. It is crucial and beneficial for financial institutions to internalize more of their own cost of risk taking, and to adsorb losses, while reducing tax-payer risk in any case of mortgage default. He further explains that home buyers can take advantage of the many competitive housing loan packages offered in the private mortgage sector. Homebuyers can therefore benefit from more choice in the private loan sector. Hess (2003) support the view and address that by introducing competition in order to raise the market share for new entrants, then more financial options to be created for homebuyers, who need to finance their housing purchases while allowing monopolies like Fannie Mae and Freddie Mac to earn profits, through any profit base on performance and on their creditworthiness rather than on legislated, government-sponsored tax and regulatory advantages, that create in the market participants' eyes an implicit federal guarantee.

In the Singapore experience, when the then Deputy Prime Minister, Lee Hsien Loong (2002), now Singapore's current prime minister, shares similar views by commenting that the implementation of the partial privatization of HDB loans would enable greater choices for homebuyers, which ultimately benefits them. Even Alan Greenspan (2004) recommends the argument that privatization helps to create new businesses opportunities for the banks, and to help them shift the market towards the adjustable-rate loan. The inference is that the willingness for the government-related financial sector to absorb risk relating to regulating fixed interest rates, and to offering default insurance and loan guarantee, will not always bring positive beneficial effects to the financial system.

Economic Efficiency

Economy theory and evidence suggest that monopolistic enterprises earn maximum profit and not so when the marginal costs equal the marginal revenues under the competitive condition, but so earn maximum profit when the marginal costs equal the average revenue. In practical terms, monopolies often well under produce below the maximum demand, and overcharge to maximize profits. The result is an inherent efficiency loss and the misallocation of scarce resources. Albon (1985) finds that monopolies like the public enterprise are expected to operate under a minimum required rate of return (i.e. the hurdle rate) but often under different degrees of inefficiency. Feldman (2001) explains that the reason for such inefficiency is that the public enterprise's performance in the absence of market discipline, manifest its inefficiency in price and quantity performances. Price wise, creditors demand an yield of the Fannie Mae and Freddie Mac debt, which approximates the risk-free rate, rather than to charge a higher rate with a risk of default, similar to Fannie Mae's and Freddie Mac's absent and implied federal support.

Quantity wise, credit support that is offered to Fannie Mae and Freddie Mac has the Treasury-like borrowing characteristic, which enables the two government state enterprises (GSEs) to raise funds in amounts and at times, when non-GSEs with similar risks cannot so raise funds. With such credit support, he required yield falls even if the two GSEs do not do well. The two GSEs continue to have sufficient funding support from the federal government significantly adverse to corporate competency and efficiency. The setback for the duopoly regime of Fannie Mae and Freddie Mac causes a severe disruption to the US housing market if ever one of the two of them should collapse. Since the potential collapse of the two GSEs requires the US Congress to "bail them out", would in effect exposes taxpayers to a large contingent liability. By introducing competition, the likelihood of such a bailout is much reduced and ensures that no one of the two GSE's collapse can be deemed to be disastrous. The federal government should do well to realize and so assume the downside risk of such a GSE collapse and should therefore perceive that such a downside risk is only eliminated, via the full privatization of the two GSEs.

The foregoing discussion may even be appropriate in the case of Singapore because it is highly unlikely that a sound statutory board like its Housing and Development Board (HDB) collapses in view of the surplus that Singapore's government sector frequently returns on the whole. It is noteworthy that the Singapore motive for privatization is a unique one because inadequate financial returns can never be the reason for privatization, unlike other nations. Nevertheless, the Singapore government should not ignore such a chance of a statutory board collapse to prepare the nation's mindset for such a contingent failure. Hess (2003) early foresees that the benefit Fannie Mae and Freddie Mac can bring to the US housing finance market is sustainable even if their "implicit guarantee" privilege is to be removed. It is because there is the large robust secondary market like for the automobile loans in the private sector to reinforce the widely held positive view for the privatization of the two GSEs. A successful privatization of Fannie Mae and Freddie Mac not only enhance the productive power of the US economy but also reduces the fiscal burden perception of loss-making GSEs to help them exercise sound fiscal discipline and control.

It is inferred that by removing government support and that by passing 'the baton' to the private sector to potentially take charge of the lending needs of HDB homebuyers, such a privatization policy may well not distort its benefits to Singapore's HDB homebuyers. A favorable privatization policy can well be an affordable private interest rate, which can be sustainably offered by private banks in Singapore to HDB homebuyers.

Long Term, Fixed Interest Rate Structure

It is readily observed in Table 3.2, the concessionary interest for the HDB mortgages is 2.60% while the mortgage interest rates for DBS, OCBC and UOB are 2.55%, 2.58% and 2.55% respectively.

These interest rates for DBS, OCBC and UOB, as labeled in full in Table 3.2, are estimated in the ballpark, based on averaging the interest rates over a 30-year loan term. These private interest rates are fixed rates although the rates in the earlier two or three years may well be set at much more competitive rates, relative to the subsequent years of the loan term.

Table 3.2 Comparison of Private Residential Mortgage Interest Rates

Home Mortgage Lenders	Interest Rates
Housing Development Board (HDB)	2.60%
Development Bank of Singapore (DBS)	2.55%
Overseas Chinese Banking Corporation Limited (OCBC)	2.58%
United Overseas Bank (UOB)	2.55%

Source: Author, 2005; 2020

It is inferred that the mortgage interest rates for private banks are generally much lower than the HDB concessionary interest rate. As such, and in terms of the mortgage interest rates, the notion that the privatization of the HDB concessionary interest-rate loans should infuse and sustain the price competitiveness among private banks in the mid to longer term, is feasible.

The Model Estimation

Albon (1985) much earlier finds that monopolies like public state enterprise are expected or required to operate under an imposed minimum required rate of return (the hurdle rate), which reflects different degrees of inefficiency. He reiterates the importance of setting a financial performance yard stick for public state enterprises and that such monopolistic enterprises should be evaluated, in terms of a single rate of return criterion, for external comparison among fellow public state enterprises, offering broadly similar economic goods in terms of their own investments, via resorting to the cost of capital as the hurdle rate. To put it simply, there is the crucial need to evaluate public state enterprises' performances with other similar private enterprises. It is essential to make a comparison with its own investment and with the use of hurdle rate. In another words, public state enterprises impose on all their activities an internal performance benchmarking in absolute terms, rather than to adopt market-wide performance benchmarking, which is often not available. To measure the efficiency of say Singapore's HDB as a mortgage lender, the HDB mortgage yield and hurdle rate are imputed to be the crucial and relevant financial performance indicators.

Mortgage yields represent a way of measuring a return on investment, expressed as a compound rate of interest, over the entire investment period (Brueggeman, 2001). First, the mortgage yield is computed over the full remaining potential life of the loan, as if the loan would not be prepaid and that the investor holds the loan to maturity. This way the effective interest cost is always be equal to the contract rate of interest. Secondly, the form of the mortgage yield does not reflect the contract interest rate if the mortgage is paid off before maturity. Most Singapore households do not stay in their first flat for their whole life and is true when HDB implements the option, whereby homeowners are free to sell their existing flat after the compulsory occupation period of 5 years. Early prepayment of the mortgage occurs in the event where the households sell their current flats prior to fully paying off their mortgages. The effective mortgage yield must be taken into consideration to better reflect the real world mortgage market and should be imputed, based on the loan repayment terms of 5 years, 10 years and 20 years, which are the assumed periods that HDB homebuyers tend to shift flats. The minority of HDB homebuyers shift their flat after 20 years staying in their existing flats is the exception and excluded in Chapter 3.

It is noted that the effective mortgage yield is likely to remain unchanged for any mortgage amount and with the same mortgage prepayment terms and prepayment penalty. The inference is that regardless of the HDB flat room type that the homebuyer is purchasing, the effective mortgage yield remains unchanged for as long as the mortgage prepayment and penalty terms are unchanged. Therefore, only the HDB 4-room flat is used to impute the effective mortgage yield and is taken to represent all other flat room types. As for the mortgage yield where no prepayment is made, then the effective yield is the same as the contract rate of interest, which would be the HDB concessionary interest rate of 2.6%. Since such a concessionary interest rate is observed to be kept fairly constant for recent few years, the contract interest rate is taken to be the fixed interest rate(s) for study purposes. The effective mortgage yields for the mortgage prepayment periods of 5, 10 and 15 years are imputed to be performance indicators, and deployed to enable comparative analysis with the HDB hurdle rate (the HDB minimum required rate of return p.a.) for the associated mortgage periods of 5, 10 and 15 years. If the effective mortgage yields 5, 10 and 15 years loan prepayment terms are lower and that the yields are equal to the HDB hurdle rates for 5, 10 and 15 years, then the notion that the HDB concessionary interest-rate mortgage be privatized is acceptable. Eq (3.1) is adopted to estimate the monthly loan payment P.

$$\frac{PVA}{(MPVIFA,\ i,\ n)} \tag{3.1}$$

, where

P	– Monthly Loan Payment
PVA	– Present Value of an Annuity (Loan Amount)
i	– Annual Interest Rate compounded monthly
n	– Number of years (Loan Period)
MPVIFA	– Present Value Ordinary annuity $1 per Period (See Appendix)

Effective mortgage yield is estimated based on eq (3.2) with no prepayment.

$$(3.2)$$

$$(\text{MPVIFA},i,n) = \text{PVA}/\text{P} \quad \left[\frac{1}{1+i/12}\right]^1 + \left[\frac{1}{1+i/12}\right]^2 + \;.....\; + \left[\frac{1}{1+i/12}\right]^{12 \;.n}$$

$$(\text{MPVIFA},i,n) = \text{PVA}/\text{P} \tag{3.3}$$

Mortgage balance (MB) is estimated in eq (3.4).

$$\text{MB} = \text{P}(\text{MPVIFA},i,n) \tag{3.4}$$

Effective Mortgage yield is estimated in eq (3.5).
(With Loan Prepayment):

$$\text{PV} = \text{P}(\text{MPVIFA},i,n) + \text{MB}(\text{MPVIF},i,n) \tag{3.5}$$

    , where

    PV   – Present Value

    MPVIF   – Present Value reversion of $1 (See Appendix)

    <u>NB</u>. i is the effective mortgage yield. Also, the factor MPVIFA is used to discount the monthly loan payment while factor MPVIF is used to discount the loan balance.

The Effective Mortgage Yield Estimation

Effective mortgage yield is estimated where no finance charges are made at the time of loan origination. The yield is estimated on the average that HDB may receive as a mortgage lender and with several assumptions:

- The loan payment pattern adopted is the Constant Payment Mortgage (CPM).
- The HDB room-flat type adopted for the estimation is the 4-room HDB flat.

- Interest rate is kept constant at say 2.6% p.a. throughout the end of the mortgage period notwithstanding that such a rate is subjected to quarterly revision in January, April, July and October of each year.
- "Fixed interest rate" is made in inflation-less environment so that the rate of return imputed is the real rate of interest, without having to factor in any risk factor.
- For prices of the HDB flat for which a homebuyer obtains a mortgage, the average valuation by HDB new town and room-flat type for say 1st Quarter 2004 is released by HDB on its web site, and that an average price for 5 HDB new towns is taken as the mortgage amount (see Appendix).
- Mortgage amount is based on 80% of the HDB valuation price and buyers' CPF ordinary account is exactly 20% of the valuation price so that the utilization of the homebuyer's CPF money from the ordinary account for its flat is not be more than 20%, so making the borrowing amount to be exactly 80% of the flat's valuation price. Utilizing CPF money belonging to the homebuyers, is a mandatory requirement of the HDB.
- Homebuyers have sufficient CPF funds in their ordinary account to pay off the additional charges like the conveyance fee, miscellaneous fees, stamp fee and registration fee and/or any other hidden cost.
- All purchasers are homebuyers from the HDB open (resale) market.
- Mortgage period is 30 years.
- Homebuyers, who purchase a HDB flat fall under the normal scheme, where no grants are taken.
- A "Prepayment Penalty" of 3% on the outstanding mortgage payment is charged to each homebuyer, who desires to prepay its loan at the time when it wants to sell its HDB flat.
- Mortgage prepayment terms of Table 3.3 is imputed based on 5, 10 and 15 years, since it is more common for homebuyers to sell their HDB flats within these periods.

Table 3.3. Mortgage Prepayment Terms

Prepayment of Mortgage	5 Years	10 Years	15 Years
Room Type:	4=Room	4-Room	4-Room
Ave. HDB Valuation Price:	S$237,920	S$237,920	S$237,920
Loan Amount:	S$190,336.0	S$190,336.0	S$190,336.0
Loan Term:	30 Years	30 Years	30 Years
HDB Concessionary Interest Rate: (Contract rate of interest)	2.60%	2.60%	2.60%
Monthly Loan Payment:	S$772	S$772	S$772
Years remaining till maturity:	25	20	15
Mortgage Balance	S$168,281	S$143,042.07	S$114,159.57
Mortgage Balance with penalty	S$173,329.43	S$147,333.33	S$117,584.35
Discounted Monthly Mortgage Payment:	S$43,159	S$80,260.28	S$113,231.00
Discounted Mortgage Balance:	S$147,604	S$110,075.01	S$77,105.61
Effective Mortgage Yield p.a.	3.218%	2.919%	2.817%
Mean value p.a.	2.98%		

Source: Author, 2005; 2020.

To solve for i, the "trial and error" i.e. a heuristic methodology, is adopted. This methodology is conducted via guessing the value for i and inserting into an MSExcel spread sheet model, as shown in the Appendix, where i = "3.22". When the correct value for i is found, the solution for the present value should be the same as the mortgage amount.

Eq (3.6) is adopted to estimate the HDB Hurdle Rate,

$$r_i = r_f + \beta (r_m - r_f) \qquad (3.6)$$
, where

r_i - Expected return

r_f	– risk free rate
β	– Beta
$(r_m - r_f)$	– Expected return on the market minus the risk free rate (market risk premium)

Estimating Beta ($\beta_{j)}$

Beta ($\beta_{j)}$ is represented by a "market security index" that measures the covariance between the returns on a particular common stock share and the returns on the common stock market (the market index portfolio). Beta is estimated under the "ex-post analysis", where the historical relationships between the return types are observed, and it is assumed that such a covariance persists into the future.

A pictorial version of the model is depicted in the Appendix. Each plot point *j* expresses the relationship between the return on the market index portfolio for a particular month, and that return on the specific share being examined in that same month,

$$\beta_j = \frac{\text{Cov}(R_j, R_M)}{\sigma 2M}$$

(3.7)

, where

β_j	– Bata of asset *j*
$\text{Cov}(R_j, R_M)$	– Covariance of asset *j* with the market portfolio
σ^2_M	– Variance of the market portfolio

Therefore,

$$\beta_j = = \quad \frac{\Delta r_j}{\Delta r_m} \quad = \quad \frac{\text{Change in } r_j}{\text{Change in } r_m}$$

(3.8)

, where

r_j	– Rate of return on the *j*th common stock share
r_m	– Rate of return on the common stock market index portfolio.

The HDB Equivalent Hurdle Rate Estimation

For Chapter 3's purposes, the beta β_j for HDB cannot be obtained, owing to the fact that HDB does not float its shares or bond investment in the Singapore Stock Exchange (SGX), unlike other real estates companies. For a more meaningful hurdle rate estimation, a reputable and large public listed real estate company, which is engaged in a similar core business as that of the HDB, is selected. The public listed real estate company β_j value relates closely with the HDB β_j value, in the event where the HDB is to expend its activities into that business, which is similar to that of a large public listed real estate company. Such a company for Chapter 3 is the largest public listed property company by asset size in Singapore, CapitaLand Limited is appropriate because it holds a market value of S\$3.7 billion in the Straits Time Index fund as early as year 2003, and that it has the largest percentage of total net assets among other Singapore public listed real estate firms. The estimation of the CapitaLand Ltd company β_j is carried out, based on 36 months' worth of its common stock share-price observations for say three years, 2002, 2003 and 2004 (in the Appendix).

Since a hurdle rate that is not estimated from HDB's own data but from CapitaLand Ltd's own SGX data, is centered on the perception that should the HDB engage in the same business as that of CapitaLand Limited. Such an HDB hurdle rate serves as an equivalent performance indicator of HDB only in respect of the cost of equity to HDB. It is deemed to be derived to be an opportunity cost to the HDB because the HDB does not venture into the private sector direct real estate development and investment business. The HDB hurdle rate so estimated is in effect that minimum required rate of return that HDB would seek to achieve. To place it in more relevant terms, we may know such a minimum required rate of return to be the HDB equivalenurdle rate.

To estimate the HDB's equivalent hurdle rate, three key assumptions are made:

- With reference to Table 3.4, the HDB β_j is secondary information and data sourced from industry practice in Singapore is 1.03. In Chapter 3, no detailed estimation is conducted for the CapitaLand Ltd β_j. Its secondary data is extracted from those detailed estimations, sourced from in its published annual reports for say a 5-year period for trend and data purposes. The estimations are accurate and recent.
- The risk-free rate is based on the return of the Singapore Government Securities (SGS) bond. The risk-free rate so obtained is 2.03%, 2.90% and 3.33% for a 5-year, 10-year and 15-year bonds, respectively. The data is sourced from say the 3rd quarter 2004 SGS data (in the Appendix).
- The Straits Times Index (STI) consist of the common-stock-market 45-stock index, which reflects the daily trading activity of common stock market shares on the Singapore Stock Exchange (SGX). The constituent common stocks account for around 78% of the daily traded value and around 61% of total common stock market capitalization. The STI is utolized to robustly represent the "expected market return" because the STI reflects the Singapore economy performance in general. Additionally, the expected market rate of return, r_m, would be that mean value of **7.53%** for the 3-year funds return from the Singapore "Straits Times Index (STI) Fund, Annual Report 2003" (in the Appendix).

Table 3. 4. Summary of the HDB Equivalent Hurdle Rate Parameters

Bond Period Type	5 Years	10 Years	15 Years
Risk-Free Rate:	2.03%	2.90%	3.33%
Beta value:	1.03	1.03	1.03
Expected Market Return, r_m:	7.53%	7.53%	7.53%

Market Risk Premium:	5.5%	4.63%	4.20%
Hurdle Rate:	7.7%	7.67%	7.66%
Mean value:	7.68%		

Source: Author, 2005; 2020.

The HDB effective mortgage yield is depicted in Fig 3.3 with a mean value of 2.98% p.a. The effective yields are 3.22%, 2.92% and 2.82% p.a. for corresponding mortgage prepayment terms of 5, 10 and 15 years, respectively. With reference to Fig 3.3, there is a gradual increment in the HDB effective mortgage yield when the prepayment is made within a shorter period. It is noteworthy that the HDB effective mortgage yield would be the same as that contract rate of return for the HDB concessionary interest rate, if there is no mortgage prepayment made by the homebuyer.

The HDB equivalent hurdle rates are 7.7%, 7.67% and 7.66% for the different SGS yield returns of bond periods 5, 10 and 15 years, respectively, and with a mean value of 7.68%. It shares a similar trend with that trend, as observed for the effective mortgage yield. The percentage difference between the effective mortgage yields and hurdle rates are 2.0%, 2.28% and 2.36% for 5, 10 and 15 years respectively. 2.22% is the mean difference between the effective mortgage yield and the hurdle rate.

Fig 3.3. The HDB Effective Mortgage Yield

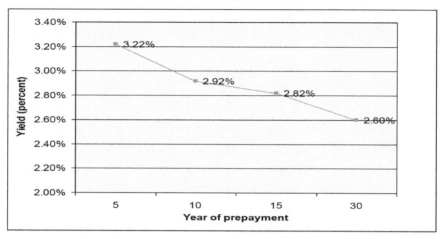

Source: Author, 2005; 2020

As early as 1989, it is so highlighted that if a public enterprise like the Singapore Housing and Development Board (HDB) earns less than a private sector enterprise in the same economic activity, then the HDB is performing more poorly than that private sector enterprise. It appears that the applicable rate for the public sector enterprises like the HDB should be closer and if not, should be the same as that applicable for the private sector enterprises (Ariff, 1989).

His notion would explain why the HDB, being a major public sector enterprise in Singapore, would not set its target lower than that, which the private sector can already perform. So, with the mean effective mortgage yield, which is estimated to be around 2.89% and is lower than the mean hurdle rate of 7.68%, then the effective mortgage yield does not meet the hurdle rate that HDB would want to set. Therefore, the notion that the privatization of the HDB concessionary interest-rate mortgages should be gradually privatized is acceptable.

Concluding Remarks

Chapter 3 examines the underlying structural relationships that affect Singapore's public housing policy to potentially privatize the HDB concessionary-rate mortgages for HDB homebuyers. It envisaged that this potential privatization would infuse and sustain price competitiveness among the domestic private banks in Singapore, and lead to improved efficiency among them as well as the Singapore economy at large. Two structural relationships are discussed in terms of the mortgage interest rate structure. First, a comparison is made between the HDB hurdle rates and the HDB mortgage yields to examine the notion of the potential privatization of the HDB concessionary rate mortgages. The examination reveals that the private banks' interest rates are lower than HDB concessionary rates on average for a 30 year-mortgage term. Therefore, it makes it more attractive for HDB homebuyers to take up the private banks' mortgages rather than the HDB mortgages. The likely reason for the lower interest rates offered by the private banks is primarily due to price competition in terms of the interest rate structure, which the individual banks face among themselves and with the HDB.

Secondly, both the HDB hurdle rates and the HDB mortgage yields are examined. The HDB mortgage yields are compared against the HDB hurdle rates to see whether-or-not the mortgage yields are higher, equal to or lower than the HDB hurdle rates. As the measure of the efficiency of the HDB mortgage financing activity, the examination reveals that the HDB mortgage yields are generally lower than the HDB hurdle rates. It is inferred that the HDB mortgage yield cannot meet the HDB minimum required rate of return, the HDB hurdle rate, which is HDB's own absolute performance benchmarking. Therefore, it is more worthwhile to pass the HDB mortgage financing activity to the private sector, where the Singapore domestic private banks are viable in generating better mortgage yields. In terms of improved efficiency to the banking sector and the Singapore economy, the notion of potentially passing the HDB mortgage financing activity to the Singapore private sector is acceptable.

Chapter 3 is not without its limitations and two are highlighted. First, the private banks' interest rates in Singapore are compared on the assumption that the interest rates would be fixed for a 30 year-loan term. This is because it is not possible to anticipate the floating interest rates offered by the private banks. Such private banks would usually offer fixed interest rate up to a maximum period of two years. Similarly, a fixed interest rate for the HDB concessionary interest rate is assumed and for a much longer 30-year mortgage term. Such a fixed HDB interest rate is not entirely accurate because the HDB offers fixed interest rate but subject to revision every 3 months.

Secondly, the estimated hurdle rates may not precisely represent the HDB hurdle rate, as the cost of equity data is solely based on "CapitaLand Limited". Estimates of the HDB hurdle rates can be sourced from other public listed real estate companies to possibly establish a more accurate cost of equity.

Acknowledgement: The Author wish to gratefully acknowledge the initial work carried out for Chapter 3 by Ms HO Suet Mei, a graduate of the NUS Department of Real Estate, and in consultation with Honorary Professor (University of Hertfordshire, Hatfield, UK), Dr HO Kim Hin / David, during their meaningful brain storming sessions before Professor HO retired from the NUS SDE Department of Real Estate in May 2019.

Chapter 3 Appendix.
The Privatization of the HDB
(Housing and Development Board)
Mortgage

Appendix. Residential Properties @ 31 March 2004

Flat Type	1-Rm	2-Rm	3-Rm	4-Rm	5-Rm	Exe	SA	HUDC	Total
Number	653	6,252	220,978	323,903	205,010	65,155	936	1,865	824,752
Percentage	0.08%	0.76%	26.79%	39.27%	24.86%	7.90%	0.11%	0.23%	100.00%

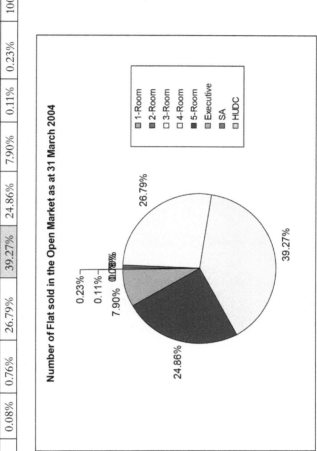

Number of Flat sold in the Open Market as at 31 March 2004

Source: HDB

<u>Appendix</u>. Average Valuation by Town & Flat Type

For 4th Quarter 2004

Town	1-Room	2-Room	3-Room	4-Room	5-Room	Executive
Ang Mo Kio	⋆	$116,300	$173,300	$237,600	$341,100	$457,000
Bedok	⋆	$104,000	$169,300	$229,600	$318,800	$390,000
Bishan	⋆	⋆	$172,000	$278,500	$364,700	$451,100
Bukit Batok	⋆	⋆	$153,200	$220,900	$312,100	$364,600
Bukit Merah	$65,800	$103,400	$176,400	$294,400	$388,500	⋆
Bukit Panjang	⋆	⋆	$156,000	$207,500	$278,200	$360,900
Bukit Timah	⋆	⋆	$199,800	$276,200	$381,100	$463,700
Central	⋆	$122,000	$203,500	$289,900	⋆	⋆
Choa Chu Kang	⋆	⋆	$148,300	$216,200	$296,600	$358,200
Clementi	⋆	⋆	$175,100	$251,400	$343,400	$408,000
Geylang	⋆	$96,900	$152,000	$239,900	$346,500	$396,700
Hougang	⋆	⋆	$161,100	$220,000	$297,900	$373,800
Jurong East	⋆	⋆	$158,500	$214,800	$287,900	$371,000
Jurong West	⋆	⋆	$150,700	$212,500	$279,600	$335,900
Kallang/ Whampoa	⋆	$107,300	$171,200	$268,300	$360,900	$402,500
Marine Parade	⋆	⋆	$201,700	$272,800	$420,100	⋆
Pasir Ris	⋆	$139,000	⋆	$241,100	$303,300	$385,600
Queenstown	⋆	$101,800	$161,100	$303,400	$417,300	$557,500
Sembawang	⋆	⋆	⋆	$222,100	$285,400	$363,800
Sengkang	⋆	⋆	⋆	$234,800	$297,900	$360,200
Serangoon	⋆	$102,000	$162,200	$227,600	$308,300	$380,200
Tampines	⋆	⋆	$184,100	$249,400	$315,200	$390,200
Toa Payoh	⋆	$114,900	$169,300	$275,800	$383,700	$411,500
Woodlands	⋆	⋆	$143,300	$213,500	$277,400	$371,000
Yishun	⋆	⋆	$153,600	$191,800	$274,900	$337,500

Footnote:
  (i)   Flat Types in Towns with asterik (★) indicates no valuation conducted
        for the quarter.
  (ii) Information contained herein is for the purpose of reference for mortgage
        financing by HDB.
Source: HDB

APPENDIX. GRAPHICAL DEPICTION OF MARKET MODEL

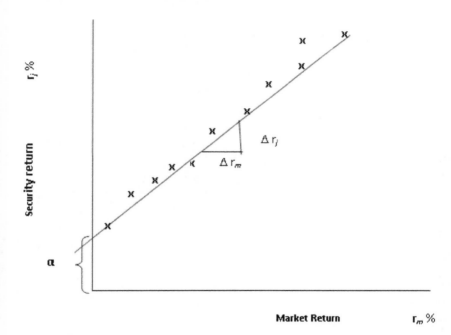

Source: HDB

Appendix. SGS Market in Review 2003 Q3

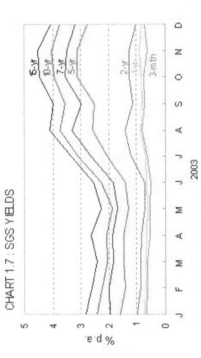

CHART 1.7 : SGS YIELDS

	Jan	Feb	Mar	Apr	May	June	July	Aug	Sept	Oct	Nov	Dec	Average
15 years SGS yield	2.90	2.75	2.50	2.70	2.30	2.50	3.10	4.05	4.00	4.50	4.65	4.00	3.33
10 years SGS yield	2.30	2.10	2.00	2.00	1.90	2.30	3.00	3.65	3.60	4.00	4.05	3.85	2.90
7 years SGS yield	2.00	2.00	1.95	1.90	1.80	1.85	2.65	3.20	3.00	3.40	3.40	3.15	2.53
5 years SGS yield	1.50	1.50	1.50	1.30	1.35	1.50	2.00	2.40	2.40	3.00	3.00	2.85	2.03
2 years SGS yield	1.00	0.90	0.85	0.85	0.70	0.70	1.10	1.30	1.00	1.10	1.20	1.00	0.98
1 years SGS yield	1.00	0.80	0.80	0.75	0.70	0.65	0.75	0.90	0.80	0.75	0.90	0.75	0.80
3 months SGS yield	1.00	0.80	0.80	0.75	0.70	0.60	0.75	0.90	0.80	0.75	0.60	0.75	0.77
Average yield	1.90												

Source: Author

Appendix. Street Tracks STI

PERFORMANCE

Ending			
June 30 2003	3 Month	6 Month	1 Year
From	**31 March 2003**	**31 December 2002**	**30 June 2002**
To	30 June 2003	30 June 2003	30 June 2003
Fund	**15.9%**	**10.1%**	**-3.4%**
Benchmark	14.2%	8.0%	-6.8%

Source: Straits Time Index Fund Annual Report

30 June 2003

Estimate average STI fund

Average of fund: $= \underline{15.9\% + 10.1\% - 3.4\%}$

Estimated base on 3

3 years

$= \underline{7.53\%}$

CHAPTER 4

ASSET VALUE ENHANCEMENT OF SINGAPORE'S PUBLIC HOUSING MAIN UPGRADING POLICY (MUP)

Real option analysis is meaningful to know and its theory has been empirically tested. The concept of real options is viewed as a paradigm shift in evaluating investment projects in terms of option characteristics. The use of real options as a tool for strategic decision-making started with the oil and gas industry as well as the mining companies, and subsequently expanded into the direct real estate, utilities, biotechnology, pharmaceutical and information technology (IT) industries. Among the first direct application of real option pricing theory to the direct real estate market is that by Titman (1985), where the option value to wait for a vacant site to be developed is examined and estimated. This has led to a new framework for evaluating direct real estate investments. With increasing popularity, the real option pricing approach is used to determine the embedded values at various stages of the direct real estate development process. It has been argued that the traditional discounted cash flow (DCF) model is inadequate for evaluating the direct real estate investment projects. A main critique is the model's inability to include changes in future cash flows and a selection of discount rates (Hodders and Riggs, 1985). As a result, the evolution of a stochastic calculus to value financial options has been extended to the evaluation of direct real estate investment projects by the early 1990s. The DCF model considers the expected value of the future cash flows during the holding period of a real asset. By discounting the future cash flows at a predetermined discount rate, the present value of the real asset is determined. However, the underlying and wider market is characterized by changes as well as uncertainties and it tends to deviate from its initial estimation or forecast, under the DCF's holding period. What are not considered include primarily the uncertainty that is to be resolved in the future and the flexibility in responding to possible future changes, which may lead to a number of potential opportunities and their opportunity costs instead of a one-off investment? Real option analysis addresses these shortcomings, in particular the possibility of developing a land today that excludes the possibility to develop it at later time. With no doubt, models for dealing with flexible interest rates, stochastic (i.e. evolving) volatilities and various advanced kinds of exchange options are all waiting to find applications in real option analysis.

The development of public housing in Singapore has distinctly evolved since 1960. In the early stage, many public housing units were produced in the shortest time at low and standardized costs, to meet the urgent need for mass housing. More comprehensive planning for public housing estates had been imposed in the later stages. Large-scale public housing facilities are developed in a highly structured and systematical manner. A quality disparity in the design and facilities among the various stages of public housing development has emerged consequently. To adopt the quality housing concept *en mass*, the Singapore government decided to introduce a long-term public housing upgrading policy. In 1992, the Main Upgrading Programme (MUP) was implemented as the major public housing policy to transform the Housing Development Board (HDB) precincts that are more than 20 years old into better quality housing, and comparable to the newer HDB estates. The HDB undertakes to implement this bold and highly targeted MUP policy to bring about a substantial improvement in the HDB living environment, as part of the government's wider agenda of wealth and asset enhancement nationwide.

The MUP is highly targeted to enhance the social and economic value of public housing in Singapore, and it is only implemented for selected public housing precincts when at least 75 percent of the HDB households in the selected precinct opt for the upgrading during a polling exercise. A schedule along the timeline of 4 years is illustrated in Fig 4.1a and Fig 4.1b for a typical HDB MUP, which targets a precinct in a public housing estate. An option to upgrade arises when a precinct that is selected for MUP is announced publicly towards the end of Year 1 together with the formation of the working committee. Design preparation, detailing and polling planning are implemented in Year 2 while polling activities are carried out at the start of Year 3.

Tender execution and the HDB MUP construction take place through Years 3 and 4, and would be completed by around the middle of Year 4. The precinct's eligible household owners are therefore envisaged to be holding American call options because they have each the right to upgrade their public housing living environment or otherwise at anytime during the upgrading period. Even without a formal real option analysis, many HDB household owners may already anticipate that their flat resale prices would rise before or upon the completion of upgrading. Yet, most of their judgments are purely intuitive and there exists little empirical evidence on the likelihood value of an upgrading opportunity (option value).

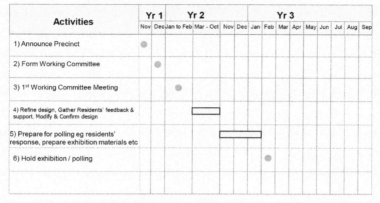

Fig 4.1a. A Typical HDB Main Upgrading Programme (MUP) Schedule

(FROM ANNOUNCEMENT TO POLLING)

Activities	Yr 1		Yr 2				Yr 3								
	Nov	Dec	Jan to Feb	Mar - Oct	Nov	Dec	Jan	Feb	Mar	Apr	May	Jun	Jul	Aug	Sep
1) Announce Precinct	●														
2) Form Working Committee		●													
3) 1st Working Committee Meeting			●												
4) Refine design, Gather Residents' feedback & support, Modify & Confirm design				▭											
5) Prepare for polling eg residents' response, prepare exhibition materials etc					▭										
6) Hold exhibition / polling								●							

Note : This is only an estimated schedule, pending ground condition of respective precinct

Fig 4.1b. A Typical HDB Main Upgrading Programme (MUP) Schedule

(POLLING TO COMPLETION)

Activities	Yr 3											Yr 4				
	Feb	Mar	Apr	May	Jun	Jul	Aug	Sep	Oct	Nov	Dec	Jan	Feb	Mar	Apr	May Jun
1) Hold exhibition / polling	●															
2) Clearances from Authorities; Tender drawings & specifications; Tender & Award		▭														
3) MUP Construction									▭							

Construction Period :
2 to 2 1/2 years depending on package adopted

Note : This is only an estimated schedule, pending ground condition of respective precinct

Source: Author, 2020

The objective of Chapter 4 is to develop a scientific estimate of the value of the embedded option in the Main Upgrading Programme so as to let HDB household owners know how much they benefit from the MUP offering, should they vote for or against the MUP implementation in their precincts and what is the optimal time to sell their flats (to exercise the option). Under the real option pricing framework, the household owner of the HDB flat may better appreciate the associated cost and gain of the MUP policy by estimating the option value to upgrade. It is also possible for this flat owner to better assess its position before any decision is made. Chapter 4 is concerned with the HDB flats at the very established Ang Mo Kio (Public Housing) New Town, which is also one of the largest in Singapore, and it falls under the announced "MUP Batch 19" scheme of the MUP policy. The corresponding criteria are imposed for Chapter 4 and outlined below:

- All flat owners are Singapore citizens, who are eligible for participation in the MUP polling.
- All flat owners are enjoying first upgrading subsidies. In another words, there is no imposition of a 10% sale's levy on the resale of a HDB flat.
- 3-room and 4-room HDB flats are focused on Chapter 4 as these two types of HDB flats form the bulk of the total flats to be upgraded.

To alternatively test the binomial option pricing model, the Samuelson-McKean model is adopted in Chapter 4 for comparative purposes. The transacted resale prices for the upgraded and non-upgraded HDB flats in the Ang Mo Kio new town are sourced for Chapter 4. The HDB Resale Price Index and relevant data are so obtained from several authoritative sources, which include the online web site of the HDB InfoWEB, HDB annual reports, the online Monetary Authority of Singapore (MAS) Data Room and press releases.

Chapter 4 should be interesting to urban economic policy researchers and makers, possibly those interested in urban renewal dynamics and within the context of public housing (HDB) stock renewal and quality sustainability. To such policy researchers, Chapter 4 offers an interesting way to estimate the policy output in terms of the embedded call option value, which enhances the existing HDB household owner's public housing apartment (or flat). Chapter 4 advances the understanding of housing economists of household behavior for investing in a potential and major upgrading of its public housing flat. It enables the household to reap a much more enhanced value in the HDB resale market later on.

Hence, Chapter 4 is organized in the following manner, with the first section providing the introduction. The next (second) section discusses the related literature with regard to real option pricing theory and the option concept. The third section provides a brief review of public housing in Singapore and the development of HDB's upgrading programme, including recent policy changes, and the responses of residents with regards to the upgrading options and the practical problems. The fourth section discusses the intuitive and explicit numerical-method solution of the binomial option-pricing model, in estimating the option values for the upgrading. The Samuelson-McKean closed-form model is then used to test the results of the binomial model. The fifth section discusses the post model findings. Lastly, the sixth section concludes the Chapter's findings and its limitations.

The Related Literature

An option is the right but not the obligation to take an action in the future. It is a contract giving a buyer a right to buy or sell an underlying asset at a specific price on or before a certain date (Brown and Ong, 2000). A call option gives the buyer a right to buy while a put option provides a right to sell. A European option is exercised on the maturity date while an American option can be exercised at any time during the holding period. The value of an option is associated with 'uncertainty" that would be resolved in the near future, or more specifically, in a give period of time. The more the uncertainties the higher the option value becomes. This options value is widely addressed and actively traded in the financial markets. A real option, as a unique and rigorous extension of the financial option, is the embedded value in strategic investments. The real option is concerned with decisions to invest in real or tangible assets. The main characteristic of the real option that distinguishes it from the financial option is the irreversibility of a real asset (or project), i.e. the project cannot be undone once it is exercised. (Further details of the comparison between the financial option and the real option are provided in Appendix I for reference.)

The binomial option-pricing model proposed by Cox, Ross and Rubinstein, CRR, (1979) is an intuitive model that models the risk-neutral process for short-term interest rates[1] and stock prices, and the model builds on their lognormal behavior. It adopts a decision tree approach, based on fundamental economic principle in a discrete–time and a discrete state–price setting. The underlying assumption of the approach is that the stock price follows the same multiplicative movement over each individual period, producing a geometric process with constant up and down multipliers. A jump process, defined by a Poisson distribution, can augment the CRR model, where the jump process denotes the discontinuous arrival of information and causes the asset value, i.e. interest rate, common stock price or the direct real estate yield, to jump. Therefore, the CRR binomial option pricing model may well be appropriate to represent the movement of the underlying HDB resale flat prices, which is subject to private market forces in HDB's large-scale public housing secondary market. In contrast, HDB's primary public housing sector directly allocates new subsidized flats to households, who purchase HDB flats for their first-time. As a result, the modification of the financial option-pricing model for the investment analysis of real assets under some representation of uncertainty is known as real option pricing. The

---

[1]   The risk-neutral process for the short-term interest rate r is defined by an ito process of the form of dr = μ r dt + σ r dz where r follows the geometric Brownian motion, μ is the mean r, σ is the standard deviation and 'σ dz' is a normally distributed stochastic term.

evolution of real option has then been widely used to evaluate the embedded options in many direct real estate investments. In Chapter 4, under the Singapore's MUP policy, the HDB flat owner is deemed as holding a perpetual American call option, which can be exercised anytime during the expiration period.

A useful option-pricing model developed by Samuelson and McKean (1965)[2] is a closed-form solution for pricing a perpetual call option that can be exercised at any time on a dividend-paying underlying asset, which is closely associated with the characteristics of the direct real estate development. It is adopted to estimate the option premium embedded in the Singapore's MUP policy. Besides, the irreversibility of the real option commands a premium and another intrinsic premium exists, owing to the variability of land use intensity. The option to develop at a variable intensity raises the volatility of the land use revenue. It is common practice in direct real estate transactions that the option fee, which is paid under a sale and purchase agreement implies a European call option, which expires when the purchaser decides to abort the transaction. Ong (1999) concludes that the implicit call option value exceeds its face value and that the seller is under-compensated in the absence of legal recourse by the seller. Sing (2002) examines the option to review land rent and the option to renew leases under the public industrial land leases in Singapore. Land rents of public leases are reviewed annually subject to a cap on the land rent increase, and lessees therefore enjoy substantial profit rents. Option premiums for such options are estimated hypothetically using a simulation approach. As a real option is a derivative of the financial option, it is imperative to define the fundamental characteristics of the financial option. The value of a real option is affected by six factors:

---

[2]   This Samuelson and McKean model is similar to the real option model developed for capital budgeting decisions by McDonald and Siegel (1986), and for land valuation by Williams (1991,1997) and Capozza (1991,1994). McDonald and Siegel (1986) use the real option model for capital budgeting decisions that applies a land use intensity variable.

1. The price of the underlying security (common stock price or an upgraded HDB flat opportunity), which represents the present value of cash flow expected from the investment opportunity.
2. The exercise price or strike price, which represents the present value of all the costs to execute the option.
3. Uncertainty, which is the unpredictability in future cash flows owing to one or more factors, such as common stock (or the HDB resale market) price volatility, taxes and dividends. It is represented by the standard deviation of the future stock (or direct real estate sector) price movement in the standard option pricing model
4. Time to expiration of the option.
5. Dividends paid.
6. The risk-free interest rate.

It is worthwhile noting that a call option is exercised when its underlying common stock price exceeds the exercise price. A call option becomes more valuable as its underlying common stock price rises and it becomes less valuable as the exercise price increases. A put option behaves in the reverse way. Uncertainty and the time to expiration are inversely related to the option value. The greater the volatility or the longer the time but prior to expiration, then the greater the option value becomes. Many valuation models are developed to estimate the option's actual price while real option analysis can deploy either the closed-form model or the intuitive model and the explicit numerical-method model solution. Nevertheless, a model is a simplified representation of reality, and so are the two models presented below. It is impossible to capture every possible variable that may influence the results of interest, so these two models capture the effects of the variables that matter the most. A limitation of every model, basically, is the possibility that something excluded from the model influences the results in a material way. For instance, it is difficult to anticipate some regulatory changes, which are totally controlled by the Government's intentions. Most often, the direct impact is on the HDB flat resale prices. That is why the traditional discount cash flows (DCF) approach is receding and the stochastic real option analysis is evolving fast, while the real option analysis can consider the volatility in HDB flat resale prices.

Both the DCF and real option analysis approaches consider all cash flows over the life of a project (for e.g. the HDB flat for resale). Both discount *ex ante* cash flows back to the present and both use market opportunity costs of capital. However, the DCF and the NPV it produces is a special case of real options analysis that assumes no flexibility in decision making. This is because the uncertainty of cash flows is not explicitly modeled in the DCF approach and its NPV. The DCF approach uses only information available today for precommitting today to a go or no-go decision. It does not map out the many paths of possible free cash flows in practice, which may be realized between project start and its finish.

Real option analysis models the flexibility of decision making by eliminating arbitrage price opportunities, and it takes a different perspective where for e.g. a call option is an expectation of maximums, given information available at the future date. For the project with such flexibility, its volatility refers to the uncertainty of the future. In other words, people who consider usages of options in the financial or direct real estate markets effectively seek to secure their financial status, to mitigate risks ahead and to gain wealth ultimately. In Chapter 4, the explicit discrete time-based and price-state binomial tree model is examined in-depth, in conjunction with the closed-from Samuelson-McKean model.

The Binomial Option Pricing Model[3]

The binomial tree approach by Cox *et. al.* (1979) is an intuitive, explicit, discrete time-based and price-state model that provides a numerical-method solution for the pricing of real options. The

---

[3] The illustrative explanation of the binomial option pricing model is shown in Appendix II.

main assumption is that the price of the underlying asset and the corresponding payoffs from the option can move up or down in a fixed and finite manner over discrete periods. The price of the asset behaves multiplicatively over each individual period, resulting in a geometric process with constant up and down multipliers. As reiterated earlier, the binomial model in Chapter 4 adequately represents the underlying HDB resale flat price movement under the MUP policy over discrete periods of time. There are three parameter values required as inputs in the Binomial Option Pricing Model:

- Risk-free interest (r)
- Time to expiration of the option (T)
- Volatility in the built direct real estate market (σ)

When modeling the simplified reality, it is allowable to make some intuitive assumptions in the scope of the real option analysis. It is imperative to note that the binomial model conforms to nine key assumptions to enable an efficient market:

1. The common stock (or an upgraded HDB flat opportunity) price follows a multiplicative binomial process over discrete periods i.e. the process is fixed with future values being log-normally distributed in continuous time.
2. The risk-free interest rate remains constant over the life of the option (T)
3. There are no dividend payments during the T period
4. There are no transaction costs, taxes or margin requirement.
5. There are no risk-free arbitrage opportunities.
6. The risk-free interest rate of buying or selling of the underlying asset remains the same.
7. Trading is continuous and there is no possibility of default on the contract.
8. The option holder will exercise the option if it is profitable.

9. A constant rate of return is continuously compounded, and that the logarithm of the underlying asset value would be normally distributed at the end of T periods.

The output of the binomial option pricing model is the option premium, which is the difference between option value (price) and current exercise value. Once the MUP is offered, the option premium is always non-negative because the option holder (household owner) is never obligated to exercise the option, and there is uncertainty in the future value of the underlying asset (the upgraded HDB flat) than it is today.

The Samuelson-McKean Closed-Form Model[4]

The Samuelson-McKean closed-form option-pricing model is an alternative model estimation of the value of a real option. Samuelson and McKean (1965) develop their model for pricing a perpetual American call option of a dividend-paying underlying asset. Subsequently, their model is extended to estimate the optimal density and the optimal timing of a direct real estate development, owing to its similarity to real option models. The Samuelson-McKean model is chosen for Chapter 4 because of its efficient closed-form solution, its simplicity and practicability in estimating the option value of a developed direct real estate opportunity, i.e. an upgraded HDB flat opportunity. The Samuelson-McKean model not only provides the strike price or land value but also some insight into the optimal timing of the development. There are three parameter values required as inputs in the Samuelson-McKean formula:

- Risk-free interest (r)
- Built direct real estate current cash yield or capitalization rate (γ)
- Volatility in the built direct real estate market (σ)

---

[4] The main components and more explanations of the Samuelson-McKean Model were shown in the Appendix III.

Various variables used in the model are assumed to be known and constant. The outputs of the Samuelson-McKean Closed-Form model are:

- Option elasticity (η): the percentage change in value of an option, which is not yet exercised, and associated with a 1% change in the value of an underlying asset
- Option value (U), the value of an upgrading opportunity
- Hurdle value (V^*), a critical value of underlying asset (an upgraded HDB flat) at and above which, it is optimal to exercise the option immediately.

The HDB Main Upgrading Programme (MUP) Policy

This section reviews related public housing policies and subsidies, inclusive of HDB's MUP policy measures and their recent developments. Public housing as a key government policy for wealth creation and redistribution in the aggregate, playing an important role in ensuring public safety and political stability in Singapore and in many countries. Governments always intervene in housing markets through a series of policies and subsidies, to achieve a set of specific goals for highly targeting HDB resident households. Major reasons for such intervention are to improve environmental and public health, social equity and justice, stimulate economic growth and to overcome any inherent market inefficiency via providing affordable and sufficient quality housing nationwide, which would otherwise be underprovided by the private sector or the free market alone (Hoek-Smit and Diamond, 2003).

There are many studies on evaluating the effects of public housing programs, which are implemented by governments and housing agencies, together with the issues relating to social welfare and individual well-being. Saugeres (2000) explains the welfare role of the government-housing agent in controlling any societal disorder, and in ensuring the cleanliness as well as tidiness of public housing and gardens via regulatory and legislative enforcement. A wide range of social housing programs like rent control and various housing subsidies are found to provide housing solutions, or to improve housing affordability in most Western European countries and the United States of America (US). Hoek-Smit and Diamond (2003) analyze the key issues of housing subsidy systems and major housing finance subsidies available in the world.

As in many cities, Singapore did face severe housing shortage and problems in the 1950s and 1960s. This housing shortage draws little attention from the Colonial Administration before Singapore's independence. Under the government of the People's Action Party (PAP), the Housing Development Board (HDB) is established in 1960. Over the past four decades, the HDB has implemented a successful, cost effective and comprehensive public housing system to efficiently manage the spatial environment, provide housing service and promoting fiscal and social equity. It is evidenced by the success of HDB in housing more than 80% of population after the 1980s from the very low base of 9% in 1960.

The HDB Main Upgrading Program (MUP) policy has been the subject of public debate as the alternative to public housing welfare, with the policy aiming to improve the tangible and intangible value of public housing assets. Within the broader context of wealth creation at the aggregate level, the MUP policy can well be construed to be the next bold and major public policy in Singapore for maximizing the allocative efficiency of scarce resources for public housing.

The HDB MUP Policy

The MUP policy is introduced by the HDB in 1989 with a pilot phase consisting of six precincts to be upgraded. Overwhelming support has come from the grassroots and residents. The MUP policy *per se* is officially launched in 1992 with the announcement of successive batches of HDB precincts selected and implemented under the MUP policy, subject to available surpluses in the government's annual budget. Appendix IV provides the details concerning the precincts that are announced for upgrading, the date of announcement of MUP poll and the date of the MUP billing. There is a total of 19 batches or 341 precincts comprising some 297,300 flats that have been identified and announced for upgrading.

MUP's key outcome is a potentially substantial enhancement of the social and economic value of Singapore's public housing stock, for selected public housing precincts, when at least 75 percent of the HDB households in a selected precinct opt for the upgrading during a polling exercise. Such a desirable outcome is closely connected in essence with studies by Nygaard et al. (2007), McKee (2007) and that by Limberes (2006), which reiterate the emerging influence of modern values and issues in general-election voting for Greece. Within the wider debate over stock transfer as a going concern from one landlord type to another, Nygaard et al. investigate housing stock transfers in the UK, where tenants vote on organizational change and with the option of the status quo, from the view point of the transfer of direct real estate rights, and the valuable underlying attributes of those direct real estate rights.

In other words, the distribution of direct real estate rights associated with the stock transfer policy primarily reflects local council and central government value extraction strategies and constraints, and that a redistribution of direct real estate rights is an essential component in re-centralizing the social housing policy and power incentive structure. Singapore's public housing MUP policy implemented by the HDB is not an exception in this regard. However, McKee (2007) argues that while the massive 2003 Glasgow housing stock transfer has enhanced local control in the decision-making process, within the limits permitted by the transfer framework, such a 2003 stock transfer has failed to deliver the levels of involvement aspired to by those actively engaged in the process. Tense central-local relations contribute to the emergence of conflict, which undermines negotiations surrounding the realization of full community ownership, via second stage transfer.

Limited local studies in Singapore relate to the MUP that assesses its impact from the physical, social, economic, maintenance and operational aspects. Many such studies focus on the MUP satisfaction level in particular precincts. Anecdotal evidence from the local press finds that about half of the residents interviewed at the Bukit Ho Swee upgrading precincts is not satisfied with the improvement works, and are intolerant with the problems encountered. Another concerning the Kim Keat public housing precinct finds that while the objectives of the MUP have been met, residents are generally satisfied and are tolerant of the adjustment difficulties with the upgrading works. Anecdotal evidence further reveals that there is a rise of between S$22,142 and S$32,888 in the market value of an upgraded HDB flat for the first two precincts chosen for the MUP. However, the report is carried out over a period of 3 months between May and July of 1996, and that the period may well be considered to be rather short, for analyzing the prices of upgraded and non–upgraded flats in the same area.

It can be argued that the HDB MUP policy has raised the prices of the upgraded HDB flats. The economic impact, from limited local studies, is found to vary from a 1% to a 10% increment on resale HDB flat prices, depending on the improvement work within the flats and around the precincts (The Straits Times, Aug 2003). The bundle of HDB MUP policy measures is next discussed and that it is these policy measures, which help the HDB households to address to what extent they make simple calculations, between private cost and expected private benefit.

The HDB MUP Scope and Packages

The latest revision in the upgrading program is announced in Parliament on March 2000. In terms of expected private benefits, the scope of the upgrading work concentrates on more functional items, which yield tangible benefits for the HDB households (residents) like the link–ways and lift upgrading. Works that are less functional and cost effective are scaled down or omitted. The shifting of the focus from the precinct and block works to works within the affected HDB flat is better appreciated by the flat owners. (Further details of the scope of the upgrading works are provided in Appendix V for reference). With the revision in the scope of works, the budgeted cost per HDB flat is adjusted as presented in Table 4.1.

Table 4.1. Revised Budgeted Cost per Flat under Revision in MUP

Items	Previous (S$)	Revised (S$)
Precinct & Block Works	24,800	11,600
Flat Works	10,300	14,700
Works Fully Funded By Govt	7,300	11,300
Total (without SAI)	42,400	37,600
Space Adding Item (SAI)	24,800	20,700
Total (with SAI)	67,200	58,300

Source: HDBInfoWEB, 2008; Author, 2020

There are two upgrading packages offered under the MUP.

- Standard Package - comprises improvement works carried out on the precinct, block and flat.
- Standard Plus Package - comprises all the improvement works carried out under the Standard Package plus a space–adding item (SAI).

Subsidies, Cost Sharing and the Upgrading Levy Policy Measures

In terms of the private cost at the HDB household level, the government heavily funds the MUP policy while the households (residents) only need to pay a small part of the upgrading package. In this manner, the government keeps to the minimum possible the private cost at the HDB household level. Table 4.2 shows the income and expenditure

of HDB's flat upgrading activity from 1993 to 2002. The annual deficit is equivalent to the subsidies provided to the affected residents each year. The upgrading subsidy over the past three years has stabilized at S$270 million p.a. A total of S$3 billion of subsidy is incurred by HDB between 1993 and 2002 (i.e. the deficit from HDB's upgrading operations).

Table 4.2. HDB's Flat Upgrading Activity: Income & Expenditure(1993–2002) (in S\$'000)

Year	Income	Upgrading cost	Income as % of upgrading cost	General & other expenses	Total expenditure	Income as % of total expenditure	DEFICIT
1993	NA	NA	NA	NA	-1,347	NA	-1,347
1994	2,819	NA	NA	NA	-244,746	1.15%	-241,927
1995	22,977	-237,679	9.67%	-3,046	-240,725	9.54%	-217,748
1996	21,425	-382,893	5.60%	-3,628	-386,521	5.54%	-365,096
1997	46,080	-486,791	9.47%	-6,374	-493,165	9.34%	-447,085
1998	42,009	-540,452	7.77%	-6,622	-547,074	7.68%	-505,065
1999	189,132	-548,309	34.49%	-8,102	-556,411	33.99%	-367,279
2000	74,634	-316,852	23.55%	-12,005	-328,857	22.69%	-254,223
2001	36,219	-299,977	12.07%	-13,462	-313,439	11.56%	-277,220
2002	61,603	-308,215	19.99%	-24,541	-332,756	18.51%	-271,153
	496,898	-3,121,168		-77,780	-3,443,694		-2,946,796

Source: Selected HDB Annual Reports, 2003; Author, 2020

Since its implementation, the MUP subsidies are revised twice in 1996 and 2000. Under the latest revised MUP policy, the budget for upgrading is adjusted to more affordable rates as observed in Table 6.1, enabling more precincts to be selected for upgrading. Depending on the types of the HDB flat, the government subsidies for the MUP upgrading range between 83% and 93% for the Standard Package and between 57% and 81% for the Standard Plus Package. Details of the cost sharing ratios (CSRs) for the upgrading cost to be divided by the government and the HDB household (flat owner) and the amount payable are provided in Table 6.3. According to HDB, the upgrading bills for the HDB households (flat owners) are about 25% less for the Standard Package and 10% to 20% less for the Standard Plus Package. The subsidy for the SAI (space-adding item) cost is reduced substantially for the larger flats to discourage over consumption.

Government subsidy for upgrading is meant to benefit the HDB household headed by a Singapore Citizen but not more than one upgrading subsidy is entitled to ensure an equitable distribution of such subsidies. In line with this rule, the first policy revision in 1996 rules out the reduction of government subsidies for Singapore citizens whose second or subsequent HDB flat undergoes MUP upgrading. The polling revision also stipulates the withdrawal of subsidy for Singapore permanent residents (SPRs). SPRs are to pay for the full sum of the upgrading cost if their HDB flats undergo MUP upgrading.

Polling and Payment Policy Measures

Upgrading proceeds only if 75% or more of the eligible households in the precinct are in favor of the Standard Package offered. From Table 4.3, the Standard Plus Package, the space-adding item is to be provided only if 75% or more of the eligible households in the HDB block are in favor of the space-adding item. The amended HDB Act and the Polling Rules exclude the right to participate in the poll for upgrading in the case of Singapore permanent residents (SPRs). Such a poll and the public housing MUP policy are only meant for citizen

HDB households to benefit. The upgrading cost is payable upon the completion of upgrading work and billing commences when the upgrading cost is finalized. The HDB flat owner chooses to pay the cost in one lump sum or through monthly installments over 5 or 10 years. Payment is made through the Central Provident Fund (CPF) contributions or in cash or both.

Table 4.3. Cost Sharing Ratio in % & Maximum Amount Payable, S$

Flat Type	1/2/3 Room		4 Room		5 Room		Executive	
Govt Cost Share (G) & Flat Owner Cost Share (F)	**G**	**F**	**G**	**F**	**G**	**F**	**G**	**F**
Precinct Block (S$11,600)	90%	10%	85%	15%	80%	20%	75%	25%
Flat (S$14,700)	90%	10%	85%	15%	80%	20%	75%	25%
Works Fully Funded by the Govt (S$11,300)	100%	0%	100%	0%	100%	0%	100%	0%
Standard (w/o SAI) (S$37,600)	93% (S$34,970)	7% (S$2,630)	90% (S$33,655)	10% (S$3,945)	86% (S$32,340)	14% (S$5,260)	83% (S$31,025)	17% (S$6,575)
SAI★ (S$20,700)	60%	40%	40%	60%	20%	80%	10%	90%
Standard Plus (with SAI) (S$58,300)	81% (S$47,390)	19% (S$10,910)	72% (S$41,935)	28% (S$16,365)	63% (S$36,480)	37% (S$21,820)	57% (S$33,095)	43% (S$25,205)

★SAI = Space-adding item

(Source: HDB InfoWEB; 2004 & 2005, Author, 2020))

The Public Response

Public annoyance is largely and noticeably registered through the local press and mass media over MUP project delays, contractors' money disputes and cash flow problems as well as public suspicion over quality and workmanship for MUP works. The cost and stalled upgrading works at the Marine Terrace HDB estate in June 2003, did irritate affected households there. Inconvenience, health and pollution problems during the upgrading works prompt the resident households to be hesitant in voting for the upgrading in some cases. In addition, affordability in housing purchases and expenditure is constrained owing to gloomy economic conditions, job uncertainty and the Central Provident Fund cuts in 2003. In August 2003, the unfavorable MUP poll result for the HDB Pandan Gardens Precinct is the first public housing precinct then to reject the main upgrading program since the launch of the MUP policy in 1992.

In the wake of dissatisfied public sentiment and weakening prospects of the government's budget surpluses, the polling for the latest batch of precincts under the MUP policy is likely to be postponed to the following year or to be more evenly spread out over the next several years. This postponement outcome denotes the social cost where the public housing stock deteriorates over time even under routine maintenance. Another social cost is the undermining of the HDB household's commitment to upkeep its HDB flat as a responsible stakeholder-owner. Nevertheless, and according to the HDB Sample Household Survey 2003[5], it is shown that a mere 13.2 per cent of HDB households are still considering upgrading, amounting to 108,389 households.

There is the average of about 4,400 HDB upgraded flats per year between 2003 and 2008. Yet, there is no formal empirical estimate of how many HDB homebuyers have realized the embedded options once the MUP is offered. Most HDB homebuyers in the

---

[5]   HDB conducts the SHS once every five years on residents living in HDB flats. The latest survey conducted in 2003 covered a total of 7,300 households in all the HDB towns and estates.

real world experience the intrinsic benefits of the MUP while they are not able to quantify the benefit of it accurately. So, are the HDB homebuyers rational enough to make a consistent decision based on their preferences? Accordingly, rational HDB homebuyers choose what they believe is to be the best approach to achieve their desired goals i.e. utility maximization. To simplify the real world, some unrealistic assumptions are made:

- A HDB homebuyer has precious information about exactly what would occur under any choice made.
- A HDB homebuyer has the cognitive ability to weigh every choice against each other choice.
- A HDB homebuyer is aware of all possible choices.

Relaxation of the above assumptions causes the so-called bounded rationality, which means that the HDB homebuyer experiences limits in formulating and solving complex problems as well as in processing information. As a fast-evolving value enhancement and asset management tool, real option analysis inclusive of its option pricing is an instrumental reason to guide human behavior.

The HDB MUP Policy and Its Real Option Model Estimation

This ensuing section discusses the estimation of the option premium for a HDB flat under the HDB MUP policy. Real option analysis plays an important role in the valuation of the HDB flat upgrading opportunity. The embedded option in the MUP provides an HDB household owner with an economic flexibility. He can choose to exercise the option at any time by selling his flat on the HDB resale market, upon completion of the upgrading if he is confident that resale prices are stable or rising. He can give up the opportunity to upgrade if he considers the subsidy benefit and the possible payoffs are minimal, with respect to the upgrading cost that he must pay. A perpetual[6] American call option therefore exists for the HDB flat owner, for which his flat is within a precinct that is announced to be part of the MUP policy. It can be viewed that at any time, there are the following:

- A right to accept the upgrading and to subsequently sell the HDB flat upon the upgrading completion.
- A right to reject the upgrading during the poll or to sell the HDB flat before the completion of the upgrading work.

As HDB has identified the MUP completion stage to be one of the key reasons for the rise in resale prices of HDB flats, the option is deemed to be in the money[7]. It is widely accepted that the upgraded HDB flats command higher resale prices than non-upgraded ones in the vicinity. The divergence of price movements between the MUP and non-MUP HDB flats is deemed to occur nearer to the completion of the upgrading works. Furthermore, the substantial subsidies provided by the government enable the HDB flats under the MUP policy to be subject to capital value appreciation, upon the completion of the upgrading works. Nonetheless, four assumptions are made to minimize the practical restrictions on the MUP policy:

1. All homebuying flat owners are Singapore citizens who are eligible for participation in the MUP polling.
2. All homebuying flat owners are entitled to a first upgrading subsidy. In other words, there is no reduction in the upgrading subsidies nor the imposition of a 10% levy on the resale of the HDB flat in future. Otherwise, the upgrading cost may outweigh the value of the MUP upgrading.

---

[6] Perpetual means the underlying asset (upgraded flat) of this option pays dividends (rental) regularly.

[7] In the money: situation in which an <u>option's</u> <u>strike price</u> is below the current <u>market price</u> of the <u>underlying</u> asset (for a <u>call</u> option) or above the current market price of the underlying asset (for a <u>put option</u>).

3. The government has provided a sufficient budget for the MUP policy.
4. The upgrading items, the conditions of the upgraded flats and the HDB flats to be upgraded remain the same.

Before proceeding with the real option pricing models, it is necessary to clearly define our models' estimate of the so called "Option Premium". In the financial world, the option premium represents the amount per share that an option buyer pays to the seller. In the MUP policy, the option premium represents the value that a homebuying HDB flat owner gains from the MUP offering. In other words, this option premium can be regarded as the present value of the future net benefit from selling the upgraded flat under the real option analysis approach. The option premium is estimated as if it not only considers the current value of underlying asset (upgraded flat), the time to expiration (option holding period) and the exercise cost (upgrading cost shared by the homebuying owner), but also considers the approximated risk-free interest rate, the direct real estate dividend/capitalization yield (annual rent over the resale price) and the resale price volatility in a stochastic approach. The option premium depends on various variables, in particularly the time factor and future uncertainties.

Interestingly, the longer the expiration period (the period of upgrading works) and the higher the volatility of resale prices on the HDB flat resale market, then the higher the option premium value. Additionally, when the Samuel-McKean Closed-Form Model is adopted, the option premium is formulated as the difference between the option value and the current value of exercise[8]. The real option is deemed to be in the money if the current real option exercise value is positive. In contrast, the real option is deemed to be out of the money

---

8   Current value of exercise = current value of underlying asset − current exercise cost.

In the MUP policy, the current value of underlying asset is the current value of upgraded flat. The current exercise cost is the current upgrading cost shared by the household owner.

if the current real option exercise value is negative. The option is in the money when the current real option exercise value is zero. Furthermore, the hurdle value (a critical value of underlying asset), which is embedded in the Samuelson–McKean Formula, measures the optimal time to exercise the real option.

Study Sample and Parameters

The HDB announces 10 precincts comprising 64 blocks under Batch 19 for the MUP of May 2002, after which the polls for these precincts would be shortly conducted. For the purposes of Chapter 4, the HDB precincts in the Ang Mo Kio New Town are chosen, owing to the substantial volume of flats under the MUP, and the high availability of HDB resale flat transactions. The HBD 3-room and 4-room flats are the focus of Chapter 4 because these two types of HDB flats form the bulk of the upgraded flats. The Chapter confines the sample to those HDB flats that are upgraded or to be upgraded with the space–adding item (SAI). The MUP Standard Package is found to have minimal impact on the value of an upgraded HDB flat, as compared to the MUP Standard Plus Package (The Straits times, Aug 2003).

From observations of the HDB resale database, upgrading with the SAI would add some 6m² (65 sf) of built space to the original HDB flat. Therefore, the types of HDB flats covered in Chapter 4 include a typical 3-Room flat of 67m² (720 sf) to be upgraded to 73 m² (785 sf); and a typical 4-Room flat of 92m² (990 sf) to be upgraded to 98 m² (1,055sf). Resale prices for the upgraded and non-upgraded HDB flats in the Ang Mo Kio new town are sourced to derive the current value of the HDB flat upgrading under the MUP. Price adjustments are made accordingly using the HDB Resale Price Index (Appendix VI). Details of the public housing precincts and the areas identified for Chapter 4 are summarized in Table 4.4.

Table 4.4. HDB Blocks, Precincts and Areas Selected for Study

Upgraded		
Batch	**Precinct**	**Block & Street Name**
10	Ang Mo Kio (Ave 3)	Blks 129 to 134 Ang Mo Kio Ave 3
8	Ang Mo Kio (Ave 4)	Blks 254 to 258 Ang Mo Kio Ave 4
6	Ang Mo Kio Ave 3/6	Blks 301, 302, 322 to 329 & 348 Ang Mo Kio Ave 3
Demonstration	Ang Mo Kio	Blks 311 to 314, 343 to 347 Ang Mo Kio Ave 3
Non Upgraded ★		
Batch 19		Blks 411 to 421, 641 & 644, 642, 643, 648, 649, 645, 646 & 647,
		Ang Mo Kio Ave 4,5,6,10
★ To enlarge sample size, other blocks in the same vicinity are included if transactions are available		

Source: HDB InfoWEB; 2004 & 2005; Author, 2020

Six key parameters are deployed as basic inputs for the required models. The values are obtained from primary and authoritative data sources:

1. Current Value of Upgrading (S$_o$). The current value of upgrading is the average resale prices of upgraded and non-upgraded HDB flats. Resale prices are chosen at the time of the first MUP poll rejection of August 2003 for the 'HDB Pandan Gardens' precinct from MUP's start in 1992; of gloomy economic conditions, jobs uncertainty and the Central Provident Fund (CPF) cuts of 2004. Resale prices are so scoured from 2002Q2 to 2003Q3 of the resale database of the on-line HDB InfoWEB, and are adjusted with the use of the HDB resale price index. The current values of upgrading are estimated to be S$278 psm (S$26psf) and

S$161 psm (S$15psf) for the 3-Room and the 4-Room flats, respectively.

2. <u>Cost of upgrading (K).</u> From a homebuying flat owner's perspective, the cost of upgrading would be the same more or less at S$10,910 and S$16,365 for the 3-Room and the 4-Room HDB flats, respectively[9].

3. <u>Average option holding period (T).</u> T is taken to be the period from the time when the HDB precinct is announced for upgrading until the completion of the upgrading works. T of 4 years is inferred from the completed upgrading projects.

4. <u>Risk free rate (r).</u> "r" is the average 5-Year Singapore government bond yield in that the period of the bond maturity is as close as possible to the option holding period. The average yield from January 2002 to December 2003 is estimated to be 2.345% and that the data is sourced from the Monetary Authority of Singapore (MAS) database.

5. <u>Yield rate or capitalization rate (γ).</u> The resale price and annual rent are required to determine γ. The average resale price is imputed from the HDB resale flat transaction database, while the average rent is obtained through telephone enquiries from numerous housing agents[10]. The yield rates for the 3-Room HDB flat and the 4-Room HDB flat are found to be 5% and 4.5% respectively. The yield rate is assumed to be the same throughout the option holding period.

6. <u>Volatility (σ).</u> The quarterly standard deviation of the returns of the HDB resale flat prices is estimated using the quarterly resale database of the on-line HDB InfoWEB from 1990Q1 to 2003Q3. The annual standard deviation of returns is imputed by multiplying the quarterly standard deviation with the square root of the period of 4 quarters. The underlying volatility of the HDB resale flat prices is imputed to be 12.57%.

---

[9] Please refer to Table 3.

[10] Personal communication in during 2003Q4.

The Binomial Real Option Pricing Model

Given the values of the parameters in Table 6.5, the estimation of the option premiums for a 3-Room HDB flat and a 4-Room HDB flat is outlined stepwise in Table 4.5 and Fig 4.2.

Table 4.5. Real Option Premium Parameters

Parameter	Values
$\sigma =$	12.57%
$r =$	0.02345
$T =$	4
$n =$	4
$\Delta t = T/n =$	1
$u =$	1.13398729
$d =$	0.8818441
$p =$	0.562708
$1-p$	0.437292

Source: Author, 2008 & 2020

From Fig 4.2, the upper cell of each node denotes the value of upgrading and its subsequent likely movements upward and downward. The lower cell represents the option value once it is exercised at time t. The option values are imputed backwards from time, t = 4 and the option premium is arrived at the first node corresponding to the present time, t = 0. The option premium is estimated to be S$10,324 for the 3-Room HDB flat, while a much lower option premium of S$2,001 is estimated for the larger 4-Room HDB flat in Fig 4.3.

Fig 4.2. Binomial Model Of Real Option Premium For A Typical 3-Room HDB Flat

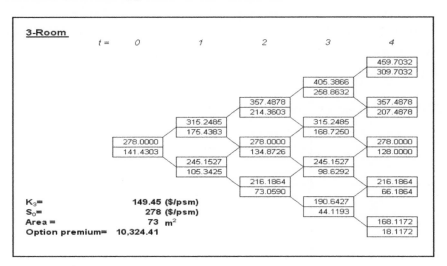

Source: Author, 2020

Fig 4.3. Binomial Model Of Real Option Premium For A Typical 4-Room HDB Flat

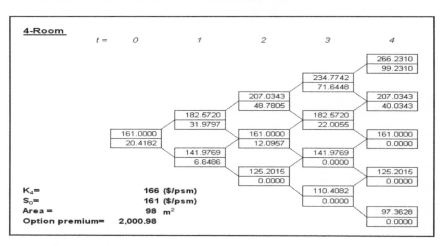

Source: Author, 2020

The Samuelson-McKean Closed-Form Option Pricing Model

Given the foregoing parameters defined earlier, the option premiums for upgrading can be alternatively estimated from the Samuelson-McKean model for the 3-Room HDB flat and the 4-Room HDB flat. Option elasticity[11] is first imputed to be 4.56 for a typical 3–Room HDB flat, which represents a 4.56% change in the value of upgrading, corresponding to a 1% change in the value of a 3-Room HDB flat. Secondly, the hurdle value V★ is found to be S$187 psm[12] and that the potential upgrading value U_3 is S$263 psm[13].

The option premium embedded in the upgrading of a 3–Room HDB flat is estimated to be S$139 psm (S$12.90 psf) or S$10,183 for the flat size area of 73 m² (or 785 sf). The associated option premium for upgrading a typical 4–Room HDB flat adopting the Samuelson-McKean model is estimated to be S$19 psm (S$1.80 psf), or S$1,905 for the flat size area of 98 m² (or 1,055 sf). The estimation details of the Samuelson- McKean model is presented in Table 4.6 and Table 4.7.

Table 4.6. Samuelson-Mckean Real Option Premium For A Typical 3-Room HDB Flat

3-Room		(Area = 73m2)	
Risk free rate	r	2.345%	
Yield rate	γ_3	5.000%	
Volatility	σ	12.57%	
Option elasticity	η_3	4.9569453	
		S$/psm	S$/psf
Potential upgrading value	U_3	268.04	24.90

---

[11]   Formula (8) under the Appendix III.
[12]   Formula (9) under the Appendix III.
[13]   Formula (10) under the Appendix III.

Current value of upgrading	V_3	278.00	25.83
Cost of upgrading	K_3	149.45	13.88
Hurdle value	$V^\star_3$	**187.22**	**17.39**
Option premium		**139.49**	**12.96**
Option premium of a typical 3-Room HDB flat		S$10,182.67	

Source: Author, 2020

Table 4.7. Samuelson-Mckean Real Option Premium For A Typical 4-Room HDB Flat

4-Room (Area = 98m2)

Risk free rate	r	2.345%
Yield rate	γ_4	4.500%
Volatility	σ	12.57%
Option elasticity	η_4	4.4001771

		S$/psm	S$/psf
Potential upgrading value	U_4	13.45	1.25
Current value of upgrading	V_4	161.00	14.96
Cost of upgrading	K_4	166.99	15.51
Hurdle value	$V^\star_4$	**216.10**	**20.08**
Option premium		**19.44**	**1.80**
Option premium of a typical 4-Room HDB flat		S$1,905.04	

Source: Author, 2020

The Post Model Findings

The HDB flat upgrading option premium from the binomial real option-pricing model is consistent with the option premium from the Samuelson–McKean model, in terms of the same order of magnitude. It shows that both models are useful in valuing the embedded real option. The slight difference between the two model results may well lie with the variable inputs and underlying assumptions. First, the capitalization rate is omitted in the binomial model and is critical to Samuelson–McKean model. Secondly, the binomial model is intuitive and determines the option value via discrete time steps of up to t = 4 years, while the Samuelson–McKean model provides a closed form solution as opposed to the binomial model's numerical-method solution. Table 4.8 summarizes the option premium (value) results for the two models and the percentage difference between them by the HDB flat type. Differences in the results are within an acceptable random-error measurement range of ±5%. The difference is relatively larger for the 4-Room HDB flat. A likely reason can be the much fewer transaction records in the case of the 4-Room HDB flat.

Table 4.8. The Binomial and Samuelson-McKean Option Premiums for Upgrading

	3-Room	*4-Room*
Binomial model	$10,324	$2,001
Samuelson–McKean model	$10,183	$1,905
% Difference	1.37%	4.80%

Source: Author, 2020

The total cost of upgrading is the same for all types of HDB flats but the upgrading subsidy falls by the flat size. A homebuying 3-Room HDB flat owner pays 9% less for a Standard Plus Package than a homebuying 4-Room HDB flat owner. In other words, the upgrading cost or the cost of the real option is lower in the case of a 3-Room HDB flat, while its upgrading value is higher when compared to a 4-Room HDB flat in relative terms. However, these subsidies have no bearing on the resale prices of HDB flats. Consequently, the homebuying 3-Room flat owner benefits from a relatively high option premium.

Table 4.9 compares the upgrading values (S_0), upgrading costs and option premiums by HDB room flat type. The option premiums as a fraction of the upgrading value are found to be 50.6% and 12.42% for the HDB 3-Room and the HDB 4-Room flats, respectively. Therefore, the option to upgrade for a smaller HDB 3–Room flat is more favorable. The option premium is substantially smaller and is less attractive for the larger 4-Room HDB flat.

Table 4.9. Comparison of Upgrading Value, Upgrading Cost and Option Premium according to Flat Unit Type

	3-Room (psm)	*4-Room (psm)*
Average upgrading value (S_0)	$278	$161
Estimated upgrading cost paid by owner	$150	$167
Option premium★	$140	$20
Option premium%	50.60%	12.42%

★ <u>NB.</u> The average value of the 2 models.

Source: Author, 2020

Concluding Remarks

Real option analysis, inclusive of its option pricing, is widely debated in the finance and economic literature. It helps to resolve the deficiency of the traditional DCF approach to mitigate risk and enhance the flexibility in investment decision making. The consequential development of real option models and the advancement in computing power enable the growing deployment of these models to direct real estate investment opportunities. Chapter 4 highlights the binomial option-pricing model, proposed by Cox, Ross and Rubinstein, CRR (1979), which can model the risk-neutral process for short term interest rates[14], common stock prices and even the HDB resale flat prices. The CRR binomial option pricing model may well be appropriate to represent the movement of the underlying HDB resale flat prices, subject to private market forces in HDB's large scale public housing secondary resale market. In other words, the HDB resale activities exist in a hypothetical market without regulatory constraints.

It is imperative to note that the binomial model conforms to several key assumptions.[15] Nevertheless, the underlying assumptions of the model may not hold in practice. It can be argued that the use of option pricing theory may not necessarily minimize risk and produce a more accurate estimate. It is reasonable to merely observe the sensibility of the model's result to changes in the model's assumption and parameters, when real option models are introduced, according to Oppenheimer (2002).

Singapore's highly effective public housing policy has housed an overwhelming proportion of about 87 percent of the population. The Housing and Development Board (HDB), the national housing authority, is shifting its wealth redistributive focus to more allocative efficient housing policy initiatives in the presence of scarce resources for public housing. The HDB Main Upgrading Program (MUP) is therefore a heavily subsidized and highly targeted public housing policy. Since its inception in 1992, the HDB has budgeted some S$3 billion to finance the MUP policy. Revisions in the MUP policy are made regularly to keep it closely relevant to the general public's expectation and feedback. Limited local and anecdotal evidence have shown that the HDB MUP policy affects public housing households and the affected areas. One positive impact is the asset value enhancement of the HDB flats within the upgraded public

---

[14]

[15]   Assumptions are shown in the second section of Chapter 4.

housing precincts. The value of the upgraded HDB flat, particularly with the space–adding item (SAI), has improved considerably. The embedded real option premiums for HDB flats under the MUP policy are found to be around S\$10,300 for a 3–Room HDB flat and S\$2,000 for a larger 4–Room HDB flat. These real option values are estimated from both the binomial real option pricing model and the Samuelson–McKean model.

The estimation of the real option value to upgrade may help the homebuying HDB flat owner to better assess his enhanced flat value, and to better appreciate the cost and gain involved. It enables the homebuying HDB flat owner to make a better decision to hold or to unlock the underlying value of his HDB flat, affected by the MUP policy. Chapter 4 shows that the MUP subsidies have a significant impact on the corresponding option premium. A 3–Room homebuying HDB flat owner is more inclined to opt for upgrading while the option premium is deemed to be less attractive for upgrading in the case of the homebuying 4–Room HDB flat owner. In addition, some bias may be induced by an inadequate amount of transaction data available for the 4–Room HDB flats. The public housing sector may well require more time to stabilize in tandem with the revision to the MUP policy, in particularly the secondary HDB resale market. Flats in different locations may well command different values. Finally, the resale price index of HDB flats may not be representative of the Ang Mo Kio public housing estate. Therefore, Chapter 4's findings can be extended to estimate the value of upgrading at other HDB housing estates like the Bedok, Telok Blangah and Marine Parade HDB estates, provided that there are sufficient transaction data available. It is also possible to examine the option values for more HDB room flat types and their impact on the hold–sell decision.

Acknowledgement: *The author wishes to gratefully acknowledge the initial work carried out for Chapter 5 by Associate Professor Muhammad Faishal Bin Ibrahim (Singapore Minister of State) (National University of Singapore, Department of Real Estate); by Ms Ngo Sie Yin, a graduate of the NUS Department of Real Estate; and in consultation with Honorary Professor (University of Hertfordshire, Hatfield, UK), Dr HO Kim Hin / David, during their meaningful brain storming sessions before Professor HO retired from the NUS SDE Departments of Real Estate and Building in May 2019.*

Appendix I

Comparison of Financial Option and Real Option

Financial Options	Real Options
Short maturity, usually in months.	Longer maturity, usually in years.
Underlying variable driving its value is equity price or price of a financial asset.	Underlying variables are cash flows, which in turn are driven by market, personal and unknown factors.
Cannot control option value by manipulating stock prices.	Can increase option value by personal decisions.
Values are usually small.	Values can be quite large.
Competitive or market effect are irrelevant to its value and pricing.	Outside factors drive the value.
Have been around and traded for more than four decades.	A recent development in corporate finance, but not currently used in personal financial planning.
Usually solved using closed form partial differential equations and simulation/ variance reduction techniques for exotic options.	Usually solved using closed form equations and binomial lattices with simulation of the underlying variables.
Marketable and traded security with comparables and pricing information	Not traded and proprietary in nature, with no market comparables.
Business and personal assumptions and actions have no bearing on valuation.	Personal actions and assumptions drive the value.

The Binomial Option Pricing Model

The binomial tree below depicts the possible movements of price over one period of time.

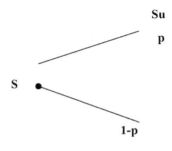

The current price of the underlying asset, S, may move upward to Su with probability p or downward to Sd with probability 1-p, where u–1 and d–1 are the rates of return of the asset over one period when the prices are expected to move upward or downward (u >1 and d<1). At the end of one period t, the option value of the underlying asset, C, is depicted below as if the option is a call option that has a strike price K.

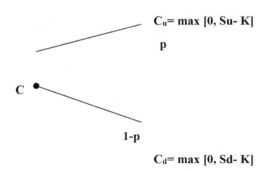

If the option value of the underlying asset is depicted as if the option is a put option that has strike price K, then the option value of the underlying asset is depicted below:

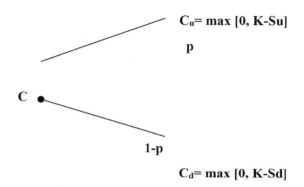

C_u= max [0, K-Su]

p

C

1-p

C_d= max [0, K-Sd]

Assuming that a risk-free arbitrage does not exist, the option value of a portfolio over one period is

$$C = [p\ C_u + (1\text{-}p)\ C_d]\ /r \qquad \text{------------} (1)$$

where $p \equiv \dfrac{r-d}{u-d}$ and $1-p \equiv \dfrac{u-r}{u-d}$, with r being the risk-free interest rate.

However, in a binomial process with multiple periods T and n sub-periods, a 2–step Binomial tree is depicted below:

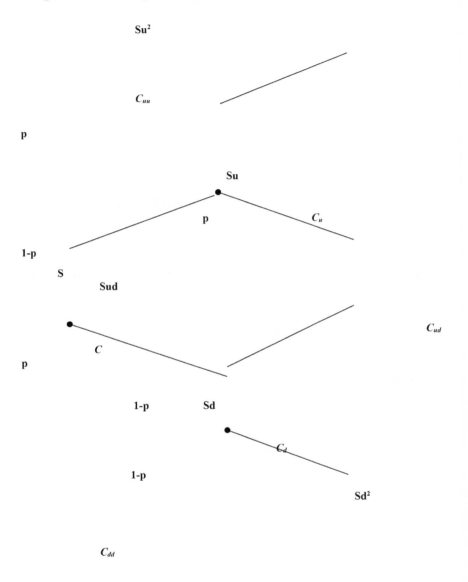

The volatility per period, σ, is assumed to be constant and thus the underlying asset would have a constant rate of return, which is continuously compounded. The logarithm of the underlying asset value would be normally distributed at the end of T periods with the cumulative variance $\sigma^2 T$. Then,

$$u = e^{\sigma (\Delta t)^{1/2}} \qquad \text{------------ (2)}$$

$$d = e^{-\sigma (\Delta t)^{1/2}} \qquad \text{------------ (3)}$$

where $t = T/n =$ the length of one sub-period in n number of periods.

At $t = 1$, the option values are given by:

$$C_u = e^{-r\Delta t}[p\, C_{uu} + (1-p)\, C_{ud}] \qquad \text{------------ (4)}$$
$$C_d = e^{-r\Delta t}[p\, C_{ud} + (1-p)\, C_{dd}] \qquad \text{------------ (5)}$$

At $t = 0$, the option value is given by:

$$C = e^{-r\Delta t}[p\, C_u + (1-p)\, C_d] \qquad \text{------------ (6)}$$

, where the probability p of an upward move is expressed as:

$$P = \frac{e^{r\Delta t} - d}{u - d} \qquad \text{------------ (7)}$$

Appendix III

The Samuelson-McKean Closed-Form Model

As stated earlier, there are three parameter values as inputs in the model,

- Risk-free interest (r)
- Build direct real estate current cash yield or capitalization rate (γ)
- Volatility in the built direct real estate market (σ)

These three required inputs are used to measure the option elasticity (η). The option elasticity is defined as the percentage change in value of an option that is not yet exercised, and associated with a 1 % change in the value of an underlying asset. It is expressed as

$$\eta = \{\gamma - r + \sigma^2 / 2 + [(r - \gamma - \sigma^2 / 2)^2 + 2 r \sigma^2]^{1/2}\} / \sigma^2 \qquad \text{------- (8)}$$

Let V be the stock (or an upgraded HDB flat opportunity) price of an underlying asset and K be the cost of exercising a real option. Applying to the direct real estate context, more specifically, a land development as an example, then V is the value of the newly developed direct real estate asset while K, the strike price is the construction cost of a direct real estate development project. The option value, or the current land value, U, is given by

$$U = (V^\star - K) (V / V^\star)\eta \qquad \text{-------------------------------------- (9)}$$

where $V^\star$ is the hurdle value that indicates a value which reaches the optimal time to exercise the option. In other words, it is optimal to exercise a real option at the time when the stock price is above the hurdle value; otherwise the option should be put on hold. The hurdle value is a function of the option elasticity that in turn is defined by the following expression:

$$V^\star = K \eta / (\eta - 1) \qquad \text{---------------------------------- (10)}$$

, where $\eta / (\eta - 1)$ is called the (hurdle benefit/cost) ratio that represents the ratio of the built direct real estate asset value divided by the construction cost exclusive of the land cost, thus triggering immediate optimal development. Therefore, the Samuelson-McKean model not only provides the strike price or land value but also some insight into the optimal timing of the development. Also, the various variables used in the model are assumed to be known and constant.

Precincts Announced for Upgrading, Date of Announcement of Successful Poll and Date of Billing
Demonstration to Batch 19 Precincts

Batch	Precinct	Block & Street Name	Date of Announcement of Successful Poll for MUP	Date of Billing
19	Bedok North St 1 / Chai Chee St	Blks 41 to 45 Chai Chee Street Blks 201 to 203 Bedok North St 1		
	Ang Mo Kio Ave 10	Blks 411 to 421 Ang Mo Kio Ave 10		
	Bedok North Ave 4	Blks 98 to 106 Bedok North Ave 4		
	Telok Blangah Heights / Drive	Blks 62, 63, 68 & 69 Telok Blangah Heights Blks 64 to 67 Telok Blangah Drive		
	Marine Terrace	Blks 51 to 59 Marine Terrace		
	Clementi Ave 4	Blks 315 to 320 Clementi Ave 4		
	Sago Lane / Banda Street / Kreta Ayer Road	Blk 4 Sago Lane Blk 5 Banda Street Blks 333 & 334 Kreta Ayer Road		
	Upper Boon Keng	Blks 19, 38 & 39 Upper Boon Keng		
	Ang Mo Kio Ave 4/5/6	Blks 641 & 644 Ang Mo Kio Ave 4 Blks 642, 643, 648, 649 Ang Mo Kio Ave 5 Blks 645, 646 & 647 Ang Mo Kio Ave 6		
	Teck Whye Lane / Ave	Blks 8 to 14, 25 & 26 Teck Whye Lane/Ave		

18	Geylang Bahru	Blks 53, 54, 55 & 56 Geylang Bahru	24 Oct 2002	
	Boon Lay Gardens	Blks 198 to 206 Boon Lay Drive	14 Nov 2002	
	Marine Terrace	Blks 1 to 8 Marine Terrace	21 Nov 2002	
	Lorong Limau	Blks 76 & 77 Lorong Limau Blks 82 & 86 Whampoa Drive	28 Nov 2002	
	Chong Boon View	Blks 422 to 425 Ang Mo Kio Ave 3	3 Mar 2003	
	Toa Payoh Lor 8	Blks 225 to 235 Lor 8 Toa Payoh	6 Mar 2003	
	Merah Heights	Blks 115 to 117 Bukit Merah Central	15 Mar 2003	
	Ang Mo Kio Ave 1	Blks 205 & 206 Ang Mo Kio Ave 1	27 Mar 2003	
	Clementi Ave 4	Blks 301 to 310 Clementi Ave 4	6 Jun 2003	
	Holland Oasis	Blk 6 Holland Close Blks 8 & 9 Holland Ave	10 Jul 2003	
	Pandan Gardens	Blks 401 to 408 Pandan Gardens	NA	
	Paya Lebar Way	Blks 120 to 124 Paya Lebar Way		
	Bedok Reservoir Road	Blks 709 to 715 Bedok Reservoir Road		
	Marsiling Drive	Blks 201 to 206 Marsiling Drive		
	Bedok North	Blks 512, 513, 515 to 518 & 554 Bedok North Ave 2/St 3		
	Bedok South	Blks 1 to 8, 19 to 21 Bedok South Road/ Ave 1		
17	Holland Park View	Blk 2 Holland Avenue Blk 4 Holland Close	10 Dec 2001	
	Bedok South	Blks 31 to 35 Bedok South Avenue 2 Blks 60 & 61 New Upper Changi Road	17 Jan 2002	
	Dorset Road	Blks 48 & 48A Dorset Road	31 Jan 2002	
	Dover Road/ Dover Close East	Blks 1 to 4 Dover Road Blk 5 Dover Crescent Blks 12 to 14 Dover Close East	9 Feb 2002	
	Depot Villa	Blks 113 & 114 Depot Road	9 Feb 2002	

	Kallang Basin	Blk 22 Boon Keng Road	11 Apr 2002	
		Blks 23 to 28, 30 to 33 Bendemeer Road		
		Blk 34 Whampoa West		
16	Marine Crescent (Batch 16)	Blks 43 to 47 Marine Crescent	24 May 2001	
	Kim Keat Avenue	Blks 194 & 195 Kim Keat Avenue	31 May 2001	
	Faber View	Blks 1 & 3 to 6 Telok Blangah Crescent	7 Jun 2001	
	Sims Drive/ Place	Blks 41, 44, 45, 50 & 51 Sims Drive	14 Jun 2001	
		Blks 46, 47, 48, 52 & 53 Sims Place		
	Commonwealth Drive	Blks 89 to 95 Commonwealth Drive	28 Jun 2001	
	Fengshan	Blks 111, 112, 115, 116 & 117 Bedok North Road	8 Aug 2001	
		Blks 113, 114 & 118 Bedok North Street 2		
15	Ghim Moh Precinct 2	Blks 7, 8, 13 to 19 & 21 Ghim Moh Road	3 Nov 2000	
	Toa Payoh North / Central	Blks 199 to 204 Toa Payoh North	10 Nov 2000	
	Brickworks	Blks 1, 2, 3 & 28 Jln Bukit Merah	24 Nov 2000	
		Blk 28 Hoy Fatt Road		
		Blk 37 Jln Rumah Tinggi		
	Indus	Blks 77 to 79 Indus Road	30 Nov 2000	
	Whampoa Drive / Jalan Tenteram	Blks 74 & 75 Whampoa Drive	4 Dec 2000	
14	Ang Mo Kio (Ave 1)	Blks 207, 208, 215 & 216 Ang Mo Kio Ave 1	19 Apr 2000	
	Toa Payoh (Lor 7)	Blks 17 to 21 Lor 7 Toa Payoh	20 Apr 2000	
		Blk 23 Toa Payoh East		
	Mei Ling	Blks 155, 156, 160 to 162 Mei Ling Street	27 Apr 2000	
		Blks 163 & 164 Stirling Road		
	Kallang Basin	Blks 57, 61, 62 & 68 Geylang Bahru	11 May 2000	
		Blks 66 & 67 Kallang Bahru		

	Marine Terrace	Blks 12 to 20 Marine Terrace	2 Aug 2000	
13	Ang Mo Kio (Ave 1)	Blks 303 to 306, 318 to 321 Ang Mo Kio Ave 1	7 Oct 99	
	Ho Ching Road	Blks 116, 117, 119 & 120 Ho Ching Road	15 Oct 99	
		Blk 118 Corporation Drive		
		Blks 121 & 122 Yuan Ching Road		
	Bukit Merah	Blks 104 to 107, 110, 113, 115, 116 & 117 Jln Bukit Merah	21 Oct 99	
	Bedok	Blks12 Bedok South Ave 2	5 Nov 99	
		Blks 13, 15, 17 & 18 Bedok South Road		
	Blangah View	Blks 50 to 55 Telok Blangah Drive	9 Dec 99	
		Blks 56 & 57 Telok Blangah Heights		
12	Kelantan Centre	Blks 25 to 27 Jln Berseh	24 Mar 99	
		Blks 28, 29, 30 Kelantan Road		
	Commonwealth Crescent	Blks 103, 104 to 113 Commonwealth Crescent	8 Apr 99	
	Marsiling Drive	Blks 28 to 37 Marsiling Drive	15 Apr 99	
	Toa Payoh (Lor 2)	Blks 123 to 126 & 128 Lor 1 Toa Payoh	22 Apr 99	
	MacPherson Lane	Blks 81 to 83 MacPherson Lane	29 Apr 99	20 Nov 03
11	Ping-An Gardens	19 to 24 Chai Chee Rd	9 Apr 98	20 Aug 03
	Telok Blangah Crescent	Blks 13, 15, 16, 18 to 21, 23 & 24 Telok Blangah Crescent	16 Apr 98	20 Jan 04
	Toa Payoh (Lor 4) - A & B	Blks 66, 69 to 71 & 73 Lor 4 Toa Payoh (A)	22 Apr 98	20 Feb 03
		Blk 72 Lor 5 Toa Payoh (A)		
		Blk 83 Lor 2 Toa Payoh (B)		
		Blks 85, 85A, 85B & 85C Lor 4 Toa Payoh (B)		
	Dover Crescent - A & B	Blks 20 to 23 Dover Crescent (A)	7 May 98	
		Blks 26 & 27 Dover Crescent (B)		
	Selegie House	Blks 8 to 10 Selegie Rd	14 May 98	

10	Marine Crescent	Blks 27 to 35 Marine Crescent	5 Mar 98	20 Apr 03
	Ghim Moh Precinct 1	Blks 1 to 6 Ghim Moh Rd	13 Mar 98	20 Oct 03
	Ang Mo Kio (Ave 3)	Blks 129 to 134 Ang Mo Kio Ave 3	19 Mar 98	20 Aug 03
	Commonwealth Drive / Queen's Close	Blks 55, 56, 58 to 60, 62 to 66 Commonwealth Drive Blks 23A & 23B Queen's Close	26 Mar 98	20 Jul 03
	Boon Lay Place	Blks 207 to 215 Boon Lay Place	2 Apr 98	
9	Bedok South	Blks 22 & 23 Bedok South Ave 1 Blks 24 to 30 New Upper Changi Road	4 Sep 97	20 May 02
	Bukit Ho Swee	Blks 34 & 46 Jln Bt Ho Swee Blks 36, 38, 40, 42 & 44 Beo Crescent Blk 48 Lower Delta Road Blk 50 Havelock Road	11 Sep 97	20 Oct 02
	Eunos Crescent	Blks 19 to 23 Eunos Crescent	18 Sep 97	20 Jun 01
	Queenstown (Mei Ling Street)	Blks 152 to 154, 157 & 158 Mei Ling Street	25 Sep 97	20 Jan 03
	Tanjong Rhu	Blk 1 Kg Kayu Road Blks 2 to 11 Jln Batu Blks 12 & 14 Kg Arang Road	6 Nov 97	20 Apr 03
8	Marsiling	Blks 6 to 11 Marsiling Drive Blks 12, 13, 15 to 17 Marsiling Lane	29 Apr 97	20 Mar 02
	Henderson	Blks 119, 120, 128 to 130 Bt Merah View	6 May 97	20 Jan 02
	Toa Payoh East	Blks 25 to 27 Toa Payoh East	15 May 97	20 Dec 01
	Bendemeer Rd / Whampoa South	Blks 43 to 45 & 47 Bendemeer Road Blk 49 Whampoa South	23 May 97	20 Nov 01
	Ang Mo Kio (Ave 4)	Blks 254 to 258 Ang Mo Kio Ave 4	28 May 97	20 Sep 02

7	Marsiling	Blks 1, 2, & 5 Marsiling Drive	6 Nov 96	20 Sep 01
		Blks 3 & 4 Marsiling Road		
	Toa Payoh (Lor 1, Lor 5/6 – A & B)	Blk 157 Lor 1 Toa Payoh (Lor 1)	14 Nov 96	20 May 01
		Blks 34, 38 & 47 Lor 5 Toa Payoh (Lor 5/6 A)		
		Blks 51 & 52 Lor 6 Toa Payoh (Lor 5/6 B)		
	Tanglin Halt	Blks 33 to 45 Tanglin Halt Road	21 Nov 96	20 Jul 01
	Upper Boon Keng	Blks 11, 12, 15, 16 & 18 Upper Boon Keng Road	28 Nov 96	20 Dec 00
	Everton Park	Blks 1 to 7 Everton Park	5 Dec 96	20 Aug 01
6	Upper Aljunied	Blks 2 to 5 Upper Aljunied Lane	17 Apr 96	20 Dec 99
	Toa Payoh (Lor 3/4)	Blks 91 & 96 Lor 3 Toa Payoh	25 Apr 96	20 Mar 00
		Blks 92, 94 & 95 Lor 4 Toa Payoh		
		Blks 98 & 100 Lor 1 Toa Payoh		
	Geylang East	Blks 95 to 98 Aljunied Crescent	2 May 96	20 Mar 00
	Commonwealth Close	Blks 81 to 88 Commonwealth Close	9 May 96	20 Feb 01
	Sin Ming – A, B & C	Blk 22 Sin Ming Road (A)	16 May 96	20 Mar 00
		Blks 23 & 24 Sing Ming Road (B)		
		Blk 25 Sin Ming Road (C)		
	Kim Tian	Blks 128 to 130 Kim Tian Road	23 May 96	20 Dec 00
		Blk 131 Jln Bt Merah		
	Ang Mo Kio Ave 3/6	Blks 301, 302, 322 to 329 & 348 Ang Mo Kio Ave 3	30 May 96	20 Jan 01
5	Toa Payoh (Lor 1)	Blks 158 to 161, 163, 168, 169, 173 & 174 Lor 1 Toa Payoh	10 Oct 95	20 Feb 00
	Beach Road	Blks 1 to 6 Beach Road	17 Oct 95	20 Feb 00
	Balestier / Moulmein	Blks 83 to 85, 93 to 101 Whampoa Drive	26 Oct 95	20 Sep 00
		Blk 69 Moulmein Road		20 Jun 99
	Chin Swee / Upper Cross Street	Blks 8 to 10 Jln Kukoh	1 Nov 95	20 Sep 00
		Blk 34 Upper Cross Street		
	Toa Payoh (Lor 7)	Blks 4, 5, 8, 9, 12, 13 & 15 Lor 7 Toa Payoh	9 Nov 95	20 Apr 00

4	Bukit Ho Swee	Blks 20, 26, 28 & 30 Jln Klinik	12 Apr 95	20 Dec 99
		Blk 22 Havelock Road		
		Blk 24 Beo Crescent		
		Blk 32 Jln Bt Ho Swee		
	Farrer Road	Blks 1 to 4 Queen's Road	19 Apr 95	20 Dec 00
		Blks 5 & 6 Farrer Road		
		Blk 8 Empress Road		
	Paya Lebar	Blks 15 to 23 Hougang Ave 3	3 May 95	20 Sep 99
	MacPherson	Blks 38 to 40, 61 to 67 Circuit Road	9 May 95	20 Mar 00
	Toa Payoh (Lor 1)	Blks 107 to 115 Lor 1 Toa Payoh	23 May 95	20 Nov 99
		Blks 205 to 209 Toa Payoh North		
3	Balam Road	Blks 19 to 24, 30 to 32 Balam Road	5 Oct 94	20 Oct 00
		Blks 34 to 36, 77 & 78 Circuit Road		
	Chai Chee	Blks 32 to 37 & 40 Chai Chee Ave	12 Oct 94	20 Jan 99
	Henderson	Blks 101 to 106 Henderson Crescent	19 Oct 94	20 Jan 99
	Toa Payoh (Lor 4/5)	Blks 56 & 58 Lor 4 Toa Payoh	26 Oct 94	20 Dec 98
		Blks 53 to 55, 57, 59 & 61 Lor 5 Toa Payoh		
	Buona Vista	Blks 10 & 12 Holland Ave	3 Nov 94	20 May 99
		Blks 11 & 13 Holland Drive		
2	Toa Payoh (Kuo Chuan)	Blks 116 & 120 Lor 2 Toa Payoh	5 Apr 94	20 May 98
		Blks 117 to 119 Lor 1 Toa Payoh		
	Taman Jurong	Blks 111, 112 & 114 Ho Ching Road	13 Apr 94	20 Jun 98
		Blk 113 Tao Ching Road		
	Queenstown (Stirling Rd)	Blks 165 to 171 Stirling Road	19 Apr 94	20 Jun 98
		Blk 168A Queensway		
	Kallang Basin	Blks 63 to 65 Kallang Bahru	27 Apr 94	20 Dec 98
	Queenstown (Commonwealth Crescent)	Blks 96 to 102 Commonwealth Crescent	10 May 94	20 Mar 98
	MacPherson	Blks 43 to 52 & 57 to 60 & 69 Circuit Road	17 May 94	20 Apr 98

1	Bukit Ho Swee	Blks 2, 4, 6, 8 & 10 Jln Bt Ho Swee Blks 12, 14, 16 & 18 Taman Ho Swee	20 Sep 93	20 Oct 97
	Bukit Merah	Blks 1 to 3 & 5 to 22 Redhill Close	21 Sep 93	20 Dec 98
	Boon Lay	Blks 167 to 173 Boon Lay Drive	27 Sep 93	20 Aug 97
	Kallang Airport	Blks 93 & 97 Jln Dua Blks 95 & 99 Old Airport Road	4 Oct 93	20 Jun 97
	St Michael	Blks 27, 28, 32 to 35 Jln Bahagia	12 Oct 93	20 Feb 98
	Queenstown	Blks 24 to 32 Tanglin Halt Road	18 Oct 93	20 Feb 98
Demonstration	Marine Parade	Blks 60 to 67 & 71 Marine Drive	30 Mar 92	20 Sep 96
	Kim Keat	Blks 1 to 3 Lor 7 Toa Payoh	30 Mar 92	20 Jul 95
	Telok Blangah	Blks 44 to 49 Telok Blangah Drive	30 Mar 92	20 Mar 96
	Ang Mo Kio	Blks 311 to 314, 343 to 347 Ang Mo Kio Ave 3	28 Apr 92	20 Jul 96
	Lorong Liew Lian	Blks 1 to 8 Lor Liew Lian	28 Apr 92	20 Mar 96
	Clementi	Blks 410 to 415 Commonwealth Ave West	28 Apr 92	20 Oct 96

NB. Under the Main Upgrading Programme, the upgrading cost is payable only when the upgrading works in the flats, blocks and precinct are completed. Billing only commences after the upgrading costs for the precinct is finalized and the lessees' share of the upgrading cost is imputed. The lessee who is the owner of the flat at the date of billing has to pay for the upgrading cost. For public precincts that do not have the Date of Billing, then the billing would not take place within the next 6 months.

Source: HDB InfoWEB

Scope of Upgrading Work offered by HDB

A) The upgrading items within the flat:

- Upgrading of existing bathroom and toilet
  - o waterproofing of bathroom and toilet floors
  - o tiling of bathroom and toilet floor and walls
  - o replacement of existing squat / pedestal pan with new pedestal pan
  - o replacement of bathroom and toilet vents
  - o provision of grab bar
  - o replacement of existing bathroom and toilet door with PVC folding doors
- Replacement of windows and grilles
- Replacement of main entrance door and grille gate

In addition, the Standard Plus Package offers the option of a space-adding item. Possible space-adding items are service balcony, bath/wc or utility room etc. (subject to site and structural constraints as well as the existing block / flat layout).

B) Possible upgrading items within the block:

- Repainting of block / facade enhancement
- Improved lift lobby
- Upgrading of lifts to stop at every floor, where technically feasible; better and faster lifts
- Re-screeding of void deck / corridor
- New designed letter boxes
- Replacement of block number plates

The actual scope of works will depend on the preference of each precinct and is subject to budget availability. Not all items may be provided. In addition, other possible specific works (to be fully funded by the Government) to be carried out if upgrading proceeds include the following:

- Replacement of soil discharge stack in bathroom and toilet
- Construction of ramps for better mobility
- Relocation/reconstruction of pump rooms/switch rooms
- Upgrading of electrical load
- Installation of dry riser
- Repair of spalling concrete (external)

C) The upgrading items within the precinct:

- Addition of covered linkways
- Entrance car porch / drop-off porch
- Reconstruction of footpath / external staircases
- Reconstruction of hardcourt
- Upgrading of children's playground
- Provision of jogging track / fitness corner
- Landscaping
- Precinct pavilion

The improvements would vary from precinct to precinct depending on the site conditions and residents' preferences.

Appendix VI

Price Index for Resale Public Housing Flats in Singapore

Resale Price Index of HDB Flats

Period		Index	Returns
1990	I	33.6	
	II	33.8	0.005952
	III	34.6	0.023669
	IV	34.1	−0.01445
1991	I	34.5	0.01173
	II	35.2	0.02029
	III	34.9	−0.00852
	IV	34.7	−0.00573
1992	I	35.7	0.028818
	II	37.9	0.061625
	III	38.7	0.021108
	IV	39.6	0.023256
1993	I	41.8	0.055556
	II	54.8	0.311005
	III	65.9	0.202555
	IV	67.8	0.028832
1994	I	69.7	0.028024
	II	71.6	0.02726
	III	75.5	0.054469
	IV	75.8	0.003974
1995	I	79.2	0.044855
	II	88.4	0.116162
	III	93.6	0.058824
	IV	101.9	0.088675
1996	I	111.4	0.093229
	II	125.7	0.128366
	III	133.3	0.060461
	IV	136.9	0.027007
1997	I	136.3	−0.00438

	II	134.9	−0.01027
	III	129.4	−0.04077
	IV	121.7	−0.05951
1998	I	113	−0.07149
	II	108.3	−0.04159
	III	103	−0.04894
	IV	100	−0.02913
1999	I	98.5	−0.015
	II	99.9	0.014213
	III	108	0.081081
	IV	110.4	0.022222
2000	I	111.1	0.006341
	II	109.7	−0.0126
	III	107.3	−0.02188
	IV	104.9	−0.02237
2001	I	101.3	−0.03432
	II	99.7	−0.01579
	III	97.7	−0.02006
	IV	96.3	−0.01433
2002	I	95.5	−0.00831
	II	95.7	0.002094
	III	96.7	0.010449
	IV	96.7	0
2003	I	98.2	0.015512
	II	100.3	0.021385
	III	102.7	0.023928

Source: HDB InfoWEB

Notes:
1) The index is based on average resale price by date of registration
2) 4Q98 is adopted as the base period with index at 100
3) Weights are based on 12-quarter moving average transactions

*The Resale Price Index of HDB flats are based on the average resale price estimated from the overall transaction records, thus it may not be representative of the Ang Mo Kio public housing estate.

HOUSING AFFORDABILITY IN SINGAPORE – A HIGHLY INTERESTING FOOD FOR THOUGHT

Chapter 5 discusses in-depth the key concerns on housing affordability of the Singapore housing system, which consists of the public housing (Housing and Development Hoard, HDB) sector, and the private residential market. The HDB sector is a mainstay and important sector of the Singapore economy that plans, designs HDB new towns and provides affordable, large scale, comprehensive and quality public housing, to accommodate overwhelmingly Singapore's resident households. The corresponding private residential market in Singapore offers quality and premium private residential accommodation for those resident households, who prefer such a private residential market than to choose to be a HDB sector homebuyer for their household-family activities. The Singapore private residential market remains a key investment asset class for private homebuying ownership either for owner occupation or for rental income investment. An underlying motive is to forecast private residential rents and capital values (CVs) for decision making by household-investors and institutional investors for private residential accommodation. There have been virtually limited studies to rigorously model the structural relationships and estimations of housing affordability for the controlled HDB sector and the private residential market Singapore.

On direct real estate (DRE) market disequilibria, the Singapore private residential market is subjected to persistent disequilibria, which is responsible for prevailing wide fluctuations around the implicit long-run steady-state equilibrium rents, CVs, rental yields and total returns (TRs). It is noteworthy that the housing system in Singapore is unique because unlike most developed counties, the Singapore government plans and then leaves it to the private sector to build. The Singapore government even benefits from its statutory boards to assist, review, direct and to execute policies like the Housing Development Board (HDB) and the government-linked companies like CapitaLand Ltd, the 'Mapletree' Investments Ltd, Sembawang Corporation Ltd and Keppel Land Ltd, which is taken private by its parent Keppel Corporation Ltd. Such statutory boards build residential assets to cater to the unique needs of the small island state of Singapore. Nowhere ese in the world can one imagine that about 85% of the Singapore population is accommodated in Housing and Development Board (HDB) apartments (flats).

Public housing (HDB) flats and their amenities are by no means poor quality because the flats and amenities are meant to provide affordable, high rise and quality housing for the masses. Public sector housing is therefore subsidized at high expense by the Singapore government, and heavily regulated to prevent abuse of the HDB sector. In Singapore, many people aspire to own private residential assets. Such an aspiration is attributed to the growth in affluence of Singaporeans in general. Average income rises moderately and steadily per year except for 1986 and 1999, when Singapore is in economic recession. Rising private residential prices as indicated by the Urban Redevelopment Authority (URA) price index, did compel many Singaporeans to purchase private residential assets in anticipation of high CV appreciation. Therefore, CV appreciation is a major component of the rate of total return in the Singapore private residential market, rather than the private residential rental yield. Ong, Ooi and Sing (2000) estimate that in the period between 1985 and 1998 the direct real estate (DRE) price appreciation did constitute as much as 60% to 70% of the total returns (TRs) for the private office, private residential and industrial sectors in Singapore. The afore mentioned DRE price appreciations and rising TRs would perhaps be the situation, owing to the fact that the direct real estate sector in Singapore is on the whole not as mature as the United States of America (US), where rental yields form the major component of the total return (TR).

Another possible reason is that Singaporeans are myopic in their TR expectations and would invest more, based on price movements. However, the Singapore government via its agent, the HDB, controls public housing prices and then to control supply and demand. Consequently, it is not practical to model the controlled sector of new HDB flats. Modeling the resale market of HDB flats is possible but subject to legislative regulations viz. the minimum occupation period of five years and would not be examined in this Chapter. It is not to say that the HDB resale market and the private residential market are not linked although the private residential market is much less regulated, and more subject to market forces. Land–scarce Singapore, which is an island–state economy of some 724 sq km (280 sq mi) and with a potential population of 5.8 million, is compelled to optimize its land use and land allocation with due care.

It should be essential to scrutinize the problem of oversupply to minimize it or to contain it, because such an oversupply problem has persisted in the last decade and to a lesser extent to date. An enhanced understanding of the oversupply problem may well help the Singapore Urban Redevelopment Authority (URA) to finetune its URA Sale of Sites Program; and help the HDB to finetune its HDB Sale of Sites Program. It may help private direct real estate developers to better time the development of their land banks, to better balance the demand and supply situation. It is not surprising that most private homebuyers in Singapore may not be well informed on the structural and behavioral dynamics of the private residential market. Information inefficiency is inherent to the private residential market, where there is the absence of a centralized marketplace. Even with widely publicized government policies, private residential homebuyers are not clear about public policy impacts and may well be inclined to follow the herd instinct.

Trends in Housing Affordability

A unique and comprehensive report *inter alia* by the Singapore Centre for Applied and Policy Economics (SCAPPE), Department of Economics (DoE), draws due attention to housing affordability in Singapore. The report briefly highlights the following trends for reference purposes:

- Housing is affordable if the affordability<=0.3.
- Housing is accessible if the accessibility ratio<=1.0.

An upward trend of the abovenamed ratios each indicates deteriorating housing affordability and accessibility. The Centre is an integral part of the DoE in the Faculty of Arts and Social Sciences of the National University of Singapore (SCAPPE, 2016, Recent trends in Housing Accessibility and Affordability). Key trends are duly observed and with Figs 1-6 depicting the trends of housing affordability and accessibility over the period from 2011 to 2016Q1. To enable trend and cyclical analysis, the HDB housing median re-sale price and the median household income are estimated. The private housing median price and the household income, at the 80th income percentile are duly estimated. Private housing median house prices are sourced from a list of regional prices. It is noteworthy that some regions in Singapore do not register any transaction in some quarters. The Figures and the required estimations across regions for different income deciles lead to three key observed trends below:

1. For young HDB resale home buyers, ta key problem with rising house prices is housing accessibility, not so much

long-run affordability. For e.g., a 4-room HDB resale flat in expensive areas is inaccessible to income groups below the 30th percentile. Even the 2-room and 3-room HDB apartments in low-priced areas like Yishun and Woodlands are inaccessible to low income groups below the 20th percentile. It is noteworthy that the estimated savings by age 29 years for the low-income groups appear optimistic. The inference is that the accessibility problem may be more severe than what the estimations indicate.

2. Private residential properties (real estate) are meant for the wealthy. Again, accessibility is a more severe problem than long-run affordability. Median priced private apartments and condominiums have become inaccessible even for those in the 80th income percentile group.

3. Rising mortgage rates obviously lower long-run housing affordability. Reduced housing affordability means reduced residual income for other living expenses.

Fig 5.1 depicts that median priced HDB re-sale units are accessible to the median-income homebuyers but that accessibility is below the level observed as early as the beginning of 2011.

Fig 5.1. Housing Accsessibility – HDB

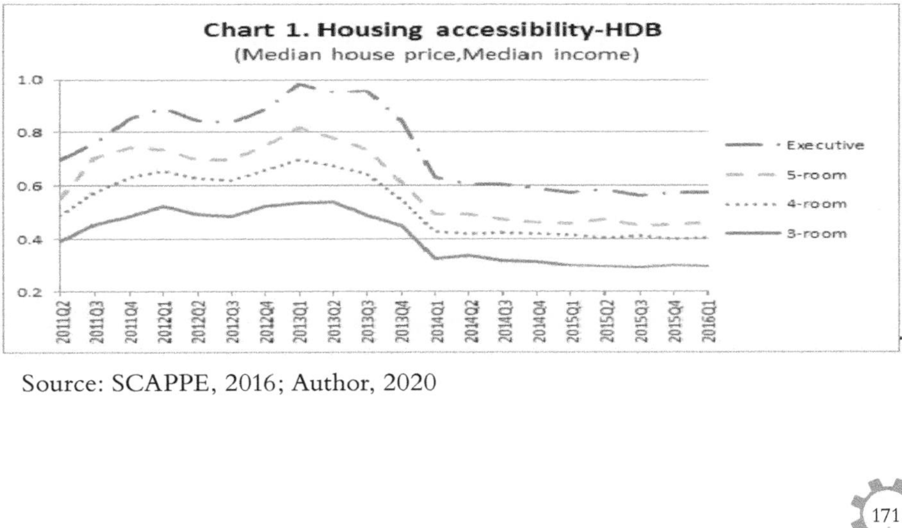

Chart 1. Housing accessibility-HDB
(Median house price,Median income)

Source: SCAPPE, 2016; Author, 2020

Fig 5.2 depicts that since 2012 median priced private residential units fall outside the accessible range even for the households in the 80th income percentile.

Fig 5.2. Housing Accessibility – Private

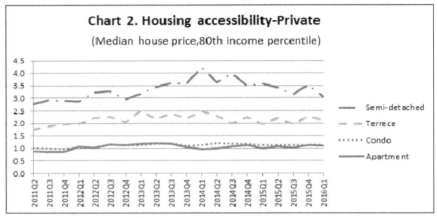

Source: SCAPPE, 2016; Author, 2020

Figs 5.3 and 5.4 depict that the median priced HDB resale units are well within the long-run affordability range for the median income group. Rising mortgage rates adversely affect affordability.

Fig 5.3. Housing Accessibility – Private

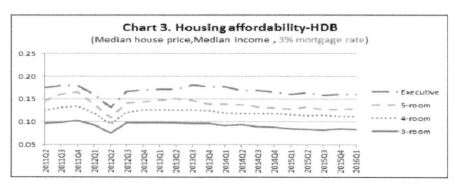

Source: SCAPPE, 2016; Author, 2020

Fig 5.4. Housing Affordability – HDB

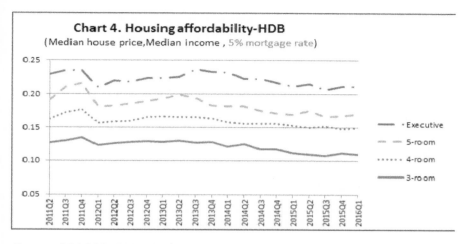

Source: SCAPPE, 2016; Author, 2020

Figs 5.5 and 5.6 depict that only the median priced private apartments and condos are within the long–run affordability range for the households in the 80th income percentile group. They are worse off if the mortgage rates go up.

Since HDB revises its resale procedures on 10 Mar 2014 to reduce the focus on Cash–Over–Valuation (COV) in negotiation with the flat homebuyer, HDB ceases the publication of its quarterly median COV by HDB new town and room–flat type from 20141Q onwards. Therefore, the expression of (10% of the HDB valuation limit+3% transaction cost) is adopted for the upfront payment by the flat homebuyer, when estimating the HDB housing accessibility from 1st Quarter 20141Q (SCAPPE, 2016; Author. 2020).

Fig 5.5. Housing Affordability – Private

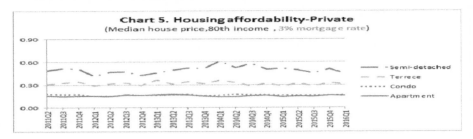

Source: SCAPPE, 2016; Author, 2020

Fig 5.6. Housing Affordability – Private

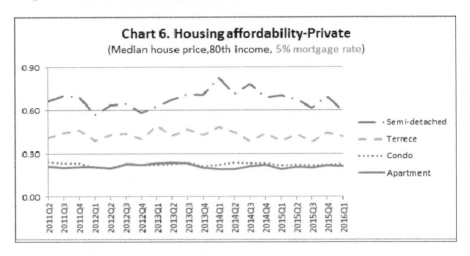

Source: SCAPPE,2016; Author,2020

Housing Affordability Definition and Estimations

Housing affordability is always an issue of concern to many Singaporean homebuying households because shelter forms one of life necessities in life. In most of the housing literature, affordability refers to the ability to rent (Bogdon and Can, 1997). Although housing prices in Singapore are relatively higher, compared to other countries, majority of households prefer to own their homes. The reason to why ownership is preferred over renting is substantiated by the fact that the homeownership rate in Singapore is almost 92%

by as early as 2000, which is a 5.5% increase as compared to 1990. Affordability in Chapter 5 refers to home ownership.

Table 5.1 Home Ownership Rate, Singapore

	1990	**2000**
Home Ownership Rate (%)	87.5	92.3

Source: Department of Statistics, MTI, 2016; Author, 2020

Before discussing the factors that affect affordability, it is important to realize that the underlying foundation that supports affordability is the rational expectations theory (RET). RET is that economics theory, which models the determinations of future events by economic actors, originally proposed by Muth (1961). RET is based on people's expectations. Expectations play an important role in consumer behavior, firm behavior, the financial sector, and the behavior of financial institutions. For e.g., expectations about income affects money demand, consumer expenditure and aggregate demand, bonds and assets demand in general. Rational expectations are formed by HDB buying households, utilizing all available information to make the possible best forecast (the optimal forecast) for the future behavior of a variable. The expectations are forward looking. However, and even though a rational expectation equals the optimal forecast, utilizing all available information, a rational expectation prediction may not always be perfectly accurate. There are two main reasons that explain why an expectation may fail to be rational:

1) People might be aware of all available information but find that it takes too much effort, to make their expectation the best guess possible.
2) People may be unaware of some available relevant information, and so their best guess of the future may be inaccurate. Accurate rational expectations are desirable and there are strong incentives for homeowning households to try to make

them equal, to become optimal forecasts by using all the available information.

One form of rational expectations is price expectations, which has a crucial role at influencing the behavior of homebuyers and sellers. To a large extent, homebuyers and sellers enter or leave the public housing (HDB) sector or the private residential market, depending on whether-or-not they expect prices to rise or fall in future. In the event of any economic recession, homebuyers form expectations, based on the available relevant information. Such information includes wage cuts, employment uncertainties, and a fall in house prices, among others. If a sharp fall in house prices occur, such fall generates expectations of further falls. Should all things remain equal, a fall in the private residential price generates more residential demand. However, utilizing all the obtainable information, the homebuyers' expectations about the fall in wages and coupled with employment uncertainties, leads homebuyers to act rationally and to hold back their residential purchases. In other words, the affordability of private residential real estate weakens.

Factors Affecting Affordability

Affordability is a crucial issue in determining public housing or private residential demand. Conventional wisdom dictates that the ability to afford depends on the homebuying household income and mortgage payments. *Cetris peribus*, the higher the household income and/or the lower the mortgage interest rates, then the more affordable is direct real estate. Predominantly, there are three factors that have a significant role in governing affordability, namely liquidity, debt and cashflow. These three factors are inter-related and are recognized as the independent variables, and with affordability being the dependent variable. Moreover, within each independent variable, there are several variables that come into play. Chapter 5 discusses the three main variables, affecting housing affordability in detail and examines the variables' relationships among themselves.

Fig 5.7. The Factors Affecting Affordability, Singapore

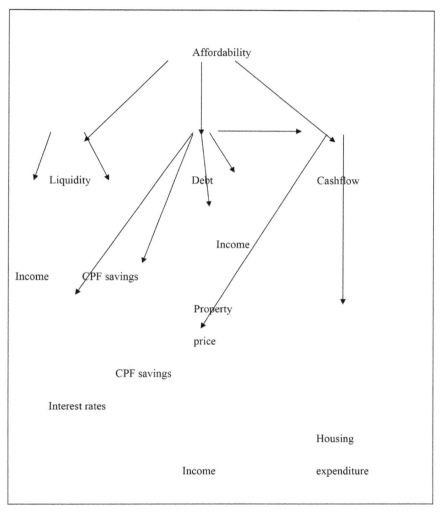

Source: Author, 2020

Debt

At the heart of Fig 5.7 is the debt variable that clearly affects affordability because debt is a major part of the capital structure of direct real estate, to enable the homebuyer's price purchase, and to enable the direct real estate (DRE) developer to fund the huge capital outlay for land and construction. Without debt, it is impossible to fund direct real estate, based on equity alone for construction and land development, or for homebuying. In fact, the amount of debt that a homebuyer or DRE developer can borrow hinges on several factors like income and employment, among others. Financial institutions assess the homebuyer or DRE developer, considering all relevant factors. The monthly debt service in turn depends on other factors like the mortgage interest rates, private residential prices and the Central Provident Fund (CPF), a government compulsory social security savings for working household employees.

Nevertheless, debt works as a double-edged sword. As prices of private residential real estate rise, and with other things being equal, prospective homebuyers need to take up higher loan amounts. Borrowing helps to improve the homebuyer's affordability of purchasing such residential real estate. In the long run, borrowing poses a problem. A higher amount of debt invariably leads to higher monthly debt service, imposing a downward pressure on homebuyer's affordability. As a result, the homebuyer must adjust his limited resources to meet other financial obligations.

Liquidity

There are various definitions of liquidity. One of them is explained by the degree to which an asset or security can be bought or sold in the market, without affecting the asset's price, and is characterized by a high level of trading activity. The other meaning, which is also the common understanding of liquidity, is the ease to convert an asset into cash quickly. For such a conversion, liquidity denotes that amount of cash savings of a homebuyer, which is augmented by income and depleted by expenditure.

Liquidity is determined as the amount of cash one has, relative to the amount of cash he wants to have, also known as target cash. The amount of target cash a homebuyer wants to have is in turn determined on the rate at which the homebuyer wants to be spending. For e.g. and if the average desired spending of a homebuyer is $2,000 per month, and that he wants to have a month's worth of spending on hand as cash, the implication is that the homebuyer wants to have $2,000 in cash on hand in that month. Servicing of mortgage loan comprises one for expenditure items among others like food, clothing, and transportation. As a matter of fact, what a homebuyer spends is determined by how much he wants to spend, as impacted by liquidity. Liquidity constrains a homebuyer's expenditure, resulting in a significant impact on affordability. With higher liquidity brought about by a rise in income (all other things remaining constant), the affordability of a homebuyer correspondingly rises and vice-versa. There are a few factors that affect a homebuyer's liquidity like income and CPF savings. The study by Phang (2001) affirms the presence of liquidity constraints from the asymmetric reaction of consumption to income increases *vis-a-vis* income declines. Under liquidity constraints, agents cannot borrow when income is temporarily low, so that consumption should be more strongly correlated with predictable income increases than declines – liquidity constraints impede borrowing but not saving (Shea 1995).

Cashflow

Cashflow is denotes the amount of cash that an individual generates and uses. The main source of cash inflow for a homebuyer is derived from income, while components of cash outflow include housing, food, beverage, clothes and transportation, among others. When planning the long-term funding of a private residential purchase, it is important to forecast the likely cash requirements to analyze the homebuyer's affordability.

Cashflow affordability measures the mortgage payments relative to the income of the homebuyer. As income is fixed in the short run, rising cash outflow on the expenditure of any items affects the affordability of the homebuyer. Being homeowners, more favorable gains of cashflow affordability from reduced financing costs seem unlikely, and that the major responsibility falls on improved income growth, or lower house price inflation if cashflow affordability is to improve much more. In fact, inflation in Singapore is relatively low and such, improvement in cashflow affordability entirely falls on income growth.

Homebuyer's Income

Effective demand, which is defined as the ability and willingness to buy, is closely related to the homebuyer's income level. Income plays a significant role in affecting liquidity, debt and cashflow. A rise in income has a corresponding rise in effective demand and vice-versa. Similarly, such an income rise also results in a rise of liquidity as it enhances the homebuyer's cash reserves. Other than improving the homebuyer's liquidity with the build-up of cash reserves, a rise in homebuyer's income helps to ease the burden of the monthly debt service. As the Central Provident Fund (CPF) funds from the working homebuyer (employee)'s ordinary account can be used to repay the monthly mortgage instalment, a rise of the homebuyer's income inevitably means that more CPF can be withdrawn. Besides, the homebuyer's cashflow is also improved.

Studies infer that changes in the homebuyer's income level have a direct impact on housing affordability (Feins and Lane 1981). However, only permanent income is considered. In other words, any transitory component of current income like the striking win of a lottery prize should be ignored in the determination of affordability. For this transitory reason, the average earnings of the population are utilized. It is established that personal wages alone may not be a sufficient measure of the affordability for private residential real estate. One main reason is that the appropriate unit for the "number of buyers" for housing is not the individual homebuyer but the household as the basic decision-making unit. A household may be defined as a person or a group of people who occupy a dwelling and constitute a single economic decision-making unit, with respect to housing expenditure. Households may be families or non-families not related by blood or marriage. Non-families comprise the singles or individuals living together.

Another reason is that the average household income consistently rises faster than personal wages. According to the Singapore Census of Population 1990, the average monthly household income from work rises by 60.7% between 1990 and 2000 in Table 5.2., while the average monthly personal income from work rises by a lesser proportion of 15.6%. Healthy economic growth of the early 1990s accounts for rising household income. Moreover, it is observed that the number of working women is growing steadily, which explains why the household income is rising faster than personal wages. According to the Census of Population 1990, Singapore, the percentage of dual-income families spikes rather early from 29.4% of the workforce in 1982 to 39.8% of the workforce by as early as 1990, a 35.4% rise over that period. The purchasing power of dual-income families is existential in terms of wealth that is accumulated in the Central Provident Fund (CPF) balances; and in the double-barreled income that enables dual-income families to take on greater debt (Ng, 1993). The combined income also enables these families to share the financial burden and better able to afford private residential real estate.

Table 5.2. Average Monthly Personal Income
Vs Average Monthly Household Income

	1990	**2000**	**% Change**
Average Monthly Personal Income	S$1,414	S$1,635	15.6%
Average Monthly Household Income	S$3,076	S$4,943	60.7%

Source: Census of Population, Singapore, 1990; Author, 2020

CPF Savings

Central Provident Fund (CPF) home financing scheme is a relatively unique system of housing finance in Singapore. It is created in 1954 with the purpose of providing funds for the needs of working employees in their retirement. Since then, the fund evolves many functions like providing the means of meeting healthcare needs, owning a direct real estate, insurance coverage and investment, among others. CPF becomes an important non–inflationary source of wealth, which facilitates effective demand.

In 1981, the CPF Board liberalized the use of CPF funds by allowing working employees (its members) to purchase private residential real estate under the 'Approved Residential Real Estate Scheme (APRS)'. Under this scheme, CPF savings can be utilized to not only pay for the down-payment but also to service monthly mortgage service, subject to the rules and regulations set out by the CPF Board. With the introduction of APRS, the CPF savings have become a major source of funds for buying a home in Singapore. The accumulated CPF savings, for instance, are often used to lower the mortgage amount taken up by the homebuyer while the monthly CPF contributions service the outlay. By lowering the mortgage amount with the utilization of CPF funds, the debt position of the homebuyer is enhanced. Over the years, the CPF Board has made various amendments to the APRS in response to economic conditions and related government policies, resulting in favorable impact on the affordability of its homebuying members. In September 1993, the homebuying members can withdraw their CPF savings to repay their outstanding home loans up to 80% of their gross CPF savings that is excess of the minimum sum. From Fig 5.8, CPF withdrawals under the APRS steadily spike to about S$7,000 million in 1999 from the low base close to S$1,500 million in 1993. Thereafter, the CPF withdrawals fall steadily from the peak to about S$2,500 million by end 2003, and are expected to return to the base level till the present.

Additionally, the cap on the CPF withdrawal limit for the purchase of private residential real estate financed with bank loans is reduced from the current 144% to 138% of the 'Valuation Limit' starting from 1 January 2004. Thereafter, such withdrawal is cut by six percentage points every year to reach 120% on 1 January 2008. Prudence is encouraged in using CPF savings to purchase a home so that homebuying members have ample CPF savings to meet their future retirement needs. Such prudence affects the affordability of homebuyers for private residential real estate, in particularly the first-time homebuying members. The reduction of the CPF withdrawal limit is meant to advise the homebuying CPF members to raise their cash payments.

Fig. 5.8. CPF Withdrawals Under The Approved Residential Real Estate Scheme

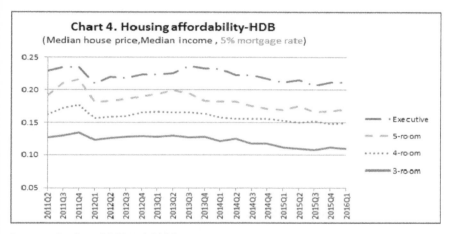

Source: Author, 2003and 2020

The CPF Interest Rates

The amount of wealth accumulated via CPF savings is largely affected by the CPF interest rates. The CPF Board makes several adjustments to its interest rates with effect from 1 Jul 1999. The CPF Board changes its frequency of adjusting the CPF rates and revises its interest rate formula. Instead of a six-monthly adjustment, the CPF interest rates are revised quarterly, bringing CPF interest rates closer to the prevailing market interest rates. The CPF interest rates are enabled to move in tandem with market conditions to enhance their competitiveness. The interest rate formula is also revised to enhance the rate of return on CPF savings, and to better reflect the long-term nature of CPF savings. Instead of the simple average of the 12-month fixed deposit and the month-end savings, the deposit rates of the four major local banks, the new formula assigns 80% weightage to fixed deposits and 20% to savings deposits.

The CPF Contribution Rate

The CPF contribution rate is another contributing factor in the formation of CPF savings. Besides amending the CPF interest rates, the CPF Board adjusts both the employer and employee's contribution rates. During the period of 1986 to 1999, the employer's contribution rates varies from 10% to 25%. The employee's contribution rates varies from 20% to 25% to help companies cut costs during the mid-1998 economic crisis, So, the government announces a 10% reduction in the employer's contribution, effective 1 Jan 1999 to Dec 2000. Prevailing CPF contribution rates for workers aged 35 years and for workers aged below are 13% and 20% respectively, and for employers and employees from 1 Jan 2005 onwards respectively.

Post 1 Jan 2005, the CPF contribution rate for workers aged above 50 to 55 years is reduced from 33% to 30%. The employer contribution rate is reduced from 13% to 11% while the employee contribution rate is reduced by 1 percentage point to 19%. The 3% reduction in CPF contributions comes from the CPF ordinary account. In other words, contributions to the special and "medisave"' accounts remain at 7% and 8% respectively. Effective 1 Jan 2006, the CPF contribution rate for workers aged above 50 to 55 years is reduced to 27%. Such a reduced CPF contribution rate for workers aged above 50 to 55 years is specifically targeted at the older employees' competitiveness to make them more employable and to save employment. The reduced CPF contribution rate helps the employer's ability to service their existing mortgages. The Singapore government permits CPF members, who face difficulty to meet their shortfall in monthly housing instalments owing to insufficient funds in the CPF members' ordinary account contributions, and to use their special account contributions to meet the shortfall.

Property Prices

Property (direct real estate, DRE) prices have a direct impact on the amount of debt, taken up by the homebuyer. Owing to high DRE prices, a homebuyer must rely on debt to finance his DRE purchase. Based on the expected monthly payment of debt service, it determines how much the homebuyer can afford a private residential real estate. According to Lee (1993), a homebuyer's affordability is dependent on the DRE project's price range. According to Singapore's Urban Redevelopment Authority (URA) and its residential property price index (RPPI), the prices of residential real estate more than doubled with a 217% increase as early as from 1991Q1 to 1996Q2, before experiencing a downturn. The 1996 residential slump is triggered by the anti-speculative measures, introduced by the government in May 1996. The 1997 Asian financial crisis also results in a sharp residential price fall of -45%, lasting till 1998Q4. After ten quarters of falling prices, residential values spike by 26% within three quarters. Within just nine months, the private residential market transforms from a buyer's market to a seller's market. Private residential real estate once again becomes out of reach for homebuyers. Therefore, and given that other factors remain unchanged, the volatility of DRE prices affects the monthly mortgage payments.

Mortgage Interest Rates

Changes in the mortgage interest rate inevitably affects private residential real estate demand because a lower mortgage interest rate is translated to a lower debt service (all things being equal), and therefore improves the homebuyer's affordability. The servicing of mortgage loan constitutes one of the major items of housing expenditure for most homebuying owner-occupiers. The burden of mortgage loan servicing is exceptionally demanding in the mortgage loan's early years when the debt service ratio (DSR), is typically at its highest. Therefore, a rise in the cost of borrowing adds to the total cost of owning DRE, which dampens residential real estate demand.

It is observed that the mortgage interest rates on private residential real estate fall tremendously as soon as the 1980s and 1990s. The average prime rate of the major banks in Singapore peaks as early as 1980 to 14.2%. Thereafter, such an average prime rate stabilizes in the range between 5.3% p.a. and 9% p.a. and as early as end 1999, to a low of 5.8% p.a. (see Fig 5.9). Additionally, a low mortgage interest rate environment is conducive, particularly in the early 1990s. In conjunction with easier mortgage repayment terms stretching 25 years in the 1980s to 30 years in the 1990s, the result is to alleviate the huge burden of residential mortgage servicing. The mortgage term may even be stretching 35 years. In general, finetuning the mortgage term and mortgage interest rates over the years, may well help to alleviate the residential mortgage servicing burden to a large extent, amidst rising direct real estate prices.

Fig 5.9. Prime Lending Rates, Singapore Major Banks

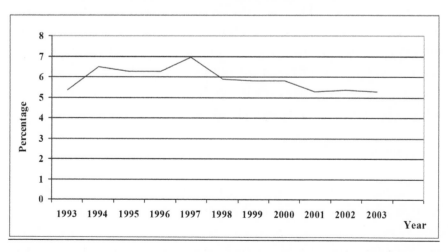

Source: Department of Statistics, Singapore Ministry of Trade & Industry, 2004; Author, 2020

Housing Expenditure

Housing expenditure constitutes a major part of the typical homebuyer's cash outflows among other financial obligations, that include food, clothing education and health. Housing expenditure consists of monthly mortgage payment, improvements, property tax and insurance, in all of which the housing item (i.e. for mortgage debt service) is the second largest housing expenditure by weight of 2,292 points or about 23% by weight .of the consumer price index (CPI) of Table 5.3. The CPI results are sourced from the Household Expenditure Survey.

Table 5.3. Consumer Price Index (CPI), Singapore

	Weights
All Items	**10,000**
Food	2,752
Clothing	443
Housing	2,292
Transport and Communication	1,803
Education	729
Health	305
Miscellaneous	1,676

Source: Household Expenditure Survey, Department of Statistics, 2004; Author, 2020

Measures of Affordability

Measures of affordability are of vital importance because of their indicator role. Adopting a set of standards, the observed patterns of housing expenditure can be measured, after which the set of standards acts as the gauge to affirm whether-or-not affordability is reasonable, is high or low. Several methods measuring affordability ranging from the simple rule of thumb measure to more complex measures, which incorporate all the factors affecting affordability. Traditionally, the key method deployed for measuring housing affordability is the rule of thumb. For instance, it is generally accepted that families can and should spend about one-fourth of their disposable income for shelter (Feins and Lane 1981). Another rule of thumb measure is the (housing/expense) ratio (Rosenberry and Hartman 1989). Such rule of thumb measures each is intuitively more appealing because they are straightforward and simple to deploy. However, the problem with such rules of thumb measures lie in their inadequacies like such rules failling to address other important factors, and that such rules are unadjusted for quality changes.

The Basic Correlation

Another simple measure of affordability is the basic correlation of the average earnings index with the URA residential property price index (RPPI) (Ng, 1993). If the rise in household income is much slower relative to the rise of the RPPI, then affordability falls and vice-versa. Nevertheless, there are several limitations with the basic correlation measure. First and although the average household income rises, it does not mean that real income also rises. Second, it is important to look at the income level of each household as different household size has an effect each on the amount of income needed (Bramley, 1990). Third, it is discerned from the literature that there are numerous factors affecting affordability, other than the income level. These numerous factors include the type of financial arrangements available and accumulated wealth in the form of CPF savings. Moreover, a direct real estate price index depends on its constituents put together. For instance, the URA RPPI takes account of all private residential transactions into the URA RPPI estimations. Movement of the URA RPPI depends on the type of direct real estate transacted during a particular time. The resultant index can be skewed either towards the high-end or towards the low-end of the private residential market, depicting an inaccurate picture of the URA RPPI.

Minimum Monthly Mortgage Payment

The minimum monthly mortgage payment for the purchase of a private direct real estate (DRE) is often used as a measure of affordability. First and foremost, to use this indicator, it is required to assume a debt service ratio to work out the minimum housing loan qualifying income that homebuyers need to purchase a typical property. As CPF funds is an important source of funds for buying a home, the estimation of the mortgage payment usually takes account of the use of CPF funds. Therefore, affordability is tracked by observing the trends of the minimum monthly mortgage payment. However, such a measure does not enable the measure of real affordability because it does not consider the comparison of income levels of the homebuyers.

The Debt Service Ratio

According to Feins and Lanes (1981), the ratio of housing expenditure to household income (i.e. debt service ratio, DSR) can be a relevant housing affordability model indicator, because DSR measures the proportion of income allocated to housing related expenditure. Affordability is defined as the relationship of monthly debt service requirements to monthly household income. The DSR can be used to compare with the market standard to estimate the affordability level(s). The advantage of the DSR is that the debt coverage ratio need not be assumed, because all factors affecting the mortgage instalment can be incorporated into the DSR model, and can be allowing simultaneous changes in the factors to be accounted for. A resultant model can be developed, taking account of the various factors affecting affordability, and to also measure the affordability of private residential real estate in Singapore, as against other countries. For such an affordability model, the study period should be long enough for trend and cyclical purposes like over 10 years. The Debt Service Ratio (DSR) affordability model takes into consideration five parameters, namely the average monthly household income, direct real estate prices, mortgage interest rates, the loan term and CPF savings. The DSR Model is expressed in eq (5.1).

$$DSR = \frac{\text{Monthly Debt Service}}{\text{Monthly Household Income}} \qquad (5.1)$$

The required data is mainly secondary data, where the key sources can be from the Department of Statistics (DOS), Ministry of Trade and Industry, Singapore, and the Census of Population, Singapore (2000 and 2020)

The Housing Affordability Index (HAI) Model

Housing affordability denotes the ability of a homebuying household to move from one form of housing to another, be it intra-private, intra-public or between the public and private housing markets. Therefore, the appropriate multi-factor housing affordability index (HAI) model of eq (5.2) is adapted from Kamath (1988) and ANHS (1991), which considers the ability to provide down payment and to service the mortgage taken up. The model also considers housing accessibility.

HAI = monthly housing income/ (down payment of 20% + mortgage rate)

$$HAI = \frac{AI}{12*\{2.5*[(0.8 \times Price_j)*MC_{i,n}]-CPF\}} \times 50 + \frac{RG + Sav + CPF\ Sav}{0.2*Price_j + LFSD} \times 50$$

(5.2)

, where $Price_j$ = Price of housing type,

AI = Annual household income

$MC_{i,30}$ = Mortgage constant of housing loan, given n years at prime lending rate i,

CPF = Monthly CPF contributions,

LFSD = Legal fees and stamp duties,

Sav = amount of household savings,

CPF Sav = amount of savings in CPF,

RG = Resale gains from previous housing

The multi-factor housing affordability index (HAI) model traces the footsteps of a typical middle-income homebuying household that conforms to the Singapore social system of going through 16 years of education, to graduate from university with an honors degree, and who then enter the workforce for 40 years before retiring at 65 years old. Special emphasis is placed on the housing types that the homebuying household chooses at different stages of its live, say from 2008 to 2023. Fig 5.10 offers a summary of the homebuying household's housing movements at different phrases of its life, given different circumstances, based on an axis of income and age.

Model Assumptions include the following:

- The couple graduated in say 2007 with say an honors degree, at the age of 25 and 23 for the male and female respectively with no savings or CPF.
- Both start off with a gross monthly pay of S$2,750 with a constant annual wage increase of 3.7%.
- Inflation rates and fixed mortgage rates and over the next 16 years remain constant.
- There are no boom/bust economic seasons; only real averaged GDP growth rate of 7% is taken based on current data.
- Continuous work for both income earners is assumed for 40 years till retirement.
- Rates of increase in housing price levels in the various residential sub-markets are assumed constant.

- Homes are assumed to be traded at valuation price and accurately reflected in the projected increase.
- Legal fees, stamp duties and other miscellaneous fees and housing grants are not included in the model simulation
- If user(s) do not have enough Ordinary Account savings for any housing payments, the difference will come from cash.

Fig 5.10, Predicted Movements of Household Income And House Purchase

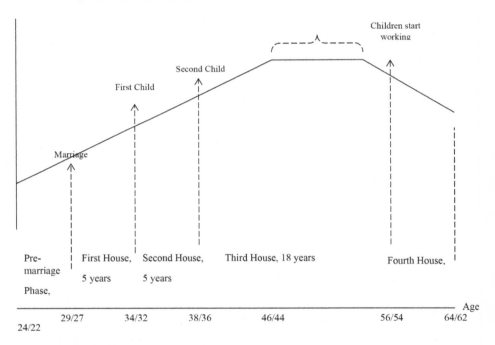

Source: Author, 2020

CPF Assumptions include the following:

- CPF contribution and allocation rates are based on those for private sector employees and government non–pensionable employees.
- The CPF interest rates remain constant over the projection period for all the CPF Accounts.

- Interest earned in the CPF Accounts is calculated and credited annually in December.
- CPF monthly contribution is subject to a salary ceiling of say $4,500.
- Except for CPF housing scheme deductions, all other uses of CPF are not included.
- Medisave Account savings are not included for the projection.
- CPF cash savings are used to meet the applicable CPF Minimum Sum at age 55.

Quarterly data for the private residential market and the public housing (HDB) sector are obtained for a long enough period, say 1990 to 2007. Simulation estimates for the HDB housing sector and the private residential market are made, upon taking the average performances of the HDB housing sector and the private residential market. The data captures the economic boom and bust cycles and is obtained from several national or reputable private sources below. The data is primarily universe–based instead of being sampling–based.

- Real Estate Information System Database from Urban Redevelopment Authority (URA)
- Monetary Authority of Singapore (Central Bank) Database
- The Singapore Department of Statistics Database
- Inland Revenue Authority of Singapore Annual Reports
- Housing Development Board of Singapore
- Singapore Ministry of Manpower
- Singapore Land Authority
- On–line Data Stream.

The HAI Simulation Estimates

Deploying the housing affordability index (HAI) model, Chapter 5 summarizes the following results in Table 5.4, based on the foregoing assumptions.

Table 5.4. The Housing Affordability Index, Singapore

Housing Affordability Index (HAI):

Housing Type/ Year	2011	2016	2017	2018	2019	2020	2021	2022	2023
4-room HDB Starter (New Estate)	2.036	4.367	4.648	4.978	5.250	5.526	5.815	7.509	7.711
5-room HDB Starter (New Estate)	1.664	3.481	3.701	3.956	4.169	4.385	4.611	5.928	6.086
Exec HDB Starter (New Estate)	1.375	2.819	2.994	3.196	3.365	3.538	3.717	4.760	4.886
4-room HDB Starter (Old Estate)	1.675	3.506	3.728	3.986	4.200	4.418	4.645	5.972	6.132
5-room HDB Starter (New Estate)	1.286	2.618	2.780	2.966	3.122	3.282	3.447	4.409	4.526
Exec HDB Starter (New Estate)	1.144	2.305	2.447	2.608	2.745	2.884	3.028	3.866	3.968
5-room HDB Resale	1.017	2.184	2.326	2.481	2.618	2.757	2.900	3.744	3.844
Exec HDB Resale	0.892	1.901	2.024	2.157	2.276	2.396	2.520	3.248	3.335
Exec Condo	0.669	1.150	1.174	1.199	1.213	1.225	1.235	1.520	1.497
Private Condo (Outside Central)	0.430	0.686	0.692	0.697	0.697	0.695	0.693	0.841	0.818
Private Condo (Rest of Central)	0.306	0.464	0.464	0.463	0.459	0.454	0.449	0.539	0.520
Private Condo (Core Central)	0.162	0.194	0.185	0.177	0.167	0.158	0.149	0.171	0.157

Source: Author, 2020

The simulation estimates focus on the steps of the hypothetical homebuying household purchasing its first HDB home, while satisfying the compulsory 5-year minimum occupancy period, before they decide to upgrade say in 2016. Private condominiums and executive condominiums are selected as the primary choice of upgrading, because they are typically the preferred choice for today's young homebuying household. The greater the HAI, then the more affordable the housing choice is for the household. It is assumed that the homebuying household buys a 5-room flat in the newer HDB estates. The homebuying household's 5-room flat choice is factored into the resale proceeds upon liquidation from say 2016 onwards when the household is given the legal freedom to upgrade. Once the compulsory 5-year minimum occupancy period is fulfilled, the hypothetical young homebuying household is comfortable with moving into a median priced resale HDB flat of their choice or purchase an executive condominium or purchase a flat under the HDB design, build and sell scheme (DBSS), if the homebuying household so chooses. Unfortunately, the price of a median private condominium or other private housing types are generally unaffordable for such a household, even with the fortuitous gains they may enjoy from liquidating their HDB starter flat. The gap between the private and public housing market widens even further, as the HAI for private condominiums within the Central area stays persistently out of the reach of the homebuying household. In the prime core central area and its prime direct real estate (DRE) developments, the homebuying household would find its HAI for a unit there to be even beyond their financial reach as time goes by.

Monte Carlo Simulation Analysis

The Monti Carlo model simulation (MCMS) is conducted using @RISK version 5.0 software program. MCMS determines the vital parameters (factors) influencing the HAI and the critical price range, which the homebuying household can pay for their housing. The results are presented in Table 5.5.

Table 5.5. TheHousing Affordability Index (HAI)

	Name	Worksheet	Cell	Minimum	Mean	Maximum	x1	p1	x2	p2	x2-x1	p2-p1	Errors
Output 1	Maximum Price of Housing**** / 2011	Simulation	F8	408458.5	501822.2	614293.1	426682.7	5%	578555.7	95%	151873	90%	0
Output 2	Maximum Price of Housing**** / 2016	Simulation	K8	479348.3	603238.8	739226.6	513609	5%	711091.8	95%	197482.8	90%	0
Output 3	5-room HDB Starter (New Estate) / HAI	Simulation	D38	1.359746	1.704643	2.388542	1.421108	5%	2.132716	95%	0.7116078	90%	0
Output 4	5-room HDB Resale (Old Estate) / HAI	Simulation	D43	0.7925804	1.043277	1.438385	0.8637562	5%	1.303271	95%	0.4395147	90%	0
Output 5	Exec Condo / HAI	Simulation	D45	0.413304	0.6940531	1.195827	0.5205896	5%	0.9252786	95%	0.4046888	90%	0
Output 6	Exec Condo / HAI	Simulation	G45	0.4392838	1.297637	3.846639	0.6295105	5%	2.303371	95%	1.67386	90%	0
Output 7	Private Condo (OCR) / HAI	Simulation	G46	0.215772	0.8131685	3.45124	0.3048197	5%	1.635004	95%	1.330184	90%	0
Input 1	***Based on fixed mortgage interest of / Mthly Mort	Simulation	C55	4.56E-02	5.33E-02	6.36E-02	4.72E-02	5%	6.10E-02	95%	1.38E-02	90%	0
Input 2	and loan term of / Mthly Mort	Simulation	C56	25.16282	30.00261	34.78122	26.55362	5%	33.38255	95%	6.828928	90%	0
Input 3	****Based on a loan-to-value ratio of / Mthly Mort	Simulation	C57	0.7124639	0.7999668	0.8878238	0.7301447	5%	0.8655759	95%	0.1354312	90%	0
Input 4	Gross Monthly Household Income	CPF and Savings	E1	2.53E-02	3.73E-02	4.87E-02	0.0287664	5%	4.58E-02	95%	1.70E-02	90%	0
Input 5	Monthly Savings as a % of income:	CPF and Savings	S1	7.73E-02	9.83E-02	0.1178557	6.24E-02	5%	0.1132083	95%	3.08E-02	90%	0
Input 6	Accumulated wealth invested at risk-free rate:	CPF and Savings	Y1	2.64E-02	4.00E-02	5.41E-02	0.0293677	5%	5.02E-02	95%	2.08E-02	90%	0
Input 7	2007 / Man	CPF and Savings	C4	2513.546	2749.661	2969.872	2578.958	5%	2915.529	95%	336.5713	90%	0
Input 8	2007 / Woman	CPF and Savings	D4	2512.367	2750.27	2993.111	2577.788	5%	2918.087	95%	340.2991	90%	0
Input 9	Loan Term (years):	Wealth Accumulation	K3	25.55247	29.99828	34.3115	26.52073	5%	33.40582	95%	6.885084	90%	0
Input 10	Avg annual increase / #NA	Trend Analysis	B149	-5.86E-02	0.0674256	0.1932855	-1.79E-02	5%	0.1489371	95%	0.1667892	90%	0
Input 11	Avg annual increase	Trend Analysis	E149	-2.36E-02	2.33E-02	7.00E-02	-1.02E-02	5%	5.58E-02	95%	6.60E-02	90%	0
Input 12	Annual Change / All	Trend Analysis	B172	-0.116412	0.1397073	0.3831438	-3.03E-02	5%	0.303185	95%	0.3334599	90%	0
Input 13	Annual Change / All	Trend Analysis	D172	-6.49E-02	8.89E-02	0.2711684	-1.47E-02	5%	0.1840116	95%	0.1987074	90%	0
Input 14	Annual Change / All	Trend Analysis	F172	-9.34E-02	7.97E-02	0.2208901	-2.00E-02	5%	0.1755692	95%	0.1956041	90%	0

Source: Author, 2008 and 2020

In Fig 5.11, the critical (maximum) price of housing at a certain period hinges largely on mortgage rates, the amount of mortgage taken and the repayment period. Gross monthly household income is another vital factor.

Fig 5.11. Regression Sensitivity Analysis for The Maximum Price Of Housing

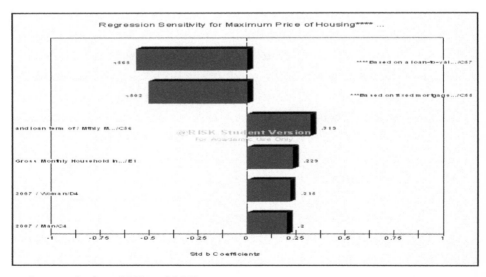

Source: Author, 2008 and 2020

Housing affordability of public housing for the middle class, represented by a HDB 5-room starter flat is heavily correlated with the maximum mortgage taken up and the rate of price rise in Fig 5.12. Regular monthly savings also play a key role in determining whether-or-not the homebuying household can pay the outlay i.e. the initial down payment of 20% of the buying flat price (including CPF).

Fig 5.12. Regression Sensitivity Analysis for HAI (HDB 5-room Starter Flat)

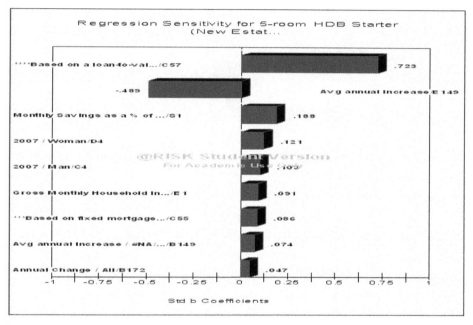

Source: Author, 2008 and 2020

For public housing and for the upper-middle income group, who qualify for an executive condominium, the expected annual price rise is more crucial than the mortgage amount taken up in Fig 5.13. Regular monthly savings are relevant but are over-shadowed by the earlier two factors of the price rise and the mortgage amount taken up.

Fig 5.13. Regression Sensitivity Analysis for HAI (Executive Condominium)

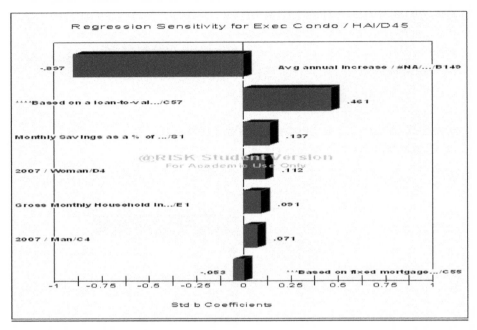

Source: Author, 2008 and 2020

In Fig 5.14, the main factors determining housing affordability for upgrading to the executive condominium comprise the rate of its annual price rise and the mortgage amount obtainable. However, the expected price rise of the HDB starter flat, which the homebuying household first purchases is a relevant factor influencing housing affordability. Because the sale proceeds of the fist flat purchase and of benefiting from the price appreciation of public housing, such sale proceeds can typically pay the down payment of the next (upgraded) flat, to improve housing affordability and accessibility.

Fig 5.14. Regression Analysis Of Upgrading To The Executive Condominium

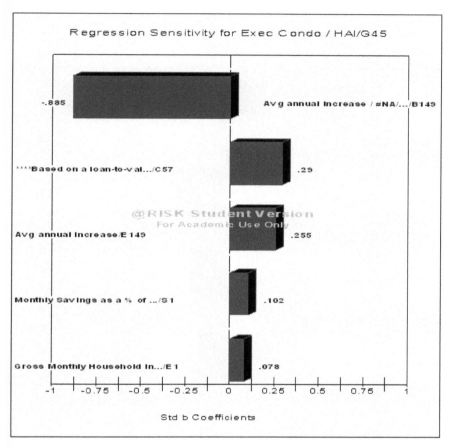

Source: Author, 2008 and 2020

For those homebuying households seeking to upgrade to private condominiums in Fig 5.15, such households also benefit from the sale proceeds of their first flat purchase and from the price appreciation of public housing. The sale proceeds can pay the down payment of the next private condominium apartment, to improve housing affordability and accessibility. The fortuitous wealth for such homebuying households is evident in selling their starter HDB housing to upgrade to better private condominium housing.

Fig 5.15. Regression Analysis Of Upgrading To The Private Condominium

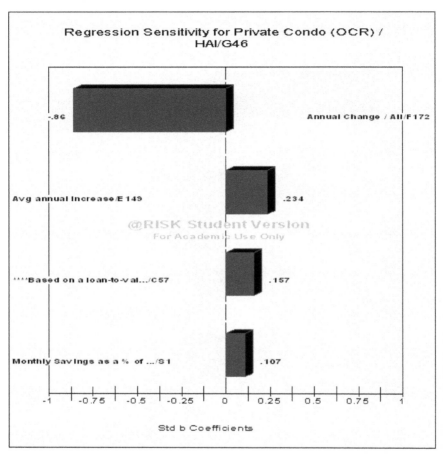

Source: Author, 2008 and 2020

Concluding Remarks

Chapter 5 brings to light that public housing (Housing and Development Board, HDB) flats and their amenities in Singapore are by no means poor quality, because HDB flats and their amenities are meant to provide affordable, high rise and quality housing for resident homebuyers. Housing affordability is always an issue of concern to many Singaporean homebuyers because shelter forms one of the basic life necessities. The corresponding private residential market in Singapore offers quality and premium private residential accommodation for homebuyers, who prefer the private residential market. Rising mortgage rates lower long-run housing affordability. Lowered housing affordability implies lowered residual income for other living expenses and so homebuyers may well choose to become HDB homebuyers for their household-family activities.

Chapter 5 finds that the appropriate affordability model is the appropriate multi-factor housing affordability index (HAI) model of eq (5.2), which considers the ability to provide down payment and to service the mortgage taken up. The model also considers housing accessibility.

HAI = monthly housing income/ (down payment of 20% + mortgage rate)

The multi-factor housing affordability index (HAI) model traces the footsteps of a typical middle-income homebuying household that conforms to the Singapore social system of going through 16 years of education, to graduate from university with an honors degree, and who then enter the workforce for 40 years before retiring at 65 years old. Special emphasis is placed on the housing types that the homebuying household chooses at different stages of its live, say from 2008 to 2023.

Deploying the housing affordability index (HAI) model, Chapter 5 presents the results in Table 5.4, based on the foregoing assumptions.

Table 5.4. The Housing Affordability Index, Singapore

Housing Affordability Index (HAI):

Housing Type/ Year	2011	2016	2017	2018	2019	2020	2021	2022	2023
4-room HDB Starter (New Estate)	2.036	4.367	4.648	4.978	5.250	5.526	5.815	7.509	7.711
5-room HDB Starter (New Estate)	1.664	3.481	3.701	3.956	4.169	4.385	4.611	5.928	6.086
Exec HDB Starter (New Estate)	1.375	2.819	2.994	3.196	3.365	3.538	3.717	4.760	4.886
4-room HDB Starter (Old Estate)	1.675	3.506	3.728	3.986	4.200	4.418	4.645	5.972	6.132
5-room HDB Starter (New Estate)	1.286	2.618	2.780	2.966	3.122	3.282	3.447	4.409	4.526
Exec HDB Starter (New Estate)	1.144	2.305	2.447	2.608	2.745	2.884	3.028	3.866	3.968
5-room HDB Resale	1.017	2.184	2.326	2.481	2.618	2.757	2.900	3.744	3.844
Exec HDB Resale	0.892	1.901	2.024	2.157	2.276	2.396	2.520	3.248	3.335
Exec Condo	0.669	1.150	1.174	1.199	1.213	1.225	1.235	1.520	1.497
Private Condo (Outside Central)	0.430	0.686	0.692	0.697	0.697	0.695	0.693	0.841	0.818
Private Condo (Rest of Central)	0.306	0.464	0.464	0.463	0.459	0.454	0.449	0.539	0.520
Private Condo (Core Central)	0.162	0.194	0.185	0.177	0.167	0.158	0.149	0.171	0.157

Source: Author, 2020

The simulation estimates focus on the hypothetical homebuying household purchasing its first HDB home, while satisfying the compulsory 5-year minimum occupancy period, before they decide to upgrade. Private condominiums and executive condominiums are selected as the primary choice of upgrading, because they are typically the preferred choice for today's young homebuying household. The greater the HAI, then the more affordable the housing choice is for the household. It is assumed that the homebuying household buys a 5-room flat in the newer HDB estates. The homebuying household's 5-room flat choice is factored into the resale proceeds upon liquidation from say 2016 onwards when the household is given the legal freedom to upgrade.

Once the compulsory 5-year minimum occupancy period is fulfilled, the hypothetical young homebuying household is comfortable with moving into a median priced resale HDB flat of their choice or purchase an executive condominium or purchase a flat under the HDB design, build and sell scheme (DBSS), if the homebuying household so chooses. Unfortunately, the price of a median private condominium or other private housing types are generally unaffordable for such a household, even with the fortuitous gains that it may enjoy from liquidating its HDB starter flat. The gap between the private and public housing market widens even further, as the HAI for private condominiums within the Central area stays persistently out of the reach of the homebuying household. In the prime core central area and its prime direct real estate (DRE) developments, the homebuying household would find its HAI for a unit there to be even beyond their financial reach as time goes by.

The corresponding Monti Carlo model simulations (MCMSs) affirm that the critical (maximum) price of housing at a certain period hinges largely on mortgage rates, the amount of mortgage taken and the repayment period. Gross monthly household income is another vital factor. Housing affordability of public housing for the middle class, represented by a HDB 5-room starter flat, is heavily correlated with the maximum mortgage taken up and the rate of price rise. Regular monthly savings also play a key role in determining whether-or-not the homebuying household can pay the outlay i.e. the initial down payment of 20% of the buying flat price (including CPF). For public housing and for the upper-middle income group, who qualify for an executive condominium, the expected annual price rise is more crucial than the mortgage amount taken up. Regular monthly savings are relevant but are over-shadowed by the earlier two factors of the price rise and the mortgage amount taken up.

The main factors determining housing affordability for upgrading to the executive condominium comprise the rate of its annual price rise and the mortgage amount obtainable. However, the expected price rise of the HDB starter flat, which the homebuying household first purchases is a relevant factor influencing housing affordability. Because the sale proceeds of the fist flat purchase and of benefiting from the price appreciation of public housing, such sale proceeds can typically pay the down payment of the next (upgraded) flat, to improve housing affordability and accessibility.

Lastly and for those homebuying households seeking to upgrade to private condominiums, such households also benefit from the sale proceeds of their first flat purchase and from the price appreciation of public housing. The sale proceeds can pay the down payment of the next private condominium apartment, to improve housing affordability and accessibility. The fortuitous wealth for such homebuying households is evident in selling their starter HDB housing to upgrade to better private condominium housing.

Acknowledgement: The Author wish to gratefully acknowledge the initial work carried out for Chapter 5 by Mr William LIM Jing Han, a graduate of the NUS Department of Real Estate, and in consultation with Honorary Professor (University of Hertfordshire, Hatfield, UK), Dr HO Kim Hin / David, during their meaningful brain storming sessions before Professor HO retired from the NUS SDE Departments of Real Estate and Building in May 2019.

CHAPTER 6

THE CONCLUSION

Chapter 6 summarises the book's findings and highlights the contributions and recommendations made. Chapter 1 develops a unique and state-of-the-art dynamic, structural public housing macroeconomic model (DSPHM), based on an open economy for several key macroeconomic variables, actual and expected, as well as the demand for new HDB flats sold. Through scenario analysis in scenario planning format, Chapter 1 readily adopts the DSPHM for simulating two scenarios, namely a "no change" first scenario and a public housing "deregulation" second scenario. In both scenarios, there is the same GDP expansion over the next 10 years. The first scenario is conclusive that beyond the optimal point of overwhelming public housing provision, the supply line of additional new HDB flats must rise at a slower pace (and in small doses) at the margin. This optimal point is favorable from an allocative efficiency perspective of scarce public housing resources. The second scenario is conclusive that the deregulation of public housing continues to sustain household affordability for new HDB flats even into the medium term (i.e. the next 6 years) at the least, and before private mortgage interest rates start to rise to become excessive. This second "deregulation" scenario also indicates the possible emergence of several new policy measures for the Singapore public housing sector – a rental HDB housing policy measure, the privatization of HDB mortgages as a new policy measure, and the private market securitization of HDB mortgages as a further new policy measure.

Chapter 2 aims at exploring the relationship between several economic factors and the demand for public housing, both in Hong Kong and Singapore. These two economies are known for their intensive government housing policies even though the manner of regulating their assisted homeownership schemes is vastly different. Therefore, two different questions have been answered subject to their respective government policy initiatives.

Chapter 2 deploys the system dynamics model, a rather innovative concept in direct real estate studies, to shed a better understanding on the policy implications of assisted ownership housing, via assessing the demand for new flats in both the Singapore and Hong Kong economies, under certain macroeconomic policy changes that are suitable for their unique situations, and instead of analyzing the effectiveness of government housing policies via the use of static models.

In Hong Kong's case, it is found that the HOS/PSPS demand would be around similar levels regardless of the performance of the economy. In a sense, the decision by the Hong Kong Special Administrative Region (HKSAR) government to cease selling HOS/PSPS flats is not justified in this Chapter, given the existing regulations of the Home Ownership Scheme (HOS) launched in 1978 by the Hong Kong Housing Authority (HA), along with another scheme known as the Private Sector Participation Scheme (PSPS). Therefore, Chapter 2 suggests a relaxation of regulations regarding the premium arrangements of the resale of HOS/PSPS flats on the open market. Similar to the Singapore government's HDB scheme, that by deferring the premium payment schedule till after the transaction, should not only ease the financial burden of the Hong Kong government HA in the construction of new flats, but also help to foster a more developed open market for the HKSAR government's HOS/PSPS flats. In the case of Singapore, Chapter 2 suggests an opening of the public housing (HDB) mortgage market to private sector loans under open competition. The fall in the demand for HDB flats shown in the Chapter can be attributed to rising demand in the secondary HDB housing market, owing to HDB's relatively lenient requirements. The Chapter offers meaningful insights on the Singapore government's aims of providing large scale public housing ownership and the potential, sustainable development of the HDB mortgage market by the private sector under open competition.

Chapter 3 examines the underlying structural relationships that affect Singapore's public housing policy to potentially privatize the HDB concessionary-rate mortgage loans for HDB homebuyers. It envisaged that this potential privatization would infuse and sustain price competitiveness among the domestic private banks in Singapore, and lead to improved efficiency among them as well as the Singapore economy at large. Two structural relationships are discussed in terms of the mortgage interest rate structure. First, a comparison is made between the HDB hurdle rates and the HDB mortgage yields to examine the notion of the potential privatization of the HDB concessionary rate mortgage loans. The examination reveals that the private banks' interest rates are lower than HDB concessionary rates on average for a 30 year-mortgage term. Therefore, it makes it more attractive for HDB homebuyers to take up the private banks' mortgages rather than the HDB mortgages. The likely reason for the lower interest rates offered by the private banks is primarily due to price competition in terms of the interest rate structure, which the individual banks face among themselves and with the HDB.

Secondly, both the HDB hurdle rates and the HDB mortgage yields are examined. The HDB mortgage yields are compared against the HDB hurdle rates to see whether-or-not the mortgage yields are higher, equal to or lower than the HDB hurdle rates. As the measure of the efficiency of the HDB mortgage financing activity, the examination reveals that the HDB mortgage yields are generally lower than the HDB hurdle rates. It is inferred that the HDB mortgage yield cannot meet the HDB minimum required rate of return, the HDB hurdle rate, which is HDB's own absolute performance benchmarking. Therefore, it is more worthwhile to pass the HDB mortgage financing activity to the private sector, where the Singapore domestic private banks are viable in generating better mortgage yields. In term of improved efficiency to the banking sector and the Singapore economy, the notion of potentially passing the HDB mortgage financing activity to the Singapore private sector is acceptable.

Chapter 3 is not without its limitations and two are highlighted. First, the private banks' interest rates in Singapore are compared on the assumption that the interest rates would be fixed for a 30 year-loan term. This is because it is not possible to anticipate the floating interest rates offered by the private banks. Such banks would usually offer fixed interest rate up to a maximum period of two years. Similarly, a fixed interest rate for the HDB concessionary interest rate is assumed and for a much longer 30-year mortgage term. Such a fixed HDB interest rate is not entirely accurate because the HDB offers fixed interest rate but subject to revision every 3 months. Secondly, the estimated hurdle rates may not precisely represent the HDB hurdle rate, as the cost of equity data is solely based on "CapitaLand Limited". Estimates of the HDB hurdle rates can be sourced from other public listed real estate companies to possibly establish a more accurate cost of equity.

Real option analysis, inclusive of its option pricing, is widely debated in the finance and economic literature. It helps to resolve the deficiency of the traditional DCF approach to mitigate risk and enhance the flexibility in investment decision making. The consequential development of real option models and the advancement in computing power enable the growing deployment of these models to direct real estate investment opportunities. Chapter 4 highlights the binomial option-pricing model, proposed by Cox, Ross and Rubinstein, CRR (1979), which can model the risk-neutral process for short term interest rates, common stock prices and even the HDB resale flat prices. The CRR binomial option pricing model may well be appropriate to represent the movement of the underlying HDB resale flat prices, subject to private market forces in HDB's large scale public housing secondary resale market. In other words, the HDB resale activities exist in a hypothetical market without regulatory constraints.

It is imperative to note that the binomial model conforms to several key assumptions. Nevertheless, the underlying assumptions of the model may not hold in practice. It can be argued that the use of option pricing theory may not necessarily minimize risk and produce a more accurate estimate. It is reasonable to merely observe the sensibility of the model's result to changes in the model's assumption and parameters, when real option models are introduced, according to Oppenheimer (2002).

Singapore's highly effective public housing policy has housed an overwhelming proportion of about 87 percent of the population. The Housing and Development Board (HDB), the national housing authority, is shifting its wealth redistributive focus to more allocative efficient housing policy initiatives in the presence of scarce resources for public housing. The HDB Main Upgrading Program (MUP) is therefore a heavily subsidized and highly targeted public housing policy. Since its inception in 1992, the HDB has budgeted some S$3 billion to finance the MUP policy. Revisions in the MUP policy are made regularly to keep it closely relevant to the general public's expectation and feedback. Limited local and anecdotal evidence have shown that the HDB MUP policy affects public housing households and the affected areas. One positive impact is the asset value enhancement of the HDB flats within the upgraded public housing precincts. The value of the upgraded HDB flat, particularly with the space-adding item (SAI), has improved considerably. The embedded real option premiums for HDB flats under the MUP policy are found to be around S$10,300 for a 3-Room HDB flat and S$2,000 for a larger 4-Room HDB flat. These real option values are estimated from both the binomial real option pricing model and the Samuelson-McKean model.

The estimation of the real option value to upgrade may help the homebuying HDB flat owner to better assess his enhanced flat value, and to better appreciate the cost and gain involved. It enables the homebuying HDB flat owner to make a better decision to hold or to unlock the underlying value of his HDB flat, affected by the MUP policy. Chapter 4 shows that the MUP subsidies have a significant impact on the corresponding option premium. A 3-Room homebuying HDB flat owner is more inclined to opt for upgrading while the option premium is deemed to be less attractive for upgrading in the case of the homebuying 4-Room HDB flat owner. In addition, some bias may be induced by an inadequate amount of transaction data available for the 4-Room HDB flats. The public housing sector may well require more time to stabilize in tandem with the revision to the MUP policy, in particularly the secondary HDB resale market. Flats in different locations may well command different values. Finally, the resale price index of HDB flats may not be representative of the Ang Mo Kio public housing estate. Therefore, Chapter 4's findings can be extended to estimate the value of upgrading at other HDB housing estates like the Bedok, Telok Blangah and Marine Parade HDB estates, provided that there are sufficient transaction data available. It is also possible to examine the option values for more HDB room flat types and their impact on the hold–sell decision.

Chapter 5 brings to light that public housing (Housing and Development Board, HDB) flats and their amenities in Singapore are by no means poor quality, because HDB flats and their amenities are meant to provide affordable, high rise and quality housing for resident homebuyers. Housing affordability is always an issue of concern to many Singaporean homebuyers because shelter forms one of the basic life necessities. The corresponding private residential market in Singapore offers quality and premium private residential accommodation for homebuyers, who prefer the private residential market. Rising mortgage rates lower long-run housing affordability. Lowered housing affordability implies lowered residual income for other living expenses and so homebuyers may well choose to become HDB homebuyers for their household-family activities. Chapter 5 finds that the appropriate affordability model is the appropriate multi-factor housing affordability index (HAI) model of equation below, which considers the ability to provide down payment and to service the mortgage taken up. The model also considers housing accessibility.

HAI = monthly housing income/ (down payment of 20% + mortgage rate)

$$
HAI = \frac{AI}{12 * \{2.5 * [(0.8 \times Price_j) * MC_{i,n}] - CPF\}} \times 50 + \frac{RG + Sav + CPF\ Sav}{0.2 * Price_j + LFSD} \times 50
$$

, where $Price_j$ = Price of housing type,

AI = Annual household income

$MC_{i,30}$ = Mortgage constant of housing loan, given n years at prime lending rate i,

CPF = Monthly CPF contributions,

LFSD = Legal fees and stamp duties,

Sav = amount of household savings,

CPF Sav = amount of savings in CPF,

RG = Resale gains from previous housing

The multi-factor housing affordability index (HAI) model traces the footsteps of a typical middle-income homebuying household that conforms to the Singapore social system of going through 16 years of education, to graduate from university with an honors degree, and who then enter the workforce for 40 years before retiring at 65 years old. Special emphasis is placed on the housing types that the homebuying household chooses at different stages of its live, say from 2008 to 2023. The simulation estimates focus on the hypothetical homebuying household purchasing its first HDB home, while satisfying the compulsory 5-year minimum occupancy period, before they decide to upgrade. Private condominiums and executive condominiums are selected as the primary choice of upgrading, because they are typically the preferred choice for today's young homebuying household. The greater the HAI, then the more affordable the housing choice is for the household. It is assumed that the homebuying household buys a 5-room flat in the newer HDB estates. The homebuying household's 5-room flat choice is factored into the resale proceeds upon liquidation from say 2016 onwards when the household is given the legal freedom to upgrade. Once the compulsory 5-year minimum occupancy period is fulfilled, the hypothetical young homebuying household is comfortable with moving into a median priced resale HDB flat of their choice or purchase an executive condominium or purchase a flat under the HDB design, build and sell scheme (DBSS), if the homebuying household so chooses. Unfortunately, the price of a median private condominium or other private housing types are generally unaffordable for such a household, even with the fortuitous gains that it may enjoy from liquidating its HDB starter flat. The gap between the private and public housing market widens even further, as the HAI for private condominiums within the Central area stays persistently out of the reach of the homebuying household. In the prime core central area and its prime direct real estate (DRE) developments, the homebuying household would find its HAI for a unit there to be even beyond their financial reach as time goes by.

The corresponding Monti Carlo model simulations (MCMSs) affirm that the critical (maximum) price of housing at a certain period hinges largely on mortgage rates, the amount of mortgage taken and the repayment period. Gross monthly household income is another vital factor. Housing affordability of public housing for the middle class, represented by a HDB 5-room starter flat, is heavily correlated with the maximum mortgage taken up and the rate of price rise. Regular monthly savings also play a key role in determining whether-or-not the homebuying household can pay the outlay i.e. the initial down payment of 20% of the buying flat price (including CPF). For public housing and for the upper-middle income group, who qualify for an executive condominium, the expected annual price rise is more crucial than the mortgage amount taken up. Regular monthly savings are relevant but are over-shadowed by the two factors of the price rise and the mortgage amount taken up.

The main factors determining housing affordability for upgrading to the executive condominium comprise the rate of its annual price rise and the mortgage amount obtainable. However, the expected price rise of the HDB starter flat, which the homebuying household first purchases is a relevant factor influencing housing affordability. Because the sale proceeds of the fist flat purchase and of benefiting from the price appreciation of public housing, such sale proceeds can typically pay the down payment of the next (upgraded) flat, to improve housing affordability and accessibility. Lastly and for those homebuying households seeking to upgrade to private condominiums, such households also benefit from the sale proceeds of their first flat purchase and from the price appreciation of public housing. The sale proceeds can pay the down payment of the next private condominium apartment, to improve housing affordability and accessibility. The fortuitous wealth for such homebuying households is evident in selling their starter HDB housing to upgrade to better private condominium housing.

REFERENCES

Chapter 1

Lim, C.Y and associates (1988). Policy options for the Singapore economy. Singapore: McGraw Hill Book Co.

Liu, T.K. (2002) Urbanizing Singapore: Optimizing Resources: Mega Cities Lecture 6, Megacities Foundation c/o S@M stedebouw & architectuurmanagement, Herengracht, 23, 1015 BA Amsterdam, The hague,The Netherlands.

D.C. Stafford (1978) The economics of housing policy. Great Britain: Croom Helm London.

Paul N. Balchin (1981) Housing policy and housing needs. London: The Macmillan Press Ltd.

P. Malpass and A. Murie (1999) Housing policy and practice (5th ed.). London: The Macmillan Press Ltd.

Balchin, Bull and Kieve (1995) Urban land economics and public policy (5th ed.). England: Macmillan Distirbution Ltd

Tan, Augustine H. H. and Phang S. Y. (1991) The Singapore Experience in Public

Housing, Occasional Chapter 1 9. Singapore: Times Academic Press for the Centre for Advanced Studies.

Tan, E.K. (2012) Public Housing & New Town Planning & Design in Singapore Lecture, MSc RE5013 Urban Policy & Real Estate Markets, Department of Real Estate, School of Design & Environment, National University of Singapore.

Tan, S.Y. (1998). Private Ownership of Public Housing in Singapore. Singapore: Times Academic Press.

Low, Linda and Aw, T.C. (1997). Housing a healthy, educated and wealthy nation through the CPF. Singapore: Times Academic Press for the Institute of Policy Studies.

Ooi, G. L. and Kwok, K. (1997). City & the State: Singapore's Built Environment Revisited. Singapore: Oxford University Press for the Institute of Policy Studies.

Yeh H. K. (1985). Households and housing. Singapore: Department of Statistics.

Joseph F. Healey (2002). Statistics A tool for social research (6th ed.) CA, USA: Wadsworth/ Thomson learning.

Hair, Anderson, Tatham and Black (1998). Multivariate Data Analysis (5th ed.) New Jersey: Prentice Hall.

George, D. and Mallery, P. (2001). SPSS for Windows step by step (3rd ed.) USA: Allyn & Bacon.

D. Fisher (2001). Intermediate macroeconomics: a statistical approach. Singapore River Edge, NJ: World Scientific.

Bénassy, J.P. (2002). The macroeconomics of imperfect competition and nonclearing markets: a dynamic general equilibrium approach. Massachusetts Institute of Technology Press, Cambridge, Mass.

King, J.E.(2002). A history of post Keynesian economics since 1936. Northampton, MA: Edward Elgar Publishing

Norusis, Marija J. (2002). SPSS 11.0 Guide to Data Analysis. New Jersey: Prentice Hall.

Norusis, Marija J. (2000). SPSS 10.0 Guide to Data Analysis. New Jersey: Prentice Hall.

Tan, Willie (2001). Practical Research Methods: With Applications in Building and Real Estate. Singapore: Prentice Hall.

Tan, Willie (2001). Practical Research Methods. Singapore: Prentice Hall.

Tan, Willie (1995). Housing Markets and Public Policy: Singapore: SBEM Book Series.

Sterman, J. (2000). Business dynamics/: System thinking and modeling for a complex world. McGraw-Hill. New York.

B. Richmond and S. Peterson (2000). An introduction to systems thinking (5th ed.). US: High Performance Systems Inc.

B. Richmond and M Paich (1997). Business applications (4th ed.). US: High Performance Systems Inc.

Economics Survey of Singapore 2002. Ministry of Trade and Industry.

Economics Survey of Singapore 2001. Ministry of Trade and Industry

Housing and Development Board annual report 1984/1985

Housing and Development Board annual report 1985/1986

Housing and Development Board annual report 1986/1987

Housing and Development Board annual report 1987/1988

Housing and Development Board annual report 1988/1989

Housing and Development Board annual report 1989/1990

Housing and Development Board annual report 1990/1991

Housing and Development Board annual report 1991/1992

Housing and Development Board annual report 1992/1993

Housing and Development Board annual report 1993/1994

Housing and Development Board annual report 1994/1995

Housing and Development Board annual report 1995/1996

Housing and Development Board annual report 1996/1997

Housing and Development Board annual report 1997/1998

Housing and Development Board annual report 1998/1999

Housing and Development Board annual report 1999/2000

Housing and Development Board annual report 2000/2001

Housing and Development Board annual report 2001/2002.

Wong K. and Yeh H.K. (1995). Housing a Nation, 25 Years of Public Housing in Singapore. Singapore: Maruzen Asia for Housing and Development Board.

Yeh H. K. (1975). Public Housing in Singapore, a multi-disciplinary study. Singapore: Singapore University Press for Housing and Development Board.

T. O'Sullivan and K. Gibb (2003). Housing economics and public policy. UK. Blackwell Science Ltd.

Ho, K.H.D; Teh, R.Y.C; Tham K.W. and Briffett, C (1997). The greening of Singapore National Estate, *HABITAL International*, Vol. 21, No. 1, pp 107-121.

Ho, K.H.D; Ho, M.W and Hui, C.M.E. (2002). Modelling the dynamic structure between port throughput and capacity policy – the port of Hong Kong.

Phang, S. Y.(2003). Housing Policy, Wealth and the Singapore Economy. *Housing Studies*, 16(4), 443-459.

Sterman, J. (2001). System Dynamics Modeling: Tools for learning in a complex world. *California Management Review*, Vol 43, No 4

Meen, G. (2003). Housing, random walks, complexity and the macroeconomy. *Real Estate Issues,* Chapter 6.

Quek, T. (2003, December, 7) If demand is bad, HDB won't build. *The Straits Times, Singapore.*

Leong, P.K.(2003, October, 10) HDB now to focus on basics. *The Straits Times, Singapore.*

2003 Centaur Communications Limited (2003, September, 8) Singapore opens its doors. *International Money Marketing*

Leong, C. T. (2003, August, 17). CPF cut will hit highly mortgaged most. *The Sunday Times.* .

Leong P. Y. (2003, August, 15). Affordability of flats a concern in this economic gloom. *The Straits Times*.

Kwak, S. (1995). Policy analysis of Hanford Tank farm operations with system dynamic approach. Ph.D thesis, Department of Nuclear Engineering, Massachusetts Institute of Technology, Cambridge, Mass.

Chapter 2
D.C. Stafford (1978). The economics of housing policy. Great Britain: Croom Helm London

Paul N. Balchin (1981) Housing policy and housing needs. London: The Macmillan Press Ltd.

P. Malpass and A. Murie (1999) Housing policy and practice (5th ed.). London: The Macmillan Press Ltd.

Balchin, Bull and Kieve (1995) Urban land economics and public policy (5th ed.). England: Macmillan Distirbution Ltd

Tan, S.Y. (1998). Private Ownership of Public Housing in Singapore. Singapore: Times Academic Press.

Low, Linda and Aw, T.C. (1997). Housing a healthy, educated and wealthy nation through the CPF. Singapore: Times Academic Press for the Institute of Policy Studies.

Ooi, G. L. and Kwok, K. (). City & the State: Singapore's Built Environment Revisited. Singapore: Oxford University Press for the Institute of Policy Studies.

Yeh H. K. (1985). Households and housing. Singapore: Department of Statistics.

Joseph F. Healey (2002). Statistics A tool for social research (6th ed.) CA, USA: Wadsworth/ Thomson learning.

Hair, Anderson, Tatham and Black (1998). Multivariate Data Analysis (5th ed.) New Jersey: Prentice Hall.

George, D. and Mallery, P. (2001). SPSS for Windows step by step (3rd ed.) USA: Allyn & Bacon.

D. Fisher (2001). Intermediate macroeconomics: a statistical approach. Singapore River Edge, NJ: World Scientific.

Bénassy, J.P. (2002). The macroeconomics of imperfect competition and nonclearing markets: a dynamic general equilibrium approach. Massachusetts Institute of Technology Press, Cambridge, Mass.

King, J.E.(2002). A history of post Keynesian economics since 1936. Northampton, MA: Edward Elgar Publishing

Norusis, Marija J. (2002). SPSS 11.0 Guide to Data Analysis. New Jersey: Prentice Hall.
Tan, Willie (2001). Practical Research Methods: With Applications in Building and Real Estate. Singapore: Prentice Hall.

Tan, Willie (2001). Practical Research Methods. Singapore: Prentice Hall.

Tan, Willie (1995). Housing Markets and Public Policy: Singapore: SBEM Book Series.

Sterman, J. (2000). Business dynamics/: System thinking and modeling for a complex world. McGraw-Hill. New York.

B. Richmond and S. Peterson (2000). An introduction to systems thinking (5th ed.). US: High Performance Systems Inc.

Wong K. and Yeh H.K. (1995). Housing a Nation, 25 Years of Public Housing in Singapore. Singapore: Maruzen Asia for Housing and Development Board.

Yeh H. K. (1975). Public Housing in Singapore, a multi-disciplinary study. Singapore: Singapore University Press for Housing and Development Board.

T. O'Sullivan and K. Gibb (2003). Housing economics and public policy. UK. Blackwell Science Ltd.

Ho, K.H.D; Teh, R.Y.C; Tham K.W. and Briffett, C (1997). The greening of Singapore National Estate, *HABITAL International*, Vol. 21, No. 1, pp 107-121.

Ho, K.H.D; Ho, M.W and Hui, C.M.E. (2002). Modelling the dynamic structure between port throughput and capacity policy – the port of Hong Kong.

Sterman, J. (2001). System Dynamics Modeling: Tools for learning in a complex world. *California Management Review*, Vol 43, No 4

Meen, G. (2003). Housing, random walks, complexity and the macroeconomy. *Real Estate Issues,* Chapter 6.

Liu, T.K. Urbanising Singapore. Optimising Resources. Megacities Lecture 2002, The hague, Nethelands, November 2002.

Quek, T. (2003, December, 7) If demand is bad, HDB won't build. *The Straits Tim.e*

Leong, P.K.(2003, October, 10) HDB now to focus on basics. *The Straits Time.*

2003 Centaur Communications Limited (2003, September, 8) Singapore opens its doors. *International Money Marketing*

Chapter 3

Brueggeman, W., Fisher J. (2005). Real estate finance and investment. (12th Edition).Boston: McGraw–Hill/Irwin.

Davis, K., Harper, I. (1993). (Ed) (1989). *Privatization in Singapore: the political and administrative implications.* Singapore: Longman.

Glen, A. (2001) Corporate financial management. (2nd Edition). New York: Prentice Hall.

Levy, H., Sarnat, M. (1994). *Capital investment and financial decisions.* (5th Edition). UK: Prentice Hall.

Housing and Development Board annual report 2000/2001
Housing and Development Board annual report 2001/2002.

Republican Policy Committee. (2003). *Problems at fannie mae and freddie mac: Too big to fall.* Jon kyl. Retrieved 28 January 2005 from http://rpc.senate.gov.

Singapore Development Board (2003/2004) Financial statement Chuang Kwong Yong: Auditor General Singapore. Retrieved 20 December 2004 from http://www.hdb.gov.sg.

Street TRACK STI. (2003) Straits time index fund annual report 30 june 2003.

PricewaterhouseCoopers. Retrieved 29 February 2005 from http://www.streettracks.com.sg

Thynne, I. and Ariff, M. (Ed) (1989). *Privatisation: the financial implications.* Sydney: Australian Print Group.

Wallison, P. (Ed.) (2001). *Serving two masters yet out of control fannie mae and freddie mac.* Washington: AEI Press.

Amram, M. and Lakatilaka, N.(1999). Real option: Managing strategic investment in an uncertain world. Harvard Business School Press.

Blanc, D. and Laferrère, A. (2001). The Effect of Public Social Housing on Households' Consumption in France. *Journal of Housing Economics,* 10(4), 429-455.

Boelhouwer, P. (2003). Social housing finance in the Netherlands: The road to independence. *Housing Finance International.* 17(4), 17-21.

Black, F. and Scholes, M. (1973). The pricing of options and corporate liabilities. *Journal of Political Economy,* 81, 637-654.

Brown, Gerald and Ong S.E.(1999). Valuing real and contractual options. *Australian Land Economic Review,* Direct real estate into the Next Millennium Ed. 99-112.

Capozza, D. and Sick, G. (1991). Valuing long-term leases: the option to redevelop. *Journal of Direct real estate Finance and Economics,* 4(2), 209-223.

Capozza, D. and Li, Y. (1994). The intensity and timing of investment: the case of land. *The American Economic Review,* 84(4), 889-904.

Chang, K.L. (1996) HDB's upgrading programme in Bukit Ho Swee. Unpublished undergraduate dissertation, School of Building and Estate Management, National University of Singapore.

Childs, P.D., Riddiough, T.J. and Triantis, A.J. (1996). Mixed uses and the redevelopment option. *Direct real estate Economics,* 24, 317-339.

Chiong, L. K. (1996). Housing Price Dynamics and the Valuation of Mortgage Default Options. *Journal of housing Economics,* 5, 18–40.

Cox, J.C., Ross, S.A. and Rubinstein, M. (1979). Option pricing: a simplified approach. *Journal of Financial Economics*, 7(3), 229-263.

Geltner, David M. and Miller, Norman G.(2001). *Commercial direct real estate analysis and investments.* Prentice Hall, Chapter 28.

Gilbert, A. (2004). Helping the poor through housing subsidies: lessons from Chile, Colombia and South Africa. *Habitat International,* 28(1),13-40.

Goh, C.T. (1995, Jan). Speech at the completion ceremony of Kim Keat Demonstration Upgrading Precinct.

Grenadier, S.R. (1995). Valuing lease contracts: a real-options approach. *Journal of Financial Economics*, 38, 297-331.

Harris, R and Giles, C. (2003). A mixed message: the agents and forms of international housing policy, 1945–1973. *Habitat International,* 27(2), 167-191.

HDB InfoWEB, Singapore. Retrieved various dates from World Wide Web: http://www7.hdb.gov.sg

Hoek-Smit, M.C. and Diamond, D.B. (2003). Subsidies for housing finance. *Housing Finance International.* 17(3), 3-13

Hull, J. (1993). *Options, Futures and Other Derivative Securities (2nd ed.).* London: Prentice-Hall.

Kautt, Glenn (2003). Real option analysis: The profession's next cutting-edge tool. *Journal of Financial Planning,* 16(2), 72-79.

Limberes, N.M. (2006) 'Mass voting behaviour: the factors that influenced the conservative vote during the 1981 Greek general election', *European Journal of Political Research,* vol. 14, issue 1-2, pages 113-137.

Lucius, D.L(2001). Real options in direct real estate development. *Journal of Direct real estate Investment & Finance*,19(1), 73-78.

McDonald, R. and Siegel,D. (1986). The value of waiting to invest. *Quarterly Journal of Economics*, 101(4), 707-727.

Merton, R.C.(1973). The theory of rational option pricing. *Journal of Economics and Management Science*, 4, 141-183.

Monetary Authority of Singapore. Retrieved 14 Dec 2003 from World Wide Web: http://www.mas.gov.sg.

Moore, W. T. (2001). *Real Options & Option-embedded Securities*. New York: John Wiley & Sons, Chapter 11.

McKee, K. (2007) 'Community Ownership in Glasgow: The Devolution of Ownership and Control, or s Centralizing Process?', *European Journal of Housing Policy*, vol. 7, no. 3, 319-336.

Nygaard, C., Gibb, K. & Berry, M. (2007) 'Ownership Transfer of Social Housing in the UK: A Direct real estate Rights Approach', *Housing, Theory and Society*, vol. 24, no. 2, pp. 89-110.

Ong, S.E. (1999). Aborted direct real estate transactions: seller under-compensation in the absence of legal recourse.. *Journal of Direct real estate Investment & Finance*,17(2),126-144.

Oppenheimer, P.H.(2002). A critique of using real options pricing models in valuing direct real estate projects and contracts. *Briefings in Direct real estate Finance*, 2(3),221-233

Priemus, H. (2003). Social housing management: Concerns about effectiveness and efficiency in the Netherlands. *Journal of Housing and the Built Environment*, 18(3), 269.

Quigg, L (1993). Empirical Testing Of Real Option Pricing Models. *Journal of Finance,* 48(2), 621-640.

Saugeres, L. (2000). Of tidy gardens and clean houses: housing officers as agents of social control. *Geoforum,* 31(4), 587-599.

Schaefer, J.P. (2003). Financing social housing in France. *Housing Finance International,* 17(4), 27-34.

Sim, L.L., Yu, S.M. and Han, S.S. (2003).Public housing and ethnic integration in Singapore. *Habitat International,* 27(2), 293-307.

Sin, A.M.(1999). The impact of housing and development board's main upgrading programme. Unpublished master thesis, School of Building and Estate Management, National University of Singapore.

Sing T. F. (2001). Optimal Timing of a Direct real estate Development under Uncertainty. *Journal of Direct real estate Investment & Finance,*19(1),35-52.

Sing T. F. (2002). Valuing renewal options in public industrial leases in Singapore. *Journal of Direct real estate Investment & Finance,*20(3),222-241.

Tahtinen, T. (2003). Financing social housing in Finland. *Housing Finance International.* 17(4), 22-26.

Tan, T. W.(1996). An in-depth study into the upgrading of Kim Keat Court. Unpublished undergraduate dissertation, School of Building and Estate Management, National University of Singapore.

Titman, S. (1985). Urban land prices under uncertainty. *American Economic Review,* 75(3), 505-514.

Williams, J. (1991). Direct real estate development as an option. *Journal of Direct real estate Economic and Finance,* 4(2), 191-208.

Wong, L. W. (2001). Application of financial option pricing models to real options. Unpublished master thesis, Smeal College of Business Administration, Pennsylvania State University.

Wong, T.C and Yap, A. (2003). From universal public housing to meeting the increasing aspiration for private housing in Singapore. *Habitat International*, 27(3), 361–380.

Press Releases (The Straits Times, Singapore)

No request made to install toilet bowls - HDB.(5 June 2003). *The Straits Times*.

Leong, P.Y.(6 June 2003).Four contractors later, and still upgrading not ready. *The Straits Times*.

Li, X.(8 June 2003). Stalled upgrading - HDB won't compensate owners. *The Straits Times*.

Tan H.Y. (10 June 2003).Upgrading delay - Many get toilet bowls, finally. *The Straits Times*.

Ho, L.C. (10 June 2003). HDB could have done better. *The Straits Times*.

Guevarra V and Tan H.Y. (11 June 2003).Contractors sink into the red after undercutting each other. *The Straits Times*.

HDB 'going all out' to complete stalled upgrading. (12 June 2003). *The Straits Times*.

When upgrading is a dirty word. (16 July 2003). *The Straits Times*.

HDB precinct says 'no' to upgrading - a first. (7 August 2003). *The Straits Times*.

Leong, P.Y.(8 Aug 2003). At least one MP to delay upgrading. *The Straits Times.*

Leong, P.Y.(14 Aug 2003). Upgrading work at Marine Terrace back on track. *The Straits Times.*

Leong, P.Y.(8 Sep 2003). Upgrading? Maybe later. *The Straits Times.*

Yeo, M. H.(18 Sep 2003). Upgrade flat? Thanks but no thanks. *The Straits Times.*

Season of HDB delays. (1 October 2003). *The Straits Times.*

HDB: One more delay. (27 Sep 2003). *The Straits Times.*

Zainol, V.(8 December 2003). Window pain. *The Straits Times.*

Chapter 5

Ang, L. 2000. Upgraders still a strong force, buying $7.7b of properties. The Business Times, (Singapore), 19 May [Google Scholar]

ANHS (Australia National Housing Strategy). 1991. *The Affordability of Australian Housing,* Canberra: AGPS. Issues Paper No. 2 [Google Scholar]

Bogdon, A. S. and Can, A. 1997. Indicators of local housing affordability. *Real Estate Economics,* 25(1): 43–80. [Crossref], [Web of Science ®], [Google Scholar]

Bramley, G. 1991. *Bridging the Affordability Gap in 1990: An Update of Research on Housing Access and Affordability,* Bristol: University of Bristol, SAUS. [Google Scholar]

Carter, T. 1997. Current practices for procuring affordable housing: the Canadian context. *Housing Policy Debate,* 8(3): 593–631. [Taylor & Francis Online], [Web of Science ®], [Google Scholar]

Chua, B. H. 1997. *Political Legitimacy and Housing: Stakeholding in Singapore*, London: Routledge. [Google Scholar]

Chua, B. H., ed. 2000. *Consumption in Asia*, London: Routledge. [Google Scholar]

Clark, W. A. V., Deurloo, M. C. and Dieleman, F. M. 1990. Household characteristics and tenure choice in the US housing market. *Netherlands Journal of Housing and Environment*, 5(3): 251–270. [Crossref], [Google Scholar]

Doling, J. 1997. *Comparative Housing Policy: Government and Housing in Advanced Industrialized Countries*, London: Macmillan. [Crossref], [Google Scholar]

Doling, J. 1999. Housing policies and the Little Tigers: how do they compare with other industrialized countries?. *Housing Studies*, 14(2): 229–250. [Taylor & Francis Online], [Web of Science ®], [Google Scholar]

Doling, J. and Stafford, B. 1989. *Home Ownership: The Diversity of Experience*, Aldershot: Gower. [Google Scholar]

Feins, J. D. and Lane, T. S. 1981. *How Much for Housing? A New Perspective on Affordability and Risk*, Cambridge, MA: Abt Books. [Google Scholar]

Fiddler, S. 2001. Who's minding the bank?. *Foreign Policy*,: 40–50. September–October [Google Scholar]

Foo, T. S. 2001. Planning and design of Tampines, an award-winning, high-rise, high-density township in Singapore. *Cities*, 18(1): 33–42. [Crossref], [Web of Science ®], [Google Scholar]

Forrest, R., Lee, J. and Chan, K. W. 2000. Editor's introduction: focus on housing in South-east Asia. *Housing Studies*, 15(1): 7–10. [Taylor & Francis Online], [Web of Science ®], [Google Scholar]

Friedrichs, J. 1988. "Affordable housing and homelessness: a comparative view". In *Affordable Housing and the Homeless*, Edited by: Friedrichs, J. Berlin: Walter de Gruyter. [Crossref], [Google Scholar]

Gibb, K. 1996. *Housing Affordability: Key Issues and Policies in OECD, Strategies for Housing and Social Integration in Cities*, Paris: OECD. [Google Scholar]

Goodman, J. (2001) Housing Affordability in the United States: Trends, Interpretations, and Outlook. Report prepared for the Millennial Housing Commission, USA. [Google Scholar]

Gyourko, J. and Tracy, J. 1999. A look at real housing prices and incomes: some implication for housing affordability and quality. *Economic Policy Review*, 5(3): 63–77. [Google Scholar]

Hancock, K. E. 1993. 'Can pay? Won't pay?' or economic principles of 'affordability'. *Urban Studies*, 30(1): 127–145. [Crossref], [Web of Science ®], [Google Scholar]

Harsman, B. and Quigley, J., eds. 1991. *Housing Markets and Housing Institutions: An International Comparison*, Boston: Kluwer. [Crossref], [Google Scholar]

Housing and Development Board (HDB) Singapore (various years) Annual Report. [Google Scholar]

Hulchanski, J. D. 1995. The concept of housing affordability: six contemporary uses of the housing expenditure-to-income ratio. *Housing Studies*, 10(4): 471–491. [Taylor & Francis Online], [Web of Science ®], [Google Scholar]

Joint Center for Housing Studies. 1994. *The State of the Nation's Housing: 1994*, Cambridge, MA: Joint Center for Housing Studies of Harvard University. [Google Scholar]

Jones, R. 1994. *The Housing Needs of Indigenous Australians, 1991*, Canberra: Centre for Aboriginal Economic Policy Research, Australian National University. Research Monograph No. 8 [Google Scholar]

Kamath, R. (1988) The measurement of housing affordability. Real Estate Issues, Fall/Winter, pp. 26–33. [Google Scholar]

Keare, D. H. and Jimenez, E. 1983. *Progressive Development and Affordability in the Design of Urban Shelter Projects*, Washington, DC: World Bank. [Google Scholar]

Kendig, H. L. 1984. "The backlog of private tenants". In *Affordable and Available Housing*, Edited by: Paris, C. Canberra: Australian Institute of Urban Studies. [Google Scholar]

Koh, G. & Ooi, G. L. (1996) Private property, social expectation & public policy in public policy and the Singapore dream, Conference on the Singapore Dream, Faculty of Architecture & Building, National University of Singapore, Singapore, 6 September. [Google Scholar]

Lane, T. S. 1977. *What Families Spend for Housing—The Origins and Uses of the 'Rules of Thumb'*, Cambridge, MA: Abt Associates. [Google Scholar]

Lee, K. Y. 2000. *From Third World to First*, Singapore: Times Editions. [Google Scholar]

Lerman, D. L. and Reeder, W. J. 1987. The affordability of adequate housing. *AREUEA Journal*, 15(4): 389–404. [Google Scholar]

Linneman, P. D. and Megbolugbe, I. F. 1992. Housing affordability: myth or reality?. *Urban Studies*, 29(3/4): 369–392. [Crossref], [Web of Science ®], [Google Scholar]

Low, L. and Aw, T. C. 1997. *Housing a Healthy, Educated and Wealthy Nation through the CPF*, Singapore: Times Academic Press. [Google Scholar]

Maclennan, D. and Wiliams, R. 1990. *"Housing subsidies and the market: An international perspective"*. York, England: Joseph Rowntree Foundation Housing Finance Series. [Google Scholar]

Miron, J. R. 1989. Household formation, affordability and housing policy. *Population Research and Policy Review*, 8: 55–77. [Google Scholar]

Muelbauer, J. 1990. "The housing market and the UK economy: problems and opportunities". In *Housing and the National Economy*, Edited by: Ermisch, J. London: Avebury. [Google Scholar]

Mulroy, E. A. and Ewalt, P. L. 1996. Affordable housing: a basic need and a social issue. *Social Work*, 41(3): 245–248. [PubMed], [Web of Science ®], [Google Scholar]

Murray, M. S. 1998. Housing condition of nuclear and extended household in the Miami–Fort Lauderdale area. *Population and Environment*, 20(1): 55–75. [Google Scholar]

Neo, P. H., Lee, N. J. and Ong, S. E. 2003. Government policies and household mobility behaviour in Singapore. *Urban Studies*, 40(13): 2643–2660. [Crossref], [Google Scholar]

Neutze, M., Sanders, W. and Jones, R. 2000. *Estimating Indigenous Housing Need for Public Funding Allocation: A Multi-measure Approach*, Canberra: Centre for Aboriginal Economic Policy Research,

Australian National University. Discussion Paper No. 197 [Google Scholar]

Noll, P. F., O'Dell, W., Smith, M. T. and Sullivan, J. 1997. Florida's affordable housing needs assessment methodology. *Journal of the American Planning Association*, 63(4): 495–508. [Taylor & Francis Online], [Web of Science ®], [Google Scholar]

Renaud, B. 1991. *Affordability, Price–Income Ratio and Housing Performance: An International Perspective*, Washington, DC: The World Bank. Working Paper [Google Scholar]

Saunders, D. 1984. "Beyond housing classes". In *International Journal of Urban and Regional Research* Vol. 8, 202–227. 2 [Google Scholar]

Suchman, D. R. 1995. *Manufactured Housing: An Affordable Alternative*, Washington, DC: Urban Land Institute. [Google Scholar]

Teo, S. E. and Phillips, D. R. 1989. Attitudes towards service provision in public housing estates and new towns in Singapore. *Singapore Journal of Tropical Geography*, 10(1): 74–94. [Google Scholar]

UNCHS. 1994. *National Experiences with Shelter Delivery for the Poorest Groups*, Nairobi: UNCHS. [Google Scholar]

UNCHS. 1999. *Guidelines on Practical Aspects in the Realization of the Human Right to Adequate Housing, including the Formulation of the United Nations Housing Rights Programme*, Nairobi: UNCHS. Progress Report of the Executive Director to the 17th Session of the Commission on Human Settlements [Google Scholar]

UNCHS. 2001. *Position Paper on Housing Rights*, Nairobi: UNCHS. [Google Scholar]

URA (Urban Redevelopment Authority). 1996. *Real Estate Statistics Series—Stock and Occupancy*, Singapore: URA. [Google Scholar]

URA. 1999. *Living the Next Lap*, Singapore: URA. [Google Scholar]

US Dept of Housing and Urban Development. 1994. *US Housing Market Conditions*, Washington, DC: US HUD. 3rd Quarter 1994 [Google Scholar]

Whitehead, C. 1979. Why owner occupation?. *CES Review*,: 33–42. May [Google Scholar]

Wallace, J. E. 1995. Financing affordable housing in the United States. *Housing Policy Debate*, 6(4): 785–814. [Taylor & Francis Online], [Web of Science ®], [Google Scholar]

Whitehead, C. M. E. and Cross, D. T. 1991. Affordable housing in London. *Progress in Planning*, 36: 1–91. [Crossref], [Google Scholar]

Wong, A. and Yeh, S. K. H. 1985. *Housing a Nation*, Singapore: Maruzen Asia. [Google Scholar]

Wong, T. C. and Yap, A. 2003. From universal public housing to meeting the increasing aspiration for private housing in Singapore. *Habitat International*, 27(3): 361–380. [Crossref], [Web of Science ®], [Google Scholar]

World Bank. 1993. *Enabling Housing Markets to Work*, Washington, DC: The World Bank. A World Bank Policy Paper [Crossref], [Google Scholar]

Yuen, B., Teo, H. P. and Ooi, G. L. 1999. *Singapore Housing: An Annotated Bibliography*, Singapore: National University of Singapore. [Google Scholar]

Yuen, B., Kwee, L.K. and Tu, Y. 2006. Housing Affordability in Singapore: Can We Move from Public to Private Housing? Urban Policy And Research Vol 24, Issue 2.

Ziebarth, A., Prochaska-Cue, K. and Shrewsbury, B. 1997. Growth and locational impacts for housing in small communities. *Rural Sociology*, 62(1): 111–125. [Crossref], [Web of Science ®], [Google Scholar]

Lightning Source UK Ltd.
Milton Keynes UK
UKHW041959010922
408190UK00001B/92